EVERY PERSPECTIVE HAS A VOICE, EVERY VOICE HAS A PERSPECTIVE

Copyright © 2023 by Larry Buttermore

All rights reserved.
This book, or parts thereof, may not be
reproduced in any form without permission.

Paperback ISBN: 978-1-63337-748-6
Ebook ISBN: 978-1-63337-749-3

Printed in the United States of America
1 3 5 7 9 10 8 6 4 2

EVERY PERSPECTIVE HAS A VOICE, EVERY VOICE HAS A PERSPECTIVE

13 Compelling Stories
as Told by Combat Veterans

LARRY BUTTERMORE

After much thought, I dedicate this book to the thirteen fine men I had the privilege of interviewing. They each served their country during the Vietnam era. They and their loving families paid a high price to protect us while there. They are still paying, as are countless other fine veterans. I (we) owe them a huge debt of gratitude.

TABLE OF CONTENTS

Opening Author's Note..1
Foreword by Capt. Gut Gruters..15

1. Bob Kuhn...16
2. Charles William (Gus) Shackson..22
3. William (Bill) Cooper..28
4. John Keir..44
5. Bill (Arnie) Lamp...74
6. Jack Ernest..110
7. Fred Seese...122
8. Sherman Mosley...156
9. Tim Young..168
10. Steve Morris..186
11. Doug Hammond...212
12. Bob Cross..286
13. Guy Gruters...328

Closing Author's Note..358
Acknowledgments...363
About the Author...364

OPENING AUTHOR'S NOTE

If you read my novel; "Over and Back," you certainly picked up the fact that the beginning took place during the Vietnam conflict. The two main characters, Trey and I offer a perspective on the time period, for sure.

As I finished writing I began to see that this time period was one where there could be many perspectives. You the reader only saw two of them. One was Trey. He chose to become a draft dodger. He never went to Vietnam. He went to Canada. While he became a productive citizen of that country, the only conflict he had to endure was being estranged from his family for about ten years. Call it "collateral damage." All the while, he was forging ahead, establishing himself. He found a mate, started a family, ran a successful business, and never looked back. After 1977, President Jimmy Carter pardoned him, with no preconditions and freedom to return to the United States. His family took him back and even though his life was not perfect, with what happened to his family, the outcome had nothing to do with the Vietnam conflict.

Then there's me. I sought out and got a deferment, as a teacher. I did nothing wrong but presented a different perspective than Trey. I never went to Vietnam. I worried often that this break that I guess I earned, would be pulled out from under me, as it was early on, when my initial "Marital" deferment was pulled. I dwelled on it less as time went on and counted it as a blessing. I went through life and never got drafted. I still have my draft card and it remained 1-A throughout my life. I caught a huge break.

EVERY PERSPECTIVE HAS A VOICE, EVERY VOICE HAS A PERSPECTIVE

Recently I saw a great little illustration on my phone. It was either on Facebook or on an Email. It showed a can of Raid Wasp and Hornet killer. It told about a man picking it up, looking it over, then taking it to the checkout area. He decided to ask the young lady working there a question.

"Is this stuff good for wasps?"

She looks it over and hands it quicky back to him.

"Oh no sir. It's terrible for wasps. It kills them on contact!"

Laughable, but perfect as an illustration of perspective. A bit later, I was scheduled to teach at a weekly church service we offer at Feridean, an assisted living facility next to our church. I used the lesson learned in the Raid story and added to it several Bible based thoughts and came up with a talk that was very thought provoking. I used the story of The Prodigal Son from the Bible. In this story there are three main characters.; a wealthy father and his two sons. Short and sweet, the younger son is extremely selfish and foolhardy. Even though he knows he will eventually inherit his father's wealth, he grows impatient and asks for it immediately. His father grants it, and the son is off and running. He just as quickly squanders it all and finds himself living in squalor; realizing that the pigs he is tending to are better off than he. In desperation, he decides to go back to his father, ask forgiveness and request a job as a menial servant to the family he once was very much a part of. When his dad sees him a far off, he treats the son's return with great joy. He throws a feast and party and welcomes his long-lost son with open arms. Everyone seems happy, except for one. The older brother can't believe any of it. Here's how. The good brother who stayed on and worked daily and never asked for anything special, now must watch his no-good brother get all the attention and a feast to boot. The story showed clearly, three very different perspectives.

After delivering this message at Feridean, I went next door to our regular church service. It was then that the parallels and perspectives set me on a path back to my story and the unique time frame called The Vietnam era.

Sitting right in front of me was my dear friend Bob Kuhn. He and his wife began attending a "Small Group" that my wife Barb and I met with on Tuesday evenings. They were one of the newer and younger members of our group, but only by a few years. Our group was always doing a study. Usually, we studied from the Bible and occasionally from a book or video.

I couldn't help noticing that Bob was very emotional if a subject somehow were related to death or suffering. He would often break down and even cry. He would tell us about his Vietnam experiences. It didn't take much to realize he had been through a lot and much has stayed with him.

I also knew his perspective on that time period would be very, and totally different than my character Trey and my own. I never talked with him about it but decided it would be a good place to start on my epilogue. My biggest fear was that he would think less of me if he knew I had been deferred and that I never had to go through what he did. Nevertheless, I asked if I could interview him. He accepted and I was able to meet with him at our church. I recorded it on my phone and Bob became the first of many compelling interviews. Once I began, I decided that I would have 4 interviews: one from each of the 4 main branches of service. I thought that would be ambitious enough and that I'd accomplish my goal. The goal was simple. Get a wider perspective/ point of view on the era. As I got to interview number three, I began to tell a few close friends about what I was doing. One spoke.

"Do you remember this person from Otterbein? You really should interview him. His story will blow you away. I shared with my brother, Bob. He told me.

"I hope you plan to interview Cousin Fred." Soon I was off and running in new and exciting directions with a simple project that now had gained "A life of its own." 4 stories soon became 12. Each of them equally compelling. Here's a brief introduction/teaser of each. As is human nature, each was different. Some guys were more/less talkative, so you will find that the lengths of each are quite different. Also, I'd never qualify as a professional interviewer, so each story has a slightly different format. I asked a lot of the same questions, but; you'll see, I got what I could from each.

I also ask each to be open and candid. That was the only way some would open up. As you read, you will see a lot of unfiltered conversation. I did not stop them or try to suppress their thoughts. They were kind enough to take their time and I just let them go.

I went into the interviews thinking that their memories from 50 plus years ago might be faded. I was so wrong. Instead, the recollections were remarkable.

After Bob, I remembered a friend from my Otterbein days. He became my second interview. He also became the first of many "phone interviews." He was in Florida, and this was the only way. I found out quickly that this was a viable way to get a story, as it felt like we were in the same room.

William (Gus) Shackson

Gus and I were in the same class at Otterbein. We were also in the same frat. I'd remember us as close over our four years. He was a "Townie," as he grew up in Westerville. His dad was a renowned prof there, in the music department. After college he went in the Air Force and we were out of touch till Facebook came along, in 2004. I realized the power of Facebook as a means of keeping in touch with people far and near. He was one of them. Because of his

R.O.T.C. beginning, at Otterbein, he became an officer, an accomplished jet pilot and test pilot. His interview also exposed a love story. Almost all the men I talked to, had love stories. Gus sadly, passed away recently. I hope his family will treasure his story as much as I did.

Wm. (Bill) Cooper

Bill was a church friend. We clicked from the very beginning. At first, I did not know of his military background. Once again Facebook helped, as he often posted pictures of reunions with his shipmates, and about his time in Vietnam, during the conflict. Both Gus and Bill were in the conflict, but not in hand-to-hand combat like my friend Bob. I quickly found that this didn't diminish their contribution. It also didn't make them any less a hero. Gus felt he had no P.T.S.D. aftereffects. Bill did. Each lost close mates to the conflict, so I suspect Gus, especially downplayed the effect his time there on his memory bank.

John Keir

John's story is the longest. I started his interview with a time crunch. I got a call in the middle of it that eliminated that obstacle. I explained my schedule to him when we began, and he filled the time I originally had with an amazing story. When I told him I had more time, he simply said.

"I have more stuff." He did for sure! He was a Marine. He, like my friend Bob, saw people die right in front of him. They both epitomized the "kill or be killed" situation that so many of our fine veterans became a part of. Also, like Bob, John's health and wellbeing was altered totally by his service experience. He would say to me.

"You name it; I have it."

I also got from John, the strong bond of family that each person has. I knew a little, but he showed me so much more. It made me go back to Gus and Bill and Bob and probe deeper. It enhanced each of their stories as well. John is a true hero, and his story is compelling.

I could have stopped here, as I fulfilled my original intent. I found someone from each of the four major service branches.

People I talked to encouraged me and began to broaden my horizon about other people I might talk to before putting this part to bed. In a conversation at a golf outing, I was encouraged to add another Air Force person. It was another acquaintance from my Otterbein days.

Bill Lamp

Bill (Arnie) Lamp was killed in a plane crash during his time in Vietnam. I was talking with a cousin, and she really thought his story would be one I should pursue. I agreed. She then put me in touch with Arnie's younger brother. He was willing. During our talk, he told me that Arnie's widow had passed, but they had two daughters before his crash. He said daughter Debbie might be willing to sit down with me. Jeff Lamp was deeply affected by his brother's death. As well, he opened how this took its toll on his sister and especially their mom and dad. The conflict took the lives of over 70,000 of our best young people. Arnie's story had to be repeated so many times, as each family sent their son or daughter to the service with the expectation of them returning. The shock and grief of their death is mind blowing to me. I was able to talk multiple times to Debbie Lamp, Arnie's oldest daughter. She passed on how her mom and sister's lives were forever altered by this incident. Both sets of parents helped, and the kids were insulated as much as they could have been. They are now both happy and productive young women. I also got a bonus that you will read about. Debbie had a copy of her father's voice from a reel-to-reel tape. He and his wife exchanged this tape back and forth many times. The technology of the day made it so that each time it was exchanged, the previous conversation was erased. This tape was approximately 30 minutes of treasured conversation where Arnie talks about what was happening in his Vietnam experience. He talked to his bride like she was there with him. He poignantly spoke to each daughter and implored them to "be good girls" while he was gone. I broke down more than once, as I listened to his words. He was a good soldier, a good friend to his mates. A wonderful husband and father.

Now I had a second story from the Air Force. This made a new goal of a second from each branch.

Tim Young

The next story was generated when I did an annual review with my financial consulting firm. Matt and Tim were in the room with me. Over the years they have given me sound advice many times over. Before getting to the nitty gritty of our appointment, they asked what new was happening in my life. I never think of this as them being anything but sincere, so I told them about my book and the epilogue part. Tim spoke up and said.

"Why don't you interview me?"

I'd been with Tim several times, but for some reason I thought he was too young to be a Vietnam vet. I was wrong and I took him seriously. I told him I'd be in touch and soon we had a phone interview.

He was guarded throughout the interview and ended with; "I'm not sure I'm all in with you publishing this, so be sure and let me know if/when this comes about so that I can decide. I did. He eventually asked for a transcript of our interview. He then rewrote it and gave it a title; calling it "Shoes." I honored this and his story will be presented in the final form he provided. He is a hero!!

Jack Ernest

One of my favorite clients as an insurance agent were the Reliford's. Cindy and Scott had been with me several years. I was summoned by a late evening phone call from my claims partners that they had experienced a major fire from a lightning strike. Even though I had been with the company for a long time, this was the first time a client of mine had such a major and traumatic event. I quickly decided to jump in my car and drive there to provide any personal help I could. When I got there, I found a chaotic scene. Scott was home in his lower-level family room when this happened. Lightning struck outside and hit the gas meter. This started then a "blowtorch" effect through their gas line. It must have had a hairline fissure that made this happen. This line ran under the main floor and above the drywall ceiling of the basement where Scott was. He saw this and was able to escape before being overcome. A cat that was in the same room panicked and was tragically killed. By the time I got there the flames were gone and the fire department was cleaning up and getting ready to leave. Cindy had arrived from an appointment and joined us. We went inside and I asked if I could pray for them. It seemed appropriate. Later we encountered the Fire chief who was at the scene. He remarked that what saved a total catastrophe was that the someone from the gas company happened by and turned the gas off at the meter. This stopped the cracked gas line from making quick work of the rest of the house. Someone of the onlookers told him that the gas company guy drove a white van and was seen by the house. The next day, Cindy called the gas company to thank them for dispatching the service person so quicky. The meter had a padlock on it and needed an official person to unlock it and turn it off. Interestingly, they were not aware of any dispatch, and no one there knew of a service person with a white van. Draw your own conclusion. An Angel; was ours.

This whole episode was amazing. They went from treating me as their agent, to making me like a member of their family. Through this new relationship I soon met Cindy's parents, Jack, and Patty Ernest. I found out that Jack was a Marine in Vietnam. He told me about many of his experiences from the conflict, and how he wanted to give back. As a result, he made many personal and group mission trips to Vietnam.

I thought of him immediately as a person I should interview, even though I hadn't talked with him for several years. Cindy set it up and we did both a phone interview and a face to face. You will find his story as one of personal valor and service.

Sherman Mosley

I needed a second Navy veteran. Earlier, my first Navy interview person, Bill Cooper could not think of anyone local that he knew. After I learned that a phone interview was just as worthwhile, I went back to him and asked if he could broaden his circle of acquaintances. He immediately thought of his friend Sherman Mosley. They met at a reunion of the ship they shared during Vietnam. They were both on it but didn't know or have contact with each other till the reunion. Whatever brought them together was a good thing, as they and their wives have been great friends for several years.

Sherman's story, as you read, will tell of an experience in the "bowels" of a big ship, where Bill's took place mostly on deck.

Fred Seese

My brother Bob and I talked a lot about my project. He asked if I'd talked to Fred. I sheepishly answered.

"No. Hadn't really thought of him."

"Well, you should. He's got quite an interesting story."

I did so and Bob was right. His story is one of a guy who joined and found a niche that most people wouldn't have pursued. He took on the specialty area of the mortuary. He did all he could to honor the thousands who were killed. He prepared bodies, cataloged remains and their personal effects and made sure each serviceman or woman killed, made its way to the proper family. I got a double bonus, as I was able to reconnect with a first cousin who grew up just 3 houses from me, plus got to hear his story. He wasn't even sure I (or anyone for that matter) would be interested in hearing. I was and you will be, too.

Now I had at least two guys from each service group, I was able to breathe in and be done. I liked what I had accomplished. I now had properly chronicled what my novel couldn't. I had the perspective of 9 different people/families that went through the conflict as combat veterans. Job well done sir.

Steve Morris

Then one day while I was shopping in my local Kroger store, I met this guy. Steve Morris was shopping for something in the same aisle as me. I couldn't help noticing him. I had become more aware of veterans because of my research. Other guys told me that they cannot resist talking to a guy with a Vietnam Veterans hat on. They know, instinctively that this person will share a story and that the only way that happens is if they interact.

So, here's a guy right in my aisle with his hat on. He's also very imposing. Tall for sure. Wearing a huge brace on his lower leg, and a black sling as well. He had to have a story or two. As I watched, I decided to make contact.

"Sir, thank you for your service." I said, hoping to break the ice.

"May I ask what branch you were in?"

"Army; Special Forces." He responded.

"Wow; very impressive!"

"Thanks" he said back, and I left it at that. I paid my proper respect, and we parted company. I finished my shopping, checked out and was walking out. Then it hit me, that this person was worth my time to tell him about my project and see if he would be interested in being interviewed. I went back in and quickly found him. I introduced myself and briefly told him what I had done and asked him if he would consent to an interview. He said yes and we exchanged numbers. Later that day I called, and we set up a time. I live in a small community called Apple Valley. Turns out we lived on the same street, but on opposite sides of the lake. Soon we set up a time and I met him. What a bonus!! His story will intrigue you, as the "Special Forces" angle was so different than any of the other guys. Also, his experiences after retiring and even now are so different. You will love his story.

Doug Hammond

When I lived in Westerville, I got the daily Columbus Dispatch newspaper. I started my day reading the paper. One of the features of any paper is the obituary section. I read it every day. I did it for a reason. I wanted to be responsive if a friend colleague or client passed away. It served me well, and I was able to offer my condolences. After I moved, I cancelled my subscription and reasoned that I could get along without it. I would say that was true, except for the obits. More times than I care to mention, I would find out someone I knew well, passed away. One of these was Doug Hammond. Doug and I went to Otterbein together. His obituary was published either in a college periodical or on Facebook. Interestingly the stuff I read in his tribute was different than I would have suspected. I realize that people can change. I also realize that I hadn't seen or heard of Doug for over 50 years. My exposure to Doug in college was that he would have fit in to the movie "Animal House" quite well. In fact, his nickname was" The Animal." Now what I was reading portrayed him as a superhero. He distinguished himself in the military, in the business world, and as a consummate family man and caregiver to his mother and wife; both who had Alzheimer's. Then he contracted the same vile disease and had to be confined in a facility. During this stay he got Covid and died.

I decided his story needed to be part of my project. I found a mutual friend on Facebook, and he was able to put me in touch with a wonderful woman who became Doug's forever friend and caregiver after his wife passed away. She then connected me with Doug's daughter, and two friends that helped me complete the story. I hope you find it as compelling as I did.

On a family golf trip, I picked up a copy of a U.S.A. Today newspaper. In it was a whole section devoted to the Vietnam conflict. I put it in my baggage to read when I got home. As I read, I saw it used interviews like my own. I then saw two categories that I had not thought of. One was from an African American. The second was from a P.O.W.

Bob Cross

I had met Bob Cross, an African American veteran at a conference I attended earlier in the year. He was wearing a veteran's cap that caught my attention. I was able to engage him in a conversation and we hit it off immediately. I told him about my project but explained that it was basically finished. I took his business card and that was that. After reading the U.S.A. section, I hustled to find it and called him immediately. He was eager to be interviewed and we were able to complete it by phone. I'm so glad I saw that article, as his addition will enhance your reading.

Guy Gruters

My daughter, Angie had told me that her company recently held a team building event and that two P.O.W.s were there as keynote speakers. One was a Vietnam conflict P.O.W. I was able to get his name and track him down by phone. He and I got together in his current hometown in Ohio. His interview was incredible and certainly became a fitting finish.

After all of this, I made another decision. If I made this effort an "epilogue" as originally planned, it's impact might well be missed. Who's going to spend time reading an epilogue that's as big as the novel they just finished? I talked this over with a few close friends and they agreed. I presented this thought to my publisher, suggesting it is worthy of becoming its own book. They agreed.

Now I'm done. I hope you get as much from reading about these heroes and their families, as I did. I also realize that even though I broadened my own perspective on this era, as well as yours, one thing is certain. For every person I interviewed there are countless others that either made it home with their own special story; or were a casualty. I would ask that you pray with me that each of them be honored and treasured. Lastly, perspectives can't exist without opinions. In each of the interviews are contained the opinions of the person I was talking to. As I re-read them, I saw in each, the opinions held by the one who owned them. I didn't try to suppress them. So, you as the reader may find a thing or two that you don't agree with. You may even find that not every word or thought would stand up to a 'fact check.' I think the unfiltered approach I took was the right one. As a result, some of the language used will be "R-Rated, and/or colorful" I hope, in advance that you'll be full of grace for me and each of my wonderful new (and old) friends!

FOREWORD BY CAPT. GUY GRUTERS

When Larry asked me to participate in his project, I readily accepted. He came and met me at my favorite restaurant, in Piqua, Ohio. He talked to me for at least two hours. I heard what he was doing and began to offer my perspective. He didn't try to suppress me at any time, which helped me open up and tell my story. Later, I saw what he wrote about me. It was totally accurate from our talk. I then was given his introduction and a short informational piece about each of the men and women he interviewed. He captured what each said, and presented it in a way that was easy to read and understand. I was there, so the stories are very familiar. I think you, as the reader, will see what I did. The title fits very well. One of his interviews stated that every veteran and every family attached to them carried their memories and their perspectives from the day they entered the service until today. Read; reread and enjoy what Larry has written. When you are finished, I predict that you will definitely have a much broader "prospective."

Capt. Guy Gruters
Former P.O.W. Vietnam
Published Author
Public Speaker
Veteran's advocate

BOB KUHN

AGE WHEN ENTERED MILITARY: 20
DATE OF ENTRY TO MILITARY: 06/1967
VIETNAM TOUR DATES: 05/1968-05/1969
YEARS OF DUTY/RESERVES: 2

BOB KUHN

Bob was drafted. The year was 1967. He trained for a year, then spent a year in Vietnam. While he was there. The Tet offensive was on, and Bob was a "replacement" for a company that had several members who were killed. This was foreboding. He recalled that he was on a troop plane and having the pilot come on and say,

"We'll be landing in 5 minutes."

A half hour goes by, and they still hadn't landed. He would find out quickly that the airfield was being shelled, thus causing the delay.

"This was not good news" Bob explained.

He related a few times that were so horrifying that they became part of his ongoing "memory bank" of his time there. First, he told me that his officers explained that you are in a war. You protect your fellow soldiers at all costs. You do what you are told and "keep it together." Soon he would find out what was so important about that.

He was sent out to retrieve 13 bodies of men he was "replacing." They had been killed a day or two earlier.

"The first thing I (we) had to overcome was the stench. One or two days in a tropical climate with often 100% humidity takes a quick toll on a dead body. Throwing up and retching became normal. The men were covered with flies, Larry. You don't forget something like that."

I nearly retched just listening. It was the first experience of many that made Bob what he is today. What he is; pure and simple.

He's a HERO.

The next thing he told me was that Kathy (then his fiancé') told him she would be waiting for him to return and that they would be married. They met on a blind date. It was New Year's Eve. 1966/67. They dated for 6 months. Bob got drafted in June of 67. They got engaged in May of 1968.

"Larry, her letters were my only contact with the outside world. I don't know what I would have done without them. One of my regrets was that because of the humidity and filthy conditions, I couldn't save them."

On a lighter note, some were laced with her perfume.

"I could smell the perfume and dream, Larry. I would hold them close for a few minutes before opening them and just close my eyes and see her face. I read them at least three times and kept them till the aroma wore off."

This made me both smile and cry. My only relatable tale was that I relished getting letters from my Barb when I was a counselor at a Boy Scout camp for the summer.

"Larry, I was lucky. Not everyone got letters."

"I purposely tried not to get close to the other soldiers. I just knew that things change in a heartbeat in such a place. I made one exception and got burned. I was talking to my closest friend. He was right there beside me when there was a blast. We were near a crater that had been carved out by a bomb. Larry: he was there and then gone. I couldn't believe it. The blast came out of nowhere and it spared me and killed him. Why?"

He then explained that this probably was a terrible accident. The troops used sandbags to put garbage in. The filled bags were thrown in the crater and burned. The bags were also utilized to put used hand grenades in. He thinks an unexploded hand grenade accidentally got in a bag and then exploded from the fire.

He also told me of another incident he witnessed.

"It was just a normal day. There were two Chinook helicopters coming into land. They probably both were loaded with munitions. All of a sudden, one flipped, over and crashed. The ammunition on board exploded and however many were in the Chinook were killed instantly. Larry, you don't forget."

Every night, some were on guard duty. It was always 2 hours. The noises must have been many and frightening. When Bob was on such duty, his mind was always on high alert, and his attitude was "be prepared for the worst." When his mind did drift, here is where it often went.

"All my friends are in college. They're having a ball and I'm out here laying my life on the line. What's wrong with this picture?"

After he came home. He encountered stuff that no soldier should have to. He was never welcomed and revered. He was made to feel bad that he was a part of a conflict he didn't have a thing to do with personally.

After Bob got out, he enrolled at Franklin University in Columbus. The G.I. bill paid for this entirely. He graduated with a business degree in 1973. He began working for the Gas Company. For whatever reason, they did not give him the opportunity he was expecting. Deciding what was best for his family, he started working for Coca Cola, as a delivery route driver. This then led him to a similar post with U.P.S. where he eventually retired. Bored, he tried bussing incorrigible kids to a special school, north of Columbus. They drove him crazy quickly and he fully retired at age 65.

He and Kathy have 2 kids and several grandchildren. Their son lives in Cincinnati, and they have a daughter here in Columbus.

Fifty years later, it's not easy to distinguish him from anyone else. That is till you spend time with him. He's not as healthy as most, but trudges on. In talking with him, he feels his health maladies which include skin cancer, are most likely related to his year in Vietnam. I believe he suffers from the ravages of Agent Orange. He was a foot soldier. The chemicals that were used, made his time there more feasible, as the area they were in would have little visibility from the air, as well as on the ground. As I found out, roughly five times as many Vietnam vets have died from the exposure to Agent Orange, then died in the conflict. I didn't ask him about P.T.S.D. but he certainly displays many common symptoms.

A recurring conversation with Bob always includes………

"I get angry. They don't understand. They don't have a clue. They never had to go through it. It makes me upset. Nobody wants to hear it. Nobody wants to get out of their comfort zone. I had to get out of mine. They think their better than me. You can't forget what went on. You can't forget how we were treated when we came home."

He related that just after 9/11 two ladies from his former church were talking about what had happen and he overheard: (In a whiny voice)

"I certainly don't want my Johnny to have to go, be in the service and maybe get hurt or even killed."

"Larry, I had to hold myself back. I wanted so bad, to slap both. What makes them better than me. I served my country."

After talking to him, all his emotions are deserved. He even accused the folks in my small group of "rolling their eyes when I start up." I quickly learned that could happen. His conversations were always heavy and hard to listen to. As for me, I totally respected him and often felt guilty when he finished. I also assured him that all his friends were uncomfortable when he talked, but zero of them ever attempted to slow him or stop him. Respect had been earned. He seemed glad to hear this.

He added.

"I think it's all on us as parents and grandparents to teach our kids and their kids about Vietnam, to love their country, and to be willing to serve. Otherwise, they'll never know. Larry, as a Christian man, I try to forgive. But it's hard. Something will pop up and I just get mad all over again."

Forgiveness is hard for sure. I see this as something Bob has much trouble with. I pray that he will realize that to forgive is Godly and that it is more freeing to him than to the person being forgiven.

Bob was able to go on an "Honor Flight" trip. He was humbled and honored. I'm so glad he did. He went to the Vietnam wall and the Korean War Memorial. He asked his Guardian.

"Why are you doing this. I'm a total stranger. You took the time and spent over $400 on this, and you never even met me."

She replied.

"Bob; you're a hero. Pure and simple."

I totally agree!!

CHARLES WILLIAM (GUS) SHACKSON

AGE WHEN ENTERED MILITARY: 23

DATE OF ENTRY TO MILITARY: 07/1965 (RESERVE DUTY 02/1960-07/1965)

VIETNAM TOUR DATES: 05/1969-01/1972

YEARS OF DUTY/RESERVES: 30

CHARLES WILLIAM (GUS) SHACKSON

Gus and I were classmates at Otterbein. We pledged the same fraternity, so we got to know each other well. His dad was a professor and head of the music department. He was an outstanding student and eventually was elected V.P. of the frat in our senior year. I always remember him as a R.O.T.C. guy. He wore the uniform proudly and I'm certain he was an outstanding member.

After Otterbein he enlisted in the Air Force. He completed O.T.C. and became a 2nd. Lieutenant. As he explained to me, he immediately asked for an "Educational Delay" which allowed him to enroll in The University of Florida business school where he obtained a master's degree in economics. While in school he was also promoted to First Lieutenant.

He told me he had dreamed of being a jet pilot since he was a young boy.

"If I happened to fail in my attempt to be a pilot, I wanted something concrete to fall back on."

As it turned out, he didn't fail and began a distinguished career as a pilot, serving two concurrent tours of duty in Vietnam.

"I flew F-16's and mostly F-4's. The first tour I was stationed in Korat, Thailand. My second was at the base in Ubon, Thailand. I was part of "F.A.S.T." F.A.C. (Forward Air Controller) played a very important part in the conflict. The F.A.S.T. part came during Gus's time in and over Vietnam. Early on, prop planes were used. By the time he entered in the fray, his F-4 became one of the go-to planes. Along with F-9's and F-100's.

He explained.

"After receiving my intel around 6 A.M. each morning we would meet up with a fuel tanker and then fly with an assignment to drop bombs on targets, usually tanks. Occasionally we targeted bridges. We were using laser guided bombs. They blew the shit out of whatever they hit."

I asked.

"Did you consider that people were also being hit by these bombs?"

"Hell yes………"

"Didn't that bother you?"

Gus answered this directly and left me no doubt that this was business that had to be done and was a necessary collateral damage part of war.

"Did you ever have a 'dog fight' type battle in the air?"

"Never, but we were always getting ground fire. We never had to jump out!!"

"What about damage to your jet?"

"We were hit four times during my tenure."

"Where did your missions take you?"

"North and South Vietnam and Laos."

"What was in Laos?"

"Bad Guys"

I pursued no further.

"Gus, did you lose any planes while you were there?"

"When you lose a plane, you lose 2 people, Larry. This happened to me twice."

"Did you know them personally?"

I wanted to retract that question as soon as I blurted it out.

"Of course."

After his 2 tours, he chose to stay in the Air Force and probably make a career out of it. He next was stationed at Lakenheath Royal Air Base in England and had no more combat time. He met his wife; Carmel there and was married at the base Chapel. Gus continued his role as a pilot and became the chief test pilot for the F-4 jets.

Two common things happened to Vietnam veterans. P.T.S.D. and Agent Orange.

"Did you suffer from either, Gus?"

"No to P.T.S.D., and yes to Agent Orange."

"How did you contract Agent Orange as a pilot?"

"We flew through it all the time and couldn't help but contract it."

"Do you have any lingering effects today?"

"I was awarded 100% disability."

"But do you have any remaining effects?"

"No."

Gus came backs to the U.S. and moved to Centerville, Va. (near D.C.) and stayed in the Air Force till 1992.

"Many veterans get in and get out. You chose to stay and make the military your career. "

"Larry, I wanted to be a pilot since I was a little kid. As it turned out, I never thought of it as work. It was a passion from the beginning to end."

"My original plan was to do 30 and out. At 28 years I decided it was time to hang it up, so I retired."

"I just retired 3 years ago my friend. You've been out for near 30 years. Must be a pretty good gig?"

"My bride and I have 2 kids. Our son lives in Raliegh and has 2 kids. My daughter lives on the same street we do, in Cape Coral, Florida."

"One last question. When you returned to the U.S., did you ever get any negative treatment? Many Vets from the war were greeted with boos, spit on and made to feel more like villains than heroes."

"Larry, I read and heard about that shit, but never had it happened to me. I'm sure that was because I didn't' come back immediately and by the time I got out all that sentiment was pretty much gone."

"Gus, if I treated you as a hero, would you accept the role? If you do, good for you. If you don't, you should!"

As a sad postscript, I found out through Facebook that Gus passed away from an illness; August 6, 2022. His obituary gave proper credit to his service, stating that he made his "Final sweep" on his final day. The obit also added a few details to what he told me.

Gus was an esteemed Fighter Pilot who flew 417 Combat Missions in Southeast Asia flying the F-4. His 32 years of distinguished service took him to many positions around the world including several US Bases as well as Iceland, Canada, Korea, Japan, and The Pentagon. In 1989 he was selected as Commander of 475th Air Base Wing in Yokota, Japan and it was in Osan, Korea where he began flying F-16's.

With over 2900 hours of flying time some of Gus's military awards and decorations include the Distinguished Flying Cross with six oak leaf clusters, Meritorious Service Medal with three oak clusters, Air Medal with 28 oak leaf clusters, Air Force Commendation Medal, Air Force Achievement Medal, and the Republic of Vietnam Gallantry Cross.

Gus was proud to be a member of the Red River Valley Fighter Pilots Association. ("River Rats" as he would say). Also, he was a supporter of several philanthropic organizations including one dear to his heart, the Shackson Memorial Endowment fund in honor of his father Lee Shackson.

Gus obviously downplayed his military life with me. I understand that, as many who served thought of their time and effort as far less than it deserved.

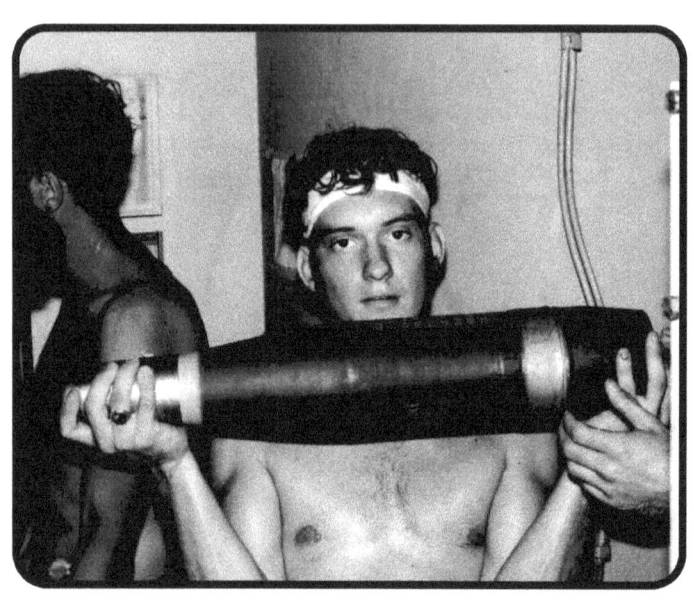

WILLIAM (BILL) COOPER

AGE WHEN ENTERED MILITARY: 20

DATE OF ENTRY TO MILITARY: 06/1971

VIETNAM TOUR DATES: 01/1972-08/1972

YEARS OF DUTY/RESERVES: 6

WILLIAM (BILL) COOPER

Bill and Paula have been friends for many years. We met at church. They were clients of mine for some time as well. Recently, I followed them on social media. I knew Bill was in the Navy by some things he posted on Facebook. I decided he would be a great addition to my research. I suspected his perspective would fall somewhere in between Bob's and my friend Gus. I was right, as you will see. Bill grew up in Columbus and described his family life as a young man. At the time of the Vietnam conflict, he was dealing with two things that contributed to his reality. He and his father were at odds. Also, he had a serious girlfriend he found cheating on him. His inclination was to get rid of both those frustrations and run from them. As a boy, he dreamed of being a Navy fighter pilot. One day during this critical time he was driving in East Columbus and passed the Navy recruiting center. He detoured that day and decided to see what they had to offer.

What Bill wanted, of course was to fulfill his childhood dream and become a Navy fighter pilot. The first assessment he took looked good, but the pilot part was short circuited by him not having 20-20 (non-correctible) vision. After learning that, they still offered the opportunity of him joining. He accepted and went home to tell his parents. His parents' response was totally negative, but Bill was determined. He told them he was leaving, and they couldn't stop him, as he was of age. He was running away and joining the Navy, and that was that.

Here's his response.

"Larry, I wasn't a warmonger. I would call myself a patriot though, for sure. I watched John Wayne and other famous actors of the day; portray military heroes and I admired them for what they stood for. I was 1-A but had a rather high number, so that part was not an eminent threat. I was enrolled in courses at O.S.U., but due to the complications with my girlfriend, I was in a bad place emotionally and it came out on my focus, and I was not doing well in my grades. I just felt I'd be better off in the Navy than in Columbus. Once in, I went to Great Lakes Naval Station, north of Chicago. There I took basic training and was evaluated for any aptitude I might have for things to come. From there I went to California and was put in school for electronics, specifically guided missiles. I must have showed them something special; Larry, as they called me aside and I began training in heat seeking missiles. Soon I was on a ship to Hawaii. "Join the Navy, see the world." The advertisements I saw on T.V. were unfolding right in front of me. So, I thought! Two weeks in Pearl Harbor was lovely, but anything like a vacation. Orders came out and we were back on a ship again. This time we were headed for Vietnam. Vacation over!! We left there in a convoy. Any ships heading west traveled with as many as 7 others, for protection. We stopped in Guam, Manilla, and the Philippines. Each stop was brief but unique. Finally, we're along the coast of Nam. Not much to report about the early days there. Getting adjusted to the extreme heat and humidity for sure was a daily matter. In 1968, things were still calm. There was an armistice, and we couldn't cross the D.M.Z. There were small skirmishes in the south, but nothing major. We provided cover fire support for small battles in the south.

This relative lull would be short lived, as the North Vietnamese were amassing troops and preparing for what was known as The Easter Offensive. This started in March, shortly after our arrival and for sure, 'all Hell broke loose' on Easter when things escalated. We were in Taiwan getting some repairs done when we were assigned to accompany an aircraft carrier. We were called 'search and rescue.' When things got quickly heated, we were called back the coast. We fired more than two thousand rounds over the next few days.

Here's an important story, Larry. There were 5 Marines that were in a forward fire base of observation post. They were going down through a valley where there was a bridge that led to all the major cities of the south. One of them was Captain Ripley. He would later become the head of the Naval Academy. He and one of the other of the five, single handedly set charges and blew up the bridge, making a huge difference in the outcome of the offensive. We were providing suppression fire support for these guys. Up until that moment, I was still struggling with the notion of just why I was there. Besides the obvious of running away from my past life, I still hadn't figured on any greater purpose. It hit me between the eyes as this was going on. I was providing support in a life and death situation. If I(we) weren't there at that time and place, the 5 Marines would not have been able to carry out their important mission and probably would not have survived."

All I could say was.

"Wow Bill!"

He continues.

"Now I'm on the bridge and we're receiving messages from them. "We're getting shelled and can't raise our heads!" They called for "Danger close" We were firing from 5 miles offshore and hitting within 1000 yards of their position. They were very complimentary of our accuracy and all, but what I heard that the South Vietnamese troops who were supposed to be protecting them and assisting, had abandoned them, leaving them totally unprotected except for our fire support. The weather conditions prevented any help from air support. We weren't the only ship in the area. Our ship: The U.S.S.

Joseph Strauss was major in this event, but another ship; The U.S.S. Buchannon got most of the accolades. Their C.O. was an Ex-Navy Seal who was bucking for a promotion and (I shouldn't even have mentioned that Larry), as it really shouldn't have mattered. That's the kind of petty shit that gets in my mind years after it happened. That became the epiphany for me, Larry. At that point, I knew that I was here to do anything possible to bring my boys (the 5 Marines) back safely. I also became jaded about the war, as here we were trying our best for a country (South Vietnam) that was basically turning its back and abandoning us and all our effort. 'Why in the Hell are we continuing to be here and putting up with such shit?' (Pardon my French) From that point on I realized I had a purpose. From April to the end of August, we were in constant battle mode. Often having multiple skirmishes, a night."

"Bill, what about the 5 Marines. Did they all make it?"

"No. We found out later there were originally 7. One died early on. And a second was M.I.A. A helicopter was able to evacuate the other 5. Here's another irony of this event. Several years ago, I got to attend a reunion of my shipmates in Ft. Wayne Indiana. I was wearing my Strauss ballcap. A Marine who was there asked me about it. We talked and he revealed that he was one of the five marines and that 2 others were there with him. As he and I recounted the time, he freely admitted that he and the others would not be alive that day if it hadn't been for our presence and the suppression fire support, we were able to provide. Larry, we were their only option for survival."

Once again, I'm touched to say.

"What a significant moment!"

"You bet. It further solidified my belief about just why I was there. My epiphany made clear. Larry, our ship was nearly hit several times. Some shells came within 50 feet of where I was on deck. My 'general quarters' responsibility was to be the last line of defense for my ship."

"Bill, explain the term 'general quarters.'"

"Yes sir, that was when we were in full battle mode, under fire, or in any threat of eminent danger. Hatches were battened and the ship was basically sealed and ready for anything incoming. For me, that meant I was one of 12 that were out on the deck. If a threat came our way, the big guns we had were basically unusable, as they were meant for more long-range targets. I (we) had shoulder launch missiles and 50 caliber guns that could manage an incoming plane, a patrol boat, or any other short-range stuff. "

"How close were you to the shore?"

"We got as close as 2000 yards of the shore. We would come into a position, then travel parallel to the shore, shell our targets, then go out as much as 20 miles to take on more armaments and do any repairs necessary. Our ship was called a guided- missile destroyer. We carried a crew of about 350. We were considered a 'special war class destroyer,' which meant we had 2 boilers, two separate power plants, two 5" mounts, tarter missiles, anti-aircraft missiles and torpedoes."

"Did you have any formal training with the weaponry you were using, or did you just learn on the fly?"

"We used a simulator that had us blowing commercial jets out of the sky at an airport. Because we were dealing with heat seeking missiles, this worked, as the commercial jets gave off a heat pattern that our missile sensors could lock on to."

"Almost like todays video games?"

"I guess you could say that. Anyhow, us guys got good at it in a hurry. Good thing, too, as we were called upon daily for stuff that only the 12 of us could handle. The worst moment was when we had 2 mines explode. As I have explained, I'm out on the open deck.

This one, hits the bow. It was surreal. Suddenly, the bow goes up out of the water. We're already about 75 feet above the water level. A gigantic wave of water that had to be a hundred feet above my deck happened. One of my buddies basically saved me from being blown overboard, by pushing me down. I was mesmerized by all of this. As it was happening, I did recognize that my 40 lb. flak jacket would act like an anchor if I were to fall in. I was grabbing for my buck knife when I got shoved down. Very quickly another mine hit mid ship and knocked out our steerage, some electronics and one of our 5" guns. We were so fortunate that neither one caused our ship a fracture, so we were not in danger of sinking.

Ultimately, we were told that we fired off between 15 and 20K of 5" projectiles during the battles over this period. Because we were a special 'War class destroyer,' we were in on most of the battles that were happening. We also had the commanding officer of the division on our ship. We were kept in the battle area and forced to do repairs there, as opposed to going to the Philippines where most other ships would go.

We eventually left and returned to Pearl Harbor. We found out our immediate fate was to be there on a 90-day rotation. This meant that we would take on the necessary repairs and re supplies and be ready to head back to Vietnam in 90 days. We never had to go back, as we were being held in reserve. Also, during this same time, Kissinger was negotiating a truce, which at best, was tenuous, as truces had been in place before and were broken. There was still fighting going on, but there was a waiting game because truces were in place and yet violated on and off that whole time. Then I got back home. I was still in the Navy, but now considered a reservist. I was on a 2/4 situation: 2 years of active duty, then 4 years as a reservist. I was able to finish up the active part while still at Pearl. Then, as I was ready to leave the ship, we went through a normal separation. They asked me if there was anything that they hadn't taken care of. I had developed an internal bleeding medical condition. The ship's doctor said it was just a case of hemorrhoids. Then I head to Treasure Island in San Francisco, where I would then be dismissed to my 4-year reservist stint. So, I'm there for two weeks. On the last day, I'm in a room with a couple of hundred guys and towards the end of this we were asked if there was anything that hadn't been resolved/taken care of. Well, somewhere along the line, we were trained that if we stood up and declared; 'with all due respect' that we couldn't be court martialed. So, I stood up and blurted out; 'With all due respect, I'm bleeding like a stuck pig, and you haven't done a thing about it.' They immediately took me over to Oakland Naval Hospital. They attempted to do an exploratory. I was in such bad medical shape that this didn't work. They sent me back to Treasure Island and put me through 2 weeks of medical leave, feeding me mega-doses of steroids and anything else that could stabilize me. Then I went back to Oakland for 3 months. At that point, Paula and I were supposed to be married. I called my poor bride to be, and she was thinking I was dying. I got them to sign me out and I went home and got married. A month in I had a relapse, and the big problem was that I was officially out of the Navy and on my own, Healthwise. I eventually got a permanent disability granted through the V.A. and I've been treated for this from 1973. Turned out that my condition (very rare) allowed me to get treated but also was sort of a guinea pig. Another irony of this was that at a family reunion after getting home, I was talking to someone, and conversation led to a Cousin Mike. We quickly found out that he was in Army intelligence, attached to the airbase in Huei. We were providing air suppression fire for them. He was one of the last ones out. We looked at each other and 'just wow!'

When I was over there and saw the poverty in the Philippines it hit me. The young women there, used the service men as a means of making a living. Between my first and second trip to the Philippines, a devastating monsoon came through. First trip, the girls average age was around 18. The second, it had dropped to around 15. Many more girls were forced to depend on this as a way of financial survival. I never realized how much; how good we have it in America. Also, I saw how important my being there was, I think immediately of the 5 Marines and of my cousin Mike. It's also not lost on me that people lost their lives because I was there."

I added.

"So, you were aware that your actions actually took lives?"

"Of course. But it was war, and I had this resolve from early on that my purpose was to do anything and everything to get my boys home alive.

All my experiences set me up for a success that was kind of unexpected, Larry. I enrolled again at Ohio State, where I previously had an inglorious .8 G.P.A. From then on, I was focused and driven, getting near a 4 point, and finishing a minor and two majors in the next three years. I was entitled to a stipend and was on the G.I. Bill. Also, I had my aptitude reevaluated and I got some extra compensation. I wanted to be an actuary. My advisor, Dr. Brown devised a curriculum, but couldn't guarantee me a degree. So, I took business from then on, in order to have a degree that would make a living. After getting my degree, I started and M.B.A. and was working actively as well. I could see that my job experience was outweighing my studies and so dropped the program in favor of working.

Knowing about his recent career, I asked.

"Did you go with Nationwide back then?"

"No; I was with an insurance company. They were called Acceleration. The company had some bad advice and quickly went from a $250mm position to being bankrupt in just 2 years."

"So, you caused the bankruptcy?"

"Hah, funny Larry."

"Just kidding, sir."

After doing several short-term gigs, I did end up with Nationwide. I was there for 16 years. I was able to help them design and build their 'Project Management system.' My education proved to be invaluable as my combined majors and minor (Insurance) gave me a path that served me well to make a great living.

"So, what rank did you achieve in the Navy?"

"I was an E-4. Could have gotten E-6. When I was in the reserves, I never thought it was important. In retrospect I didn't approach that one right, as it would have provided more in my retirement. Also, I provided my younger brothers a benefit, in that, because I had served in Nam, they couldn't. Both also joined the Navy. Remember the story from W.W.II about five brothers from the same family that were all killed? A rule/law was enacted after that where a single family cannot have two siblings in a theatre of war at the same time. My one brother was stationed on an aircraft carrier. He served a full 4 years and then got out. My other brother made a career and was in for 20 years."

"Because you were in, and served, were you given a retirement benefit?"

"No; all I got was a small stipend because of the 10% disability I was granted. Another irony was that the B-52's that used defoliants would bomb a beachhead and the chemicals would naturally get into the water. We were just as subjected to the Agent Orange and 'other stuff' less known. All our water was taken from that water. It got 'processed' but the chemicals got through nonetheless."

"So, weren't you qualified to receive compensation because of your exposure?"

"Larry, I'm on a registry for it, but the affliction I suffered isn't on there. But we have an extraordinary number of guys on my ship that are getting sick and are now receiving compensation as the testing is revealing. Mine, because if the internal bleeding, wasn't on the list. I got the 10% and was sufficient to get me treatments and meds over the years. The Navy maintains it was stress induced. Diabetes is borderline with me, so I can get treatment for it, but probably too borderline to qualify as a claim for compensation. I'm okay with that."

After hearing, I added.

"So, I see you as a proud man as far as your Navy experience."

"Once the Memorial was built, I could not bring myself to see that wall. I was in D.C. one night on business. I called a cab and went. It was after midnight, and I could come to grips with the fact that I lost guys. I myself was at risk every day, as a local terrorist was in a fishing boat and could have shot me or bombed or mined us and me. I feel I was almost as 'front line' as an Army guy with 'boots on the ground.' How did I eventually feel about this? Unquestionably I was there for a reason, and I carried it out proudly. I did stuff that brought back guys. Did I care about Vietnam after that. Hell no! The Vietnamese people simply abandoned us, and our guys were killed because of that. My cousin was in Amry intelligence. Lord knows what they would have done with him had he been captured. I provided a way for my guys and that was enough justification for me. Years later, I realize that if God hadn't wanted me in that position. I wouldn't have been there.

Remember the book I wrote (Witnessing Made Simple)? To be an effective witness, you must live out the stuff you will witness about. To be able to relate, or have others relate to you, you must live it. I can honestly say that I came back far better than when I went in. The 5 or 6 guys on my ship that had Bible studies and influenced me probably saved my life. For sure they changed it. They made a difference. Also, the life experience helped. I saw such poverty and what it did to me was provide the determination to take all those credits and classes that others thought were impossible.

It prepared me for success, Larry. When I got an actual job after college, it was easy peasy. Nothing like the rigors of the Navy and my schooling. I was lucky in that many of my buddies got messed up. The V.A. was not as good as it is today. The things we know today are so much better now. When I was authoring my book, I was hooked up with a couple guys and it was made known that I was authoring a book. "What's it about? one asked."

"It's about witnessing."

"After the meeting, the guy stopped me and simply asked; What is witnessing" I rest my case, Larry I was in the place God wanted me and daily I was given ample proof to keep me going. Many of my associates at Nationwide were believers. This was so great, because at the company I had just left from, it was the total opposite. Staying there would have surely been a backslide. That sequence of events became my destiny. I can look at it even further because I can now relate to others and add value to their lives.

We were on a gunline 46 days in a row. We would have three nightly targets for those 46 days. At night is when we had our battles. The enemy had optically sighted weapons, meaning that they could see us. At night, their weaponry became much less effective.

During the day we would go out to a supply ship and get new armaments each day. We burned up five-gun barrels. We were in DaNang harbor and there was a special ship stationed there to provide repairs to us so that we didn't have to leave the area. That was a major lifesaver as our support was always needed. One memorable incident that showed us the total appreciation we were getting happened when the C.O. of the ship assisting us sent out a 'Mike boat' (landing type craft) with a hundred cases of beer for us guys. Every guy on the ship got 3 cans of beer. We couldn't drink on our ship, so we had to go down into the Mike boat in small groups and drink our beers there. It wasn't enough to get drunk, but it was a grand gesture. Also, little did we know, the water in that bay was brown water and full of Agent Orange.

"One curiosity Bill; you were one of just 12 guys that were constantly out on the deck. How did it work when one of you had to take a potty break; go eat; catch some Z's, etc.,"

"So, normally we were in General Quarters. When we went out away from shore we were in "relaxed" G.Q. which allowed a laxer time where we could open the hatch and use the ship. When we were in battle situation, we did what we had to. When I was a kid, I never could have done the things I did in my Navy experience. We ran on fumes and adrenaline. It prepared me for my future. When Paula first announced that she was pregnant, she was ecstatic. I, on the other hand could only think of the added responsibility that I would assume. Larry, some things just came with the territory."

As a postscript, I knew (from Facebook) that Bill had a nickname. He was known as "Crash," Recently I asked him the origin and timeframe. He responded, "2007 was the year. The short answer, I had a bike wreck and Paula's friend called me "Crash."

The long answer,

I was training for a Century ride and a triathlon in honor of and in memory of a long list of individuals with cancer. It was part of the "Team in Training" program with the Leukemia & Lymphoma Society.

That day I was going to ride 40 miles and run 4 miles for training.

Paula said I went upstairs and took a shower, left my clothes strewn all over, came downstairs and proceeded to ask her numerous times where the money came from in the bucket. We had done a wine tasting fundraiser the night before and had not deposited the money yet.

Apparently, I scared her, so she called our oldest son to ask him what to do. He spoke to me on the phone and then told Paula to immediately take me to the emergency room.

I remember nothing of all of this.

I remember pulling into a parking space.

I remember someone putting me into a wheelchair.

I remember wondering why they were taking pictures of my shoulder from the wrong direction.

I remember nothing else until much later when we got home.

Later we realized that my helmet was broken in two places. My bike was torn up on the left side. I had suffered a severe concussion and multiple torn tendons in my rotator cuff and a partially torn A.C.L.

The computer on my bike stopped at 14 miles. I later recreated what I could remember of the training ride, and I could not recall anything past a certain point in the ride that was fewer than 14 miles.

We guess that I might have been clipped by a vehicle. Who knows.

What I do know is that God sent some Angels to help me ride my damaged bike home, helped me use the keypad to open the garage and get into the house. I have permanent memory loss of at least 2 ½ hours.

After Paula told her friend what happened, she would call to check up on me and ask….

"How's 'Crash' doing?" It has stuck ever since.

And now, you know the rest of the story.

One last thing to add, that I learned during a lunch we had recently. Bill is now on the Board of Directors of a non-profit here in the Columbus area. It centers around helping two diverse groups. The first one drew him in, as it used horse riding as a means of treating and providing therapy for veterans. The second, uses the same means of helping young people with Autism. He would admit that his experiences have led him to a life of service.

JOHN KEIR

AGE WHEN ENTERED MILITARY: 17

DATE OF ENTRY TO MILITARY: 09/28/1967

VIETNAM TOUR DATES: 05/27/1968-06/13/1972

YEARS OF DUTY/RESERVES: 2

JOHN KEIR

John and I met when I we were both working for Whites Furniture in Columbus, Ohio. I was privileged to work there from 1964-1990.

He was hired to help with the opening of our new Sleep Shop on Morse Rd. This would have been around 1970-1975. He was young and strong and just the kind of guy needed to work with mattresses and hide-a-beds. At the time, I had no idea of his military background. Somehow, many years later, I heard he had health problems related to Agent Orange. When I started this project, I really wanted to include him. At first, I was thwarted, as the phone number I found was apparently old and did not connect me. I almost gave up, but then found what I knew was a "land line" from the Westerville area. I called and he answered! I told him who I was, and he immediately remembered our years together. Once I explained what I had in mind, he agreed to be interviewed. We made a date, and I asked if he wanted to meet for breakfast or lunch.

"Larry, I have severe mobility problems. Could you just come to my house?"

"Of course, John." I was saddened by what he said but had no choice.

I showed up and met he and Joanie, his wife of nearly 50 years. I brought a picture from our days at Whites. He wasn't in it, but he would recognize many of the folks. Figured it would be a good ice breaker. It was! After we reminisced a bit, he said.

"Speaking of pictures, here's one you might be interested in. This is me on May 23, 1969. That's me. I keep it for two reasons. First, look at the trees."

"Oh yeah, I can see they are bare; defoliated. That's the Agent Orange stuff."

"Yep, I also kept it because the guy who took it; a good buddy, was killed the very next day. Byron "Beetle" Bailey. I was teaching him to read maps. Next day he was gone! Yeah, you see I've got a lot of health issues. Heart problems, Diabetes from Agent Orange."

"How much of it do you attribute to Vietnam?"

"All of it. The V.A. has me on 100% disability. That stuff was bad. When they made the Agent Orange, they made it under high heat conditions. It was made with a dioxin. We were drinking water with the stuff in it; getting sprayed by it. Breathing it all the time. We didn't know! We were just trying to stay alive. A lot of us guys now get together once a year in North Carolina. We talk. Doesn't matter what the body type; fat, skinny, tall, short, they all have diabetes. The government fessed up to it finally. I found out I was diabetic in the late nineties. The doctor told me I was likely to have been this way for decades and didn't know it. "

"So, help me out, John. Go back. You were in Vietnam; when?"

"May 68 to June 69."

"So how did you get in the service in the first place? Were you drafted?"

"Nope, I joined the Marines when I was 17; young and stupid. My father had been a P.O.W. in Japan. My mom was in the Navy. They met up at the V.A. hospital in Cleveland. I tell my kids that I'm lucky (and they are as well) that we're even here. My dad was captured in New Guinea and was put on a boat for Japan. They were to be used as slaves. On the way, the boat was torpedoed by one of our ships. He was one of the very few that were rescued.

Eventually, he was sent to the V.A. hospital in Cleveland, which is where he was from. So, I just wanted to do my part. I joined the Marines because I'd heard they had the best training. They really do. They got me physically ready. They do a good job with the mental training, but Larry, there's just no way they can prepare you for the mental part. I was sent to California and entered in language school. I passed the A.L.A.T (Army Language Aptitude Test). One of the last parts of training is called staging. It's supposed to simulate the reality of being in a jungle. When I got there, they made barracks assignments. They said I'm headed to the "casualty" barracks. 'Hey, I'm not sick or injured. Why are you sending me to the casualty barracks? ' "

"Remember that language test you took? Well, you scored a 100% on it. We need you in this spot till we get enough guys to send on to language school."

"So, after we finally got about 40 guys, they sent me up the coast to language school. Spent 12 weeks there. We had North Vietnamese teachers. They were Doctors and lawyers who had to flee south when the war started."

"Guys, these will be the last English words you'll hear in this class."

"Total immersion for 12 weeks. We had 10 phrases a day. We had to be able to read them write them and speak to them. I had my own method. Every day I would buy a Hershey Bar and a Coke. I purposely would unlatch a widow in the classroom before leaving. Then I'd sneak back in after hours. I'd go to the blackboard, write the 10 phrases down. I'd study them, then erase them and see how much I could remember. After a couple of hours, I could write all 10 down and say them. When I got done; then I'd sit down and eat my candy bar and drink my Coke. I'd climb out and sneak away. After the 12 weeks, I tested out as a fourth-year student in all phrases. Now I've spent the last 50 years trying to unlearn it. I can still curse! That's what they taught us first, Larry. They didn't waste any time, as we were quicky shipped out to Anchorage Alaska, then on to Vietnam. When I got there, the first thing I noticed was how red everything was. You've been down south, haven't you? Like in Georgia. Red clay, dirt, and all? Funny thing was, all I knew was that I was going to be in the 3rd. division. Charlie Company preceded us. I reported and was told that the fourth Marine regiment needs men. So, I go there. Ok, the first battalion needs men. Go to Delta one-four. Delta one-four lost eight men yesterday. That's where you're going. I suddenly found out what 'needs men' meant. So, they sent me out to a place called the rockpile. It was kind of a neat place. It was in South Vietnam Nam near the D.M.Z. So, I went to the rockpile with my company. Then they put me in a squad. I met this guy named 'Chimp' who was a Chicano from L.A. He really looked like a chimp."

"Hey, you just got here from boot camp, so we're gonna call you 'B.C.' from now on. So, the nickname stuck. He was my squad leader. He was a real good one, too. He took me out on patrols and basically showed me how to stay alive. This was beyond any training I had before, that's for sure. Now every night we look at that rock which is probably a volcanic rock. That's what we called the rockpile. It stared us in the face every night. There's a place called Camp Caroll about half a mile away. We would mine sweep halfway there every night. It was cool because they sent a tank along with us every night. We guarded them, as minesweepers, and the tank guarded us. After about a week and a half they took us all up to Camp Carroll. Around June 5th, 1968, they picked us up and took us all there, and threw a party for us. I remarked; 'Nice of the Marines to throw us a party!' Pretty soon we learned what the party was all about. They cooked us steaks with all the fixings. Had lots of beer, quite an affair. After I was there for a while, one of the guys that had been around for a little bit grabbed me by the neck and spoke.

"You stupid M.F.; you know what this is really, pal? It's the Last Supper it's our Last Supper. They're being awfully nice to us because they don't expect us to be alive by tomorrow."

"The next day on the 5th., they put us all on helicopters and they flew us to this hill, just South of Khe Sahn. The hill was called L.Z. (landing zone) Loon. When we landed, there was shooting going on already. Delta Company arrived the day before we did. They got chopped up bad. We started digging in and I got a foxhole right next to Chimp. This was our new reality of how we would spend our time. Maybe an hour and a half or so guarding each other in our holes. Sometimes we get to sleep, and sometimes we had to watch, of course. Everything was calm, but there was a lot of movement around. We could tell there was stuff going on. Pretty soon, all hell broke loose. We had a position on a hill. The North Vietnamese were coming up in a human wave. They didn't want us on that hill, that's for sure. We would hear bugles and whistles and here's this human wave coming up the hill. They're coming up in waves, and we're killing them. So, we're up near the top of the hill. It was steep where we were. Chimp tells me I should go down the hill and help some of our buddies who were in trouble down there. So, I got out. I started low, crawling towards the place where they were. So, I pass an N.V.A. (North Vietnamese Army trooper), dead in front of me. I'm crawling down to the third hole. First, to get Marines in front of me, who were in a hole. There was one Marine in the hole that wasn't moving. I'm for sure he was scared out of his gourd. I'm also sure I killed my first N.V.A. in that hole. The scared Marine had a winning strategy. He, unlike his two buddies, who were dead, had a plan. His buddies kept popping up out of the hole and shooting, eventually getting their heads blown off.

He decided to wait till he saw an N.V.A., and then he would just shoot up at them, killing them. Turned out to be his life saver. At this point, I'd been there only about a week and a half. Yeah, I'm an 18-year-old kid, growing up fast! That's the kind of stuff that comes back to me 50 years later, Larry. Today they called P.T.S.D. Back in those days, they didn't have a name for it, but it's the same thing. Flashbacks, stuff that just comes into your head uncontrollably. Here's something, Larry. When we first got married, Joanie and I had a full-size bed. Then we got a queen size bed and finally a king size bed. I kept kicking her out of bed at night! That was as a result of the flashbacks I was having. I never could get through the night without having them, and my reaction was to thrash and kick, and poor Joanie was the recipient of many of those kicks. At night is when all the stuff would come out. At night I'd get the sweats and wake up. Sometimes my heart was racing. I thought for sure I was having a heart attack. One night I woke up and realized that I was in the jungle.

Anyway, later that day, we ran out of ammo. I found a an A.K.-47 on a dead body. I told my buddies; 'don't shoot me, I may have to use this.' Pretty soon we got some new ammo; you know, a box from one of our fellow Marines, as they brought it around and re-supplied us.

Here›s another one, Larry. Just after this, I stepped up out of the foxhole and suddenly, this huge white flash appears right next to me. My buddies in the next hole over, later told me that I flipped over in the air 2 or 3 times! It knocked me out cold. Eventually I came to. It knocked my helmet off, 10 or 15 feet away from me. Finally, I scrambled over and picked it up put it back on; and climbed back up the hill. I ended up taking the ammo can over to the next foxhole and the guys in there looked up at me and they spoke.

"Hey, we were just planning on coming down to pick you up. We figured you were deader than a doornail. Yeah, we saw a mortar round land right next to you. We figured you were gone."

"Well guys, when it blew up, it threw me in the air, and I ended up landing on some North Vietnamese bodies. They cushioned my fall and here I am. Yeah, I guess I was lucky. My flak jacket got all torn up the shredded and my helmet got beat up but I'm still here."

"I had a lot of shrapnel that hit near me. Some of it deflected off my gun as well. Then I had some a smaller shrapnel in my scalp, and yeah, I was beat up. My buddies wanted me to hang it up go to the back. Basically, I refused. I spoke.

"I still have a trigger finger. I can help, and I don't wanna leave. So, I stayed and helped, and they had me do just different things. The worst thing that I had to do was go pick up a body. I got in this foxhole and, uh, all there was left was a guy's legs. Now this guy was still standing up what was left of him, and it was, Larry; it was unbelievable. He was once up on the top of the hill which was the C.P. (the command post.) The guys who were with me said he must have gotten hit by an R.P.G. ;(rocket propelled grenade.) Those things hit and just basically vaporize everything that's in their path. Yeah, we think that's what hit him. Poor guy just was in the wrong place at the wrong time. Had to take those legs out and take them up to the landing zone. They had a cargo net that we put bodies in. So, we then would see these big helicopters come in; hook up to these nets and pull them up and take them to the back. What we saw were a bunch of arms and legs and body parts hanging out the nets. Welcome to Vietnam! Those were 18-year-old kids, Larry. Our skipper was Michael Jackson, yep Michael Jackson. Can you believe that name? Yeah, he's still alive. He's a judge up in Cleveland. Yeah, he called back to the three of us. He was back in the woods, still. Just sitting on a log. He was all messed up too. "

"Men, if you need evacuated just let me know."

I replied.

"Sir, we all have our fingers left. I don't know about them, but I wanna stay."

Jointly, they all agreed. "We do too!"

"Hey, I don't know where you find guys like you, but go back in there. Thanks a lot, here."

So, we went back in. We were surrounded, and we figured we were gonna die right there anyway. What we didn›t know was that we had already killed everybody from that human wave and the N.V.A. came back and got their ammo and got their guns and everything, but they left their bodies there. I didn't know that exclusively until much later, when I was a scout and came back into that area and there were a massive number of skeletons that proved to be the N.V.A., that we killed during that fight. Later, that day, they came and medevacked us all out of there. They took us all back to this place called L.Z. Stud. They sent me to a field hospital where I spent four or five days getting patched up. Larry, I was charmed over there. There would be long times of boredom which was good. Occasionally, we'd have a firefight, either attacking at night or in the morning. We joked with each other as a Marine, that we were just sent there to walk around the jungle till we got attacked, so we could kill somebody. Funny, but somewhat realistic. One very vivid memory was July 4th, 1968. We were on another hill next to Khe Sahn, which was just a hellhole. Khe Sahn was a base. It was real near the Laos border. You ever hear of (I'm trying to think of this name of a gunship there was a there was a dragon name.")

"Was it Puff, John?"

"Yeah, Puff. They had these long lines of tracers. They had two puffs working over, coming in there having us surrounded. These lines with tracers crossed each other. This was a gunship helicopter that we had, yep. Yeah, I remember this one time they gave us a heat tabs to cook with we would get in our holes and light up and try to cook things; but then we were getting shot at. We found out that they were using heat sensors and were locating us by these little tabs that we were cooking with, shooting the hell out of us. Sounded like a hailstorm, unbelievable hailstorm. So, we had these flares, and we were shooting them up in the air and keep in mind it's July 4th. And one of the Marines had a bottle of vodka that his wife sent so we were passing it around taking sips of it didn't take long to get tipsy, Larry. Also, some of the Marines had a radio and so they were playing, (and I'll never forget this) they had on the radio the song California Dreaming. You know that song Larry, by the Mamas and Papas? Yeah, we were all crying because we would much rather be back in California than where we were. Even to this day Larry, if I hear that song on the radio by the Mamas and Papas I must pull off and stop driving. It affects me a lot. It puts me instantly back on that hill. On that same hill, a helicopter landed. This portly Sergeant was hunting for me. So, he pulls me off to the side and speaks.

"Hey, you were in Monterey, weren't you?"

He says:

"I know that you were in school there for language, and we need you right now. We need you to be a scout." I said "Well that would be kind of nice."

"Well Sir, you won›t stand in lines."

"He didn't tell me, that most times I'd be out on the point. First, in July I did some patrols; nothing memorable. But then in August. I was promoted to Corporal. I'd only been in less than a year, and that usually takes a longer time. Yeah, on that day, they transferred me out into the scouts. My buddy, old Michael Jackson, he calls me aside and reads my ass out. He goes; "I just wasted a rank on you. Do you know there are four companies: A, B, Charlie, and Delta? Turns out he's the one that promoted me.

"I forbid you to work as a scout for Delta company."

"OK, I'll work for the other ones, then."

"From then on, I went over to be a scout. I was with field intelligence. Eventually they closed Khe Sahn, and L.Z. Stud became our main base. Eventually they changed the name of it to Vandergriff Combat Base. That was our new rear command. It was big. You could land cargo planes there. Funny thing is a little Side Story; Larry, this guy named Jack McLean. He wrote this book (Loon, A Marine Story.) It was my first battle. That was his last. He got back; got patched up and got sent home. He did his "12 and one." You have no idea how many marines died in their 13th month, Larry. Mclean's grandfather was a U. S. senator. Jack was the "chosen one." He was supposed to go to Harvard, but he joined a Marines and went to Vietnam. He was working in a supply facility out in California, because of his connections. So, one day, one of his officers came in and said, "Hey, we're putting you guys on a plane we're sending you to Vietnam. They need you over there! It's a meat grinder He was in Delta also; same reason I was. He tells his life story in this battle. Anyway, as a scout, I would walk ahead of them lead the patrol. Sometimes I was by myself, and on rare occasions there would be two scouts. Some days we had some Kit Carson scouts. They were locals. They were Montagnard's. They were wild indigenous people who lived in the jungle. They shot monkeys out of trees with crossbows. North Vietnamese treated them like we treated our slaves. Anytime I walked with them I felt safe because they could notice even a leaf being out of place. Occasionally we would even have scout dogs. Most of them were German shepherds. Myself, I managed to walk into one ambush the whole 13. It was on the last day I was there; very careless, is what I did. There were some nasty battles that I got in; that's true. One of them I picked myself in March 68. I was in R&R. While I was gone, Charlie company was almost wiped out. Larry, see that other book over there. Karl Marlantas is the author. I got the book a while back. I was recommended to read it. Things that happened in that book, were so clear to me. Just like I was there. The book is about a thousand pages, but I read it in three days. It was chilling, as it was just like I had lived it."

"John, I have a question. Did you get to use your language skills as a scout? Did you ever encounter an N.V.A. and had to listen to them speak and understood what they said?"

"Larry most of the usage of my skills was this. Occasionally, we'd find a document and I'd be able to read it and understand it, which was very helpful. Saved a lot of lives that way. The Montagnard's. had their own language, but it still is somewhat like N. Vietnamese. It helped me communicate with them. We developed almost like Pig English / Pig Montagnard's. It was funny, but we could talk to each other and pretty much understand, which was very helpful. We treated them like little Marines. Tat Tat was one of my favorites. He was 17 years old; had a wife and three littles. They had a farm out in the jungle. He came back one time with these tobacco leaves that they grew on his farm. They were already cured, and he would roll them up like cigars, and hand them out. They were so strong they almost made us heave to smoke them. We had some good laughs over that, though. Sometimes he would carry a rifle and other times he would carry his own crossbow."

"So, John did they help you or prevent you from being ambushed?"

"One time we were on this trail with Tat Tat. We sat down, and he went off to the side. He signaled for us to get down. 10-15 minutes later he comes out of the jungle carrying two A.K.- 47's. A couple of hundred yards down, we found out where he got them. There were two N.V.A.'s pinned to a tree there. He had shot them with his crossbow. One time I was leading a patrol. We came to this creek. Going around the bend we hear this big crash. We got down. Eventually, this giant lizard like a Kimono dragon comes crashing out of there. I'm sure he knows we're there. He takes this huge drink out of the creek, trudges back through the underbrush. Great stuff. We had been in a National Forest. Lots of animals. We had one Marine that was killed by a tiger. We had some nights that were as dark as could be. You couldn't see your hand in front of you, it was so dark. Must use your ears. Funny thing was they sent out a government hunter to kill the tiger. One night when we were on patrol, we had a group of guys, and we went down into this valley by a river. There's a sand river. We didn't have time to dig holes so we would just take turns sitting guarding for about an hour and a half and then resting for about an hour and a half. Hadn't seen much of the enemy. Middle of the night we hear this growling. We scooch back so we're all close to each other in a circle. Keep hearing all this growling. We were more terrified of it, than our enemy! Anyhow, eventually he went away. I wear a size 13 boot. My foot fit in the paw that sucker. Saw a few elephants too. Later, we were up on hill right in the West-northwest corner of Vietnam near the D.M.Z. We can see off in the distance a herd of elephants going in through the jungle. When we got close to them, we saw them as a herd of wild elephants. Add snakes, cobras. Lots of wildlife for sure. Lot of the stuff I saw in this book that's sitting there on the table.

    Karl Marlantas; it turns out, was a second Lieutenant and was serving in the same area I was at the same time I was. No wonder a lot of the things in this book seemed familiar. He was an officer and he ended up getting the Navy Cross. It›s funny, after I read the book. I got his name off Google on the computer, and I got in touch with him. I wrote him a letter I told him my name and that I was called B.C. I gave my email address. Joanie and I were on our 40th anniversary trip, he answered me. His response was very long and detailed. He did Remember me! How cool is that? So, he asks me if he could communicate with me about a guy in North Carolina. This kid is attempting to gather memorabilia about his father-in-law's time in Vietnam and I›d like you to maybe reach out to him see if you could add to his collection. The kid's amazing. He basically is creating a Nam Museum.

Vietnam was a real adventure. Several times I should have been killed. Several times I was injured by shrapnel. I decided many times not to report it just because I didn't want to leave the area, I wanted to serve out my full term. If I would have turned these in, I would have gotten up to three purple hearts and they would have sent me up where I would have probably been relegated to unloading luggage off the planes there. That wasn't my thing. I wanted to serve out my time. That picture I showed you of the guy that was named Beetle Bailey. He wanted to be a scout. I was teaching him how. We went up to the top of this hill. We saw this big tree at the top that looked to me like a Beech tree; smooth bark you know how they are. One had a bunch of writing on it. I wanted to see what it was and copy it down and see if I could make sense of it. So, we stopped, and I sent him just to keep watch. So, my buddy Beetle, he goes down this one trail which I wouldn't have done, and very quickly he and his buddy got shot in the head. They walk right up to a N. Vietnamese in a hole in a tunnel. They were ambushed and both were shot in the head and killed. I went down there; threw a couple of grenades in the holes and killed a couple of N.V.A.'s. It just happened, and I guess I took it out on somebody. Had to drag the bodies out, and then a helicopter came and took them away. So, I went down a trail along this Creek, to the bottom of the hill.

Our guys would do water runs down to this Creek, every day. They always came at the same time and way. The N.V.A.'s were studying them and getting to know their tendencies. Got to the very bottom of this hill. Larry, I got to the 13th. month without ever walking into an ambush. So, I went down with some canteens to fill. Very first one I filled I heard this pop. It was a Chinese Communist grenade. I turned and immediately started running. Bullets were skipping all over the place beside me. I knew I had about 40 feet to go, and I just decided to basically lay down and play dead. It worked, thankfully. Also, thankfully there were a bunch of angry ass Marines behind me, plus the N.V.A.'s. Basically, it was like laying under a firing range. There were three N.V.A.'s and a Chinese advisor that were shot up right there by my Marine buddies. I was a little teary eyed because I thought I; you know, somehow ended up abandoning my guys. I remember a lot of this, and I end up having survivor's guilt. I should have been killed and others were, and I don't know why all that happened. Another time we were going up this mountain. It was where we saw those elephants. Going along this trail and found this crude booby trap. I stopped and made a quick decision. I went up the trail another 100 yards. Next thing you know I get tapped on the back by couple of my guys, and they say that the squad leader wants to talk to me.

"Drop back and the kid right in front of me, who tapped me on the shoulder walked another few feet and got blown away by a machine gun, right in front of me. Worst thing was he was carrying a L.A.W. like a long aluminum tube. They were they were made to go through anything, up to and including a tank, carrying one of those. So, in addition to getting shot up, he got blown up by the fact that the N.V.A. set off a charge that made his L.A.W. go off. It wasn't pretty, Larry, as all the pieces and parts got blown around. The squad leader I was talking about, set off some rounds up in the air, which was done to draw fire, and it sure did. Larry, you talk about gruesome! That was another one where survivors guilt was in place because I should have been killed there and I wasn't because he was in front of me. Anyhow it was an interesting tour. We fly on Friday from DaNang to Okinawa. When I went back to Okinawa, I had to scrounge around even to find a uniform, as mine was basically blown up in my Sea bag. I was on tour, then I'm on a plane and going back to California. I picked up one souvenir while I was there. It was a Russian rifle; sniper rifle; not an automatic. Couldn't take this one, as it had a sight on it and a bayonet. I was able to keep that as a souvenir. So, when I tried to get it through customs, I met up with this Major who was there, and he looked at me and he says; 'You got papers for that Sir?' I spoke.

"Yes Sir, which I didn›t. He looked at me and he said, "next." The guy Byron, in North Carolina. I wish I would have saved it and given it to him, but I didn›t. He has my hat. I was able to give that to him."

"So, John did you stay, or did you get out after two years?"

"Well, I got out after 21 months. When we got into a group there, our sergeant was very nice. He speaks.

"Go down to San Diego and have some fun. I remember sitting on a wall watching young kids run around. I spent about two weeks down there. At the end of June, they gave me a ticket to get home."

"Hey John, I have a question. Did you get any hassle when you came home; either through the airport or after you got home? Did you suffer any of the abuse that I know a lot of soldiers did? Where the public saw them as a villain rather than a hero."

"When I was in the airport, I had my rifle with me. Nobody messed with me there, that's for sure. I ended up having a standby ticket for Columbus Ohio. Sitting there, and finally they called my name. I heard this stomp, stomp, stomp as I was walking through the airport. This guy comes up to me and says, "Sir, you can't take that gun on the plane with you."

"So, he tagged it and told me I could pick it up when I got home. It was a cool gun. I used to take it to Westerville South when I was teaching there and show it. Got on the plane and sat down. There were a few of U.S. military types. Pretty soon they were calling our names and asking us to come forward. We walk on up there and they end up putting us in first class. How cool! That's only time I ever flew first class! What I wanted to do was fly home, get in a cab, go up High Street to Dunedin, where I lived; then walk down and surprise my parents. Turns out my 'rat ass' brother, who was in the Navy out in California knew I was coming home, and he told my parents. So, there was no surprise. No, they were waiting for me. Came home; tried to assimilate. You know the idea of a baby killer that we were accused of was ridiculous. We were dealing with adults that were trying to kill us and we had to kill them. One time over there I tried suicide. Couldn't achieve it. This one Lieutenant whose nickname was Scar; old Scar, but he was called back, getting nicked all the time and he had probably must have had three purple hearts. He was a good guy. I met him on this long March up a hill into a valley. We were told the watch for the Spider holes, which the N.V.A. had carved out. So, we got up to the top of this hill, Delta company was up there. This has been a nasty hill where a lot of people got killed. But I did something you should never do. Back a way, in Delta company, I met this kid named Steve Byers. He and I became good friends. In fact, we were great friends. This you should never do in combat zone. He was a good, big old laid-back southern boy. We were together a couple of months and did all kinds of stuff. Built ourselves a little hooch with our ponchos. So anyway, I knew Steve was with this company so I asked if I could check and see if he was there. They spoke.

"Well, he›s out on patrol." I went over there, and some shooting started down the hill. I figured he›s been through a lot of those before. It›ll be okay. Then I see these guys. They tell me they had two K.I..A's. Somebody said," They got Steve, B.C." They carried him up showed me him in a poncho. I just sat there and cried like a baby. This was crushing. Scar walks up to me.

"Scar asks me what happened. I spoke.

"Hey, my best friend just got killed."

"Well, my best friend got killed this month too."

"B.C., let's go get em!"

Basically, we made a suicide pact right then and there. We got ourselves a bunch of grenades and ammo. Stupid crazy thing to do, but we walked down the hill quietly. And we found some stuff that led us to believe that we were in the right area. Walked on another 50 feet and there was a small trail. Suddenly, we walk out in this wide-open area and there were a bunch of bunkers. Heads started popping up. So, Scar and I started shooting. It was like; you know that game "whack a mole." Yep, it was like that Larry. We›d just shoot, and they›d go down. Went over the first bunker; shot down in it. Then I took a grenade I knew it had a 5 second fuse on it. I waited two seconds and loped it in the bunker; blew the whole top off the bunker. There were two N.V.A. in that bunker. I shot one in the head just to make sure. So, we were involved with all these bunkers and there were people in them and some of them were carrying packages of explosives. We kept our wits about us and rolled out of trouble three times. Last hole, I was so full of adrenaline. I shot into the hole; dropped my rifle, took out my knife, jumped down in the hole. I could see the N.V.A. soldier holding a rifle right in front of me. I just bull rushed him. I lost my knife taking his rifle away. I just grabbed his throat squeezed and twisted and pulled. Had him pinned to the wall. He tried to scratch me a few times, but I held on until he went limp. I even held on a little longer. I dragged his ass through the top of the bunker and on to the ground. I got my rifle and kept shooting him in the chest, just to make sure. I was, as you can see; I was enraged. As it turns out, I was laughing. I was in my own little world. Pretty soon I hear "B.C.! B.C.! he's dead! Come on." Pretty soon, I hear a bunch of guys coming down the hill. They were coming to save us, but they didn't need to. We didn't need saving. Turns out those N.V.A.'s were a select team that were there to kill a bunch of Marines. But hey, we got them first, so they didn't achieve anything like that. Scar was put up for a Silver Star and I was put up or a Bronze Star. That Bronze Star thing: they told me I was gonna get it, but I never really did. Kept getting all this paperwork that said I was getting a Bronze Star. People kept telling me I probably would get it when I got home, but I never did. I didn't get my Purple Heart till two years after I got out. So technically I never got it.

That little effort was the most. I got six or seven N.V.A. at one time. One thing I regretted; at that first battle at L.Z. Loon, I lost all religion. You know; I'd read the Bible in high school, and we went to Maple Grove Methodist Church on High Street.

I said to John.

"After all, you know; carrying body parts and stuff and shit, I can see you would."

"So, I was sacrilegious from that time on. So, a lot of times I would go down through a trail or a valley and I would say; "I'm the baldest M.F. in this valley."

I further asked.

"John, here's where I wanna fill in a few blanks if I may. So, you were 17 when you come in and 18 when you got out, right?"

I started to O.S.U. at 19. I found out about the lottery shortly after I got to Ohio State and turns out my number was 56, which meant I would have gone quickly anyway. So, I sort of beat that system by enlisting."

"So, John you went to Ohio State, and did you get a degree in education?"

Yep, on the G.I. bill. I Went to Westerville; got a teaching job. You know I was working, so the furniture store got me commission checks. Yeah, I was there earlier, and I was hired to open the sleep shop at Morse Rd. Ralph Defalco hired me and taught me well."

"When did Joanie come into the picture?"

"Spring of 1970; couple days before Kent State happened, we were in the same English class. We started dating, and a couple years later we got married."

"Was she from Columbus?"

"Joanie lived out on the West side. I(we)found out early that being a teacher wasn't all that it was meant to be as far as money goes. I was making $198 every two weeks and quickly found that I wasn't gonna be able to make it on that much money, so I did several things. I worked at Whites, as well as some other places and cobbled together enough money to for Joanie and I live on. So, I came back to Gordon (owner of Whites) and said, 'Hey Sir, I really need to have my job back if I can. I'm teaching, so I won't be able to work full time. If you can stand that, I'd like to come and work as much as I could."

He was great. He let me do that. I got to work at some warehouse sales, and you know how they were. You could make some big money in one day. The most I ever made in one day was 500 bucks, down at the warehouse store! That money really helped me. We had Kevin already, and so we needed money. Anyway, I got my master's degree in 1985. I finally could say bye bye to Mr.

Gordon and Whites' Furniture, as I had enough money to live on finally. That was fun, actually! I was teaching, going to school, and coaching all at once."

"John, I did that same thing too, from 65 to 70 I was a teacher, tennis coach and worked at Whites and going to school getting an M.B.A. I was like you; very driven, full of ambition trying to get done, plus I needed the money."

He told me.

"I taught about 33 years, all in Westerville. I retired about 15 years ago. Played a lot of golf. Joanie was still working. I'd come home and play golf five days a week, walking of course."

"What did Joanie do, John.?"

"She was also a teacher. Anyhow, we were able to raise our kids. Here's my son (shows me a picture). Yep, Kevin was a big boy. He still is. Here's a picture of my daughter and her family. Yeah, that's Krista on the right. She was a shot putter, and a discus thrower and she was the best in the state for a long time. Kevin was an offensive lineman in high school and college. He cleared the way for; you remember kiJana Carter? On every run he ever made, Kevin plowed the way for him. He ended up going to Carnegie Melon. Kevin's an engineer; or, more specifically a mechanical engineer. He works for a company over in the Gahanna area. His wife's name is Kristie. She's an administrator for Ohio health."

"How many grandchildren are there, John?"

"Rosie's a freshman. She's 13. She lettered for being a shot putter. He has an 11-year-old who's a soccer player. Now he's taking up diving. Krista has a 2-year-old and a 5-year-old. She started late. Kids are fun! Krista now lives near Westerville. She lives right down on the other side of Polaris. She married a Guy named John Edward Keipper. Both of our; both my dad and her dad were mail men; bunch of coincidences. Krista works up in Delaware as a school administrator. She started out teaching handicapped kids. She was at Dublin for a while. She ran Dublin Special Olympics."

"So let me ask you a couple of more questions, John. When you got out, you got your schooling, got into the work world, got married and all that. When did the Agent Orange take place?"

"It showed up in the late 90's. A doctor examined me and said that I was diabetic, and probably was ever since I left the service."

"John, what about the P.T.S.D. part?"

"That went on almost our whole marriage."

"So, for all that time in between, from the 70s to the 90's before you realize this had crept up on you; am I correct that you had a typical existence up until then?"

"One thing I did was I chain smoked 3 packs a day. A lot of my buddies that I met down in North Carolina were on their fourth or fifth wife. Me and Joanie hung in there. It was funny when I left Nam, I never looked at a newspaper or anything and I didn't know what was going on over there after I left. I found that three months after I left, they pulled the whole 3rd Marine division out. When I was down in North Carolina one of these guys came up who was in Nam. So, one quick story, Larry. I met this guy in Nam who was from Southern California, and we got together and became buddies His name was Pete. We made a friendly bet because that was a year that O.S.U. played U.S.C. in the Rose bowl. We bet 20 bucks, and it was not real money. It was government issued money and almost like Monopoly money. We bet 20 bucks and so in the meantime he gets a flesh wound and gets medevacked out of there and eventually comes back. He walks up to me and hands me 20 bucks and speaks.

" Hey, you won."

Well soon enough we both won because we got a visit in Nam from Woody Hayes. Wouldn't you know it, he comes over there and he spends some time with us. So, he shows us the film of the whole Rose Bowl game, which was cool, don't you think? "

"Well, that is totally cool, John!"

"Later on, I met Woody personally, and I would have loved to tell that story to him, but I never got a chance to. Pete made it through, too. I grew up right next to campus, so I always held old Woody in high regard. He was my hero! On game days, I used to sell programs on campus. I'd go down there, get a handful of newspapers and programs. Had this crusty old manager, but he'd give me a handful, selling for 10-15 cents each. I found out after a year or so to stand near a guy with a handful of tickets; a scalper you know. I could sell a lot of them that way. Those scalpers always had a few tickets leftover when they got done, so they'd give one to me, and I'd go to the game: great? Then on Sundays we'd get down to the stadium and with our wagons, pick up pop bottles. People would buy them and just leave them there. So, we pick them up take them up the corner store and get the deposit for them. Makes sense, easy money. Did that about every Sunday. When I was seven or eight years old, I used to play Youth League baseball on Tuttle field occasionally, Woody would come walking down to our field and he talked to us. He was a good guy."

"Also, John, I believe you were a coach, along with being a teacher. Did you just   coach golf?

"No, I coached golf, track, and softball, at Blendon middle school. Yeah Krista, she was quite an athlete. She was in the Hall of Fame, as well. She was a four-point student; has two undergraduate degrees, plus 2 master's degrees. Kinda hoping to live for another 10 years so I can see my grandkids grow up a little bit!"

"Well John, I hope you do!"

"Yeah, I played golf year-round, Larry. Played at Little Turtle. Like we'd walk 18 holes almost year-round. Larry, sometimes it had temporary greens didn't matter to me. It was great; I'd see deer and wild turkeys and a lot of times I'd be the only one out there."

"John when did your mobility start being affected?"

"When I was walking the golf course about the 13th. hole my legs would start feeling like cement around that time. Kept getting worse and worse over time. Found out I had heart trouble. They put 4 stents in there. I had some Angina issues. One day I went up to Minerva Park to play golf. They hooked me up there with 2 brothers. I was walking and they were in a cart. So anyway, I told those guys that I was having a heart procedure the next week and that; you know there's a good shot I would never play golf again. Wouldn't it be something if I'd get a hole in one on this last hole I ever played? Anyway, I had a little wedge in there and it went in the hole. Damn if I didn't get a hole in one! it was the 4th one, I ever got. About the time I retired, my health went in the dumper. From the knees down I'm just about totally paralyzed. Ever heard of "drop foot?"

"John, I see you have a van out there."

"I have a motorized wheelchair; weighs about 400 pounds. That van costs about $80,000 decked out. The V.A. got me a fancy wheelchair but there wasn't much I could do with it. It was big and heavy, and I couldn't put it in the car. So, the V.A. approved some things, and now I have it so that I can get up in it and drive it. It's very deluxe. There I have push button remotes that I can get in and out of it pull up to the driver's area I can drive it all with my arms and hands, which is great. I realized several years ago that I wasn't gonna be able to drive because my right leg just wouldn't move from the brakes to accelerator. I was able to get teaching instructions on hand controls. A little girl from the V.A. taught me all I needed to know about hand controls. Did that two hour a week, twice a week for six weeks. I was told it costs $60 for 15 minutes.

I'm so glad the V.A. was paying for it. This past year, I was certified to drive with hand controls. I had to go to the B.M.V.; get a special license, saying that I could only drive with hand controls. I had to go through a lot of B.S.s before I was totally approved but I was persistent and got it.

You know these reunions I go to down in North Carolina; there's something interesting I wanted to tell you about that. The guy that wrote this book; It's a book, by the way, that any kind of politician above the city level should have to read before they make any kind of decisions. He's a real warrior; good guy. He walks around wearing a Hawaiian shirt. His wife's some talented musician. When they come to the reunion sometimes, they come when they're in a nearby big city. I think it's Asheville where she's at. But the guy that wrote this other book, he comes to them also. When he came back, he went to Harvard. When we went to these reunions, we made a lot of friends. Joanie's made a lot of friends too. She's in a wine group. Interesting, there's one guy from up in Michigan. I think he's in Arizona now. His wife dresses like Daisy Duke. You know, the shorts. We'd always stay in the same motel. One time we encountered a bunch of Amish people staying in that same motel. Had a great time talking to them. The Amish: they get to a point in their life they can decide whether they wanna stay or go out of the Amish. They were on one of these missions and staying on our motel for a day or two.

Larry, I've got these skin cancers I've had to deal with. This one (shows me) is my 7th. and I've had two or three more pop out this year. Plastic surgeons did a great job on my nose. They said I was lucky. I might have had a blowhole if they hadn't done it right. Little things pop up. Just like the P.T.S.D. You see a psychologist that tries to cure you. Had this treatment that has a 70% cure rate. What happens to the other 30% I ask? Do they become serial killers? It gave me a questionnaire of 15 questions. All of them were rate them one to five. So, I answered them all. They looked at it and spoke.

"Hey; nothing wrong with you."

"It went through a week by week and I'm getting a higher score every week, but I think it was because I was starting to tell the truth. Now it looked like I was getting worse and worse. One of the things I had to do was write down the worst thing that happened to me, which was the L.Z. thing. Write it down and read it to yourself every night before you go to bed. Next time I go back my psychologist, I finally got done and he says; "Hey this isn't working." So, after several tries, we gave up on each other determining that I was getting worse, and he couldn't make me any better. Then I dealt with some psychiatrists. They, on the other hand give you medicine to try to cure you. Had an Indian woman, Doctor. I go in every three months and talk. First, they gave me this medicine and I slept like a baby. Took it every night. I was down at the V. A. having something else, checking my legs. So, she saw one of the medicines I was taking asked me how long I was taking this one medicine. I told her 13 months. She said, "Oh my, you're only supposed to take that for one month!" No wonder I'm feeling like a zombie. So, we stopped that. So, he pushed me into another medicine. After two or three days I couldn't even focus. Joanie had to drive me around. So, she prescribed another medicine. It was even worse.

"So, let's try this one other medicine that's been working for some of my patients."

So, she gives me a capsule. I took it and it kinda worked. I take it still. It's 5 milligrams a day. It helps me some. I still feel like I'm in the jungle every night, but I can deal with it. I got a bear sleeping next to me who snores like crazy but don't say anything to Joanie about that! She won't like the story. I'm okay. I'm in my own home.

Finally, we decided that I would come on an "as needed" basis and I haven›t been there since."

"So, John it looks like you take medicine every day for a lot of different things, right?"

"Yeah, here's all the pills I take. My blood pressure record was 220 / 120. I have diabetes medicines. I have nerve pain medicine. I used to take 20 pills every morning now I only take 13. Then I take more at lunch and dinner and then before I go to bed. At bedtime I take 5. For my prostate, one for my blood pressure two gabapentin's."

"So, John, do you have prostate problems too?"

"Oh yeah; big time. Have you ever seen these ads on T.V. for what's called the Euro Lift? Supposed to be minimally invasive no cutting. Well, Larry there's only one way to get into your bladder and you know what it is. They go in your bladder, split your prostate; put this thing in there; sort of numbed up. You don't feel what they're doing. Then they just let you down and send you home. While I was healing, I'm peeing out blood clots. I go to the bathroom and poor Joanie would think she was entering a murder scene, right? That was for about a week. Then it calmed down for a little bit. It worked for a while. You know with me, Larry, things do just work for a while and then they end up screwed up. If you ever have anybody wants to do that on you, the Euro Lift; you tell them no!! So, they look around with this scope and me and you know, it's nurses and doctors altogether. it's pretty unsettling that's for sure! Well, they get done and they look at me and he tells the nurse.

"Take him in there and show him how to use a catheter."

I saw my self-respect running down the hall and out the door. From then on, I don›t think anything would ever embarrass me the rest of my life. One time we were traveling. We were in Hilton Head. We were down with some friends and there was a hurricane warning. We had to be evacuated. So, we get in the car and here's me. I had to pee. My catheter's behind me. Finally, I got ahold of it I filled up two water bottles! I had to go. Believe me that was the only time I was ever happy to have those catheters. My new urologist finally took me off the catheters."

I was always appreciative of the Air Force guys that came in and supported us. When I was at O.S.U., I had one class; I think it was an English class during the antiwar demonstrations. There was a demonstration going on in front of my building and there was a Black Panther type guy there who told me I couldn't go in. I told him that I was an ex-marine and that I just got back from Vietnam, and I was paying for these classes, and I was, by God, gonna go in. He just opened the door and let me in. I'm not sure if he didn't wanna mess with me or if he understood that I wasn't the enemy that I was the good guy.

Krista took Joanie and I to a Varsity O event down on campus. It was a backstage look at Ohio State. I got to take my wheelchair. Took my chair down the ramp that the band comes in on. They had a lot of different athletes and former athletes that were on the field, and we took a lot of pictures. Then we went up the ramp the football players come down. Got to go up in the press box. Everybody that comes has an assigned seat. Then they took us down to the Huntington club where all the luxury boxes are. So, we›re at a table for 8 or 10. On the back of my wheelchair I have a Semper Fi Marine sticker. So, a guy yells at me. He was an officer in Vietnam, same time I was over there. He was in the First Division. I was in the Third. We chatted for a little bit. Anyhow he sat down right across from me we talked for a while. We used to play Columbus Academy in golf. John McCloy III came to Academy and suddenly were playing New Albany Country Club instead of The Gahanna Golf course. So, this Marine I was talking to on the other side of the table; he's listening to me tell all these golf stories.

"I know John McCoy. He was my boss. He was the C.E.O. of Bank One. I was the president. Now I see why you're talking about your second house in Florida and your other house here in Tartan Fields. That was the guy I was talking to. He's bitching about the price of the football tickets.

He speaks.

"Hell, I fund two scholarships here, and they still charge me full price for tickets. My mind went to; 'Wow, what a big problem you have Sir.' We were there three hours; had a great time.

"Hey John, I see you yawning. I've got to go anyway. I can't thank you enough. Not only did I get to talk with you, but I also got a bonus couple of hours. The stuff we talked about will be in my brain forever. You were and are an American hero. Thanks again."

BILL (ARNIE) LAMP

AGE WHEN ENTERED MILITARY: 22

DATE OF ENTRY TO MILITARY: 07/1964

VIETNAM TOUR DATES: 12/1966-04/13/1969

YEARS OF DUTY/RESERVES: 5

BILL (ARNIE) LAMP
FEATURING JEFF LAMP AND DEBBIE LAMP

Arnie was a year older than me, and we crossed paths many times while we were students at Otterbein. In retrospect, I wish I'd known him better. At Otterbein, we were in different frats. He was in Zeta Phi, and I was in Pi Kappa Phi. In those days, we were rivals.

Back in October of this year, I volunteered at the Otterbein "O" Club golf outing. While waiting for my assignment, I ran into Wendy Roush. I knew who she was, but never much talked with her. Somehow in our conversation, the subject of my book came up. She asked me if I'd ever heard of Arnie lamp. I told her, of course that he and I were at Otterbein together; one year apart. She spoke.

"Well, he and I are second cousins. If I could get in touch with his brother, would you be willing to talk to him as part of your investigation into what you're trying to do in your epilogue?"

I said that would be great and she began to effort in my behalf to hook me up with Arnie's brother Jeff. After a brief vacation, I was able to reach Jeff by phone and we agreed to meet at a restaurant in Granville, where his home is. He handed me an article to look at before we even started. It was in the Buckeye Lake news. Which is a local paper for Buckeye Lake. Here's what it said about Arnie.

Arnold "Arnie" Lamp Jr. was from Hebron. He was a 1960 Lakewood graduate and Otterbein College (now University) graduate in 1964. On December 4th, 1968, Captain Lamp started his second tour in Vietnam and was stationed at Tan Son Nhut Air Force Base just outside of Saigon. He was a pilot flying the RF4-C

Phantom 11, a two-man aircraft armed with cameras and infrared detection devices, but no weapons. His missions were to fly at night or during the day looking for enemy activity. On April 12th, 1969, Captain Lamp and his navigator, Charles Mattern, took off on what would be Captain Lamp's last mission. Over the jungle at 10,000 feet, the aircraft started having trouble. Lamp ordered Charles Mattern to eject, which he did, and was recovered. But for some reason, Captain Lamp was unable to eject. Search crews were sent with no avail and on April 19th, 1969, he was listed M.I.A. (missing in action) at age 27. They assumed he could not have survived under those conditions. When the war ended on April 30th, 1975, his body still had not been recovered. There was an attempt in the 1980s to recover his body with the help of Vietnam Veterans. Their search was unsuccessful. On December 13th, 1993, the Vietnamese government allowed the remains, which proved to be that of Captain Lamp, to be returned to the United States. He was laid to rest at Glen Rest Memorial Estate in Reynoldsburg. Arnold Lamp was inducted into the Wall of Fame at Lakewood High School on September 16th, 2016. This short article is one where Arnie and his life was given to us in brief. By talking to his brother Jeff, I got a lot more insight into Arnie lamp the man. Also, I got a chance to speak to Debbie Lamp, his daughter. More on her perspectives later. Now a little bit about Jeff Lamp.

Jeff Lamp

He's Arnie's younger brother. Interestingly, Jeff told me that Arnie grew up as Bill Lamp. When he went to Otterbein, he somehow became known as Arnie. Jeff thought that was kind of curious but made not too much more out of it. He and his brother and an older sister grew up in Harbor Hills, Ohio which is near Buckeye Lake, southeast of Columbus. I learned that Jeff went to Otterbein as well. Jeff was 10 years younger, but took an extra year to graduate from Otterbein, so that happened in 1975. Arnie joined R.O.T.C. and later, the Air Force. Jeff went on into the business that the family established years before which was the lumber business. As it turns out that same career was waiting for Arnie once he got out of the Air Force. Sadly, that was cut short by his untimely death, and as Jeff so aptly put it, this event was so devastating to the family, especially mom and dad. Jeff himself broke down a few times while we talked, and I could tell that he loved his brother deeply and was very proud of him. He told me that he was in military school in Florida and was talking with his mom on the phone; when she excused herself to go to the door and answer it. Turns out that whoever was at the door brought her the news that Arnie was missing in action. This later of course, changed from M.I.A. to K.I.A. That means killed in action.

Arnie married his high school sweetheart. Turns out they were next door neighbors in Harbor Hills.

"Wendy Roush was a senior when I was a freshman."

"So, Jeff; tell me about Arnie's Vietnam journey."

"Larry, here's what I know. In his first tour he was a co-pilot on big planes that were used for refueling. A KC-135. He came back from that, and I think he just had the 'need for speed.' So, he ended up getting into F-4 Phantom jets. He became a reconnaissance pilot. He loved flying. It was a real passion for him. Dad always wanted him to take over the company. The last letter: his last letter to his parents, basically told them he was going to get out of the Air Force and come back and get involved with the company, which I'm sure made them happy, of course. That also really made everything that much harder for my parents, right? Mom and dad never really recovered after this happened. I was in military school at the time in Florida. That phone call I told you about. That's when everything started. Somebody had been to the crash site and his canopy lock was intact. They couldn't do any excavation at that time, but they assumed he was dead. We had the funeral service. Maybe 7-8 years later, we get this letter. I think it was through the embassy. A family in Vietnam had his remains and wanted a mere $100,000 to have them released to us. So, mom and dad said.

"Absolutely not! We don't know if it's his."

Few more years go by, we have three or four sponsors who want to go to the crash site and excavate. Turns out they didn›t have the wherewithal or the ability to get things done, so that was unsuccessful. So, in 1994 the government got back to us and said that they had these bones; the same ones that the family had. It was a femur and a jawbone. They did some D.N.A. testing and did verify that that was indeed my brother's remains."

"Jeff, do you have any other siblings?"

"Yes, I have a sister. She passed away a few years ago from rheumatoid arthritis."

"Was she older or younger?"

"She was two years older than Bill (Arnie)"

"Sounds like your parents endured more than most parents should ever have to. I'm sure it had a profound effect on you as well Jeff, right? Me bringing it up probably opens some wounds that didn't need to be, and I apologize in advance for that."

"No problem. When he came home after his first tour; this may have no bearing on the story at all Larry, but I'm going to tell it to you. During the time he was home, between tours, he was getting back with his wife; not that they were having any problems, but just the natural stuff that would take place when guy comes home and must spend limited amount of time with his wife and two girls. Larry, when I was headed to the bus stop to go back to school. When all this was happening. I had this totally strange feeling in my heart that I'd never see my brother again."

"Wow Jeff, that's profound. Thank you. I guess I can understand Jeff; you had a brother in a wartime situation that was full of guys that already hadn't come back and for you to think like that wasn't totally unusual.

Tell me about Arnie and his bride. When did they get married and how did that come about?"

"Well, he was in flight training in Oklahoma. She (Judy) went down to visit him. Soon after that they were getting married; (obvious reasons; wink; wink). While he was in Vietnam, Arnie and Judy would converse with each other. No cell phones then, of course. They each had a reel-to-reel tape recorder. They recorded stuff that they talked about back and forth over the years. Debbie, his daughter has these tapes and converted them to a C.D. They had a younger daughter named Laura. She was a Rubella baby. So, Laura grew up with some challenges. She went to Gallaudet which is, as you know, a college for the deaf, right? She's a great girl. She works at a great job and lives with Debbie. They live together in Dayton. Debbie works for Wright state University in Dayton, and she has a job basically coordinating all the on-campus activities of the school. She deals with the frats, sorority's, clubs, etc. She manages all of that for Wright State. She also graduated from Otterbein and has a master's from Capital University. Neither Debbie nor Laura knew much about their dad except from what they learned through their mom and through the newspaper clippings that were kept of course, and especially what she learned through the C.D. that she made about the memories that they had together. Judy's father was a chemical engineer for Owens Corning in Newark. That's why they were in this area in the first place. They were our next-door neighbors in Harbor Hills. He ended up changing jobs and went to New Jersey. Judy moved out there with the two daughters to be near them and was a schoolteacher, till she retired. She went to O.U., not Otterbein. When Judy retired, she moved to Toms River N.J. and retired there. Debbie took a job with Ohio Wesleyan, in Delaware. Judy bought a house in Delaware, to be near the girls. When Debbie took the job down at Wright State, they bought a big enough house so that all three of them could live together and not run into each other. Judy passed away from cancer. She had breast cancer but beat it. Then about seven or eight years later it reappeared. She was a fireball. She wanted to do something she had in her mind, she did it. Full speed ahead! That's the kind of person she was."

"Did you have a fair amount of interaction with the Judy and the girls?"

"Yeah, some. Mom died in 04 and dad died in 07. Mom fell and broke her hip and never recovered. My dad had a series of mini strokes. TIA's, I believe they're called. He came to visit in 07. My cousin was sort of looking after him in Florida. They lived in Sebring FL. Mike; my cousin was looking into dad's wellbeing. They put him on a plane, and he came up to Ohio. Within a couple of weeks, he had another episode. This one was bad enough that we needed to get him some help, so we put him into an assisted living place called Kendall. They had him in pretty good shape for a guy that was 91 years old at the time. I would pretty much stop at least three times a week on my way home. I'd visit and read to him. I feel he just decided that he didn't want to live any longer, Larry. He was there for 100 days. At that point we knew he had to make a change. We would probably have to move and go from Kendall to somewhere less appealing."

"I understand, Jeff. That had a lot to do with the insurance that he had, I'm sure."

"We had the room ready. All the furnishings; everything was ready for his move. They called me the morning he was supposed to move and said, 'Jeff, your father passed away this morning.' He ended things on his own terms. That was my dad. He even said that you can live too long, and he thought that he had lived too long. Up to the end he was very sharp which frustrated me because I thought that he had years to live. He was so sharp mentally. My wife's father: on the other hand, had early onset Alzheimer's. He was really a smart engineer for Kraft Foods. He was physically strong, but he had Alzheimer's. Then there's dad, who was failing physically, but mentally strong. My dad had all his faculties until he died. We always kidded each other and said that if we could have put our two fathers together, they'd both probably still be alive."

"Jeff, where did you and your wife grow up?"

"Well, she was growing up in Galax, Virginia. Her father got transferred to a town on the Ohio River between Portsmouth and Cincinnati, so she went there her junior year in high school and then went on to college at Morehead State in Kentucky. She wanted to be a teacher, so she ended up being a teacher. Then he got transferred to Coshocton. She ended up moving to Granville and teaching in Newark. That's where we met. We moved, as a couple, in 1988, to Granville, and have lived here ever since.

"Larry, I do a lot of writing in my work, and I know are how hard it is to edit things especially conversation right specially if the editor doesn›t know exactly where you›re coming from."

"Jeff, remembering living on Buckeye Lake, did you like that when you lived there?"

"It was a great place to live! It was a different time. It was a brand-new community. It had its own golf course and tennis courts. Everybody their kind of knew each other. What a great place! Lot of kids grew up together. We all knew each other; classmates, etc.

The place we live right now is right across route 61, and we've lived there since 88. We stayed there, but lots of people moved out. We raised our kids there. It was a great place. Now these days it's turning back to what it was originally with younger kids there, and young families. When we were at Buckeye Lake, we had a boat. In fact, we had two boats. Dad had a Chris Craft, and we had a kind of an old beater boat. In May, while school was still in session, us guys would all get up about 4:30 in the morning. We would get the boat; go out and go water skiing and be back home; showered and on the bus in time to go to school. Pretty amazing when you get out on the boat at sunrise! It's like water skiing on glass."

"How many kids do you have, Jeff?"

"I have two daughters. Both graduated from the University of Kentucky. The oldest is an architect/commercial interior designer. The youngest; she always was outgoing; never knew a stranger. All that we heard was, she went to a job fair her senior year. The person who is doing the interviews graduated from the University of Kentucky. She worked for DFAS in Indianapolis. It's the biggest government building in the United States other than the Pentagon. It has 4100 people. That office did all the financials for all the branches of the services and all the government. They write the president's check if you know what I mean. She's an accountant there. She's not a CPA but has accounting background. People just gravitate to Her. She met a guy there and he eventually became her husband. He's in counterintelligence; took a job in Washington DC. She sure enough moves to Washington. Initially, she worked for the Marine accounting office in the Pentagon. While she was there, she got a job opportunity to go to Kuwait We questioned her when that happened, but she said,' Well gosh why wouldn't I go there? When I get my tour over, I'll have all my student loans paid off and literally hundreds of thousands of dollars that I can bank.

Pretty hard to disagree with her, wouldn't you say? They asked her to go to a certain city and pick up a dignitary. 'OK I'll do that.' While he was there, she was the liaison. She planned everything for him. He decided quickly that my daughter was the berries. This guy had a son who was my daughter age. He and she hit it off, good chemistry. When he comes back the Admiral tells everybody to ask for Ali. So, she's getting all the dignitaries that come to the base and she gets to squire them around; helicopters and everything. Next thing you know she's just moving up and up. Then her husband got transferred to Germany. She loves to travel. He was on a one-year tour but kept on re-upping because he liked it so well. So, they've been to every country in Europe except 6. She gets a little tired of this whole a business and one of her general friends found out she was looking for a job, so she gets to oversee all Northern Africa for this one general. She's a civilian contractor, while her husband is in the Reserves. Eventually her contract went through, and she had to go come back. So, she got a job with the Air Force, but eventually got out of it because she realized that this operation was about as basic as any she'd ever seen, and she didn't like it. She said they were undisciplined, and she couldn't stand that. Once again, word got out that she was looking for a job and now she is the Asian director to the secretary of the Navy. She just loves it. She just had a baby a year and a half ago. Her husband now works for Deloitte. He's an expert in setting up systems and they use him for that. He goes in. He has all the levels of security, so he goes in ahead of an office to see how it runs, through their questions and answers he feeds this back to Deloitte, and they set up the accounting systems so that's what he does. He hates it but it's a means to an end and he does it.

So, my oldest; she's off the charts. She floundered in Kentucky. She got good grades, but she didn't know what she wanted to do. I tried to talk her into going into the Army or something, just to get some discipline; get some idea of what she wanted. So, we spent six years at the University of Kentucky to the tune of $175 grand. She ended up with a marketing degree. If she would have just said; 'I wanna go into architecture, I could have gotten her scholarships just with my influence. So, finally, she decides she wants to be an architect. I told her if you do this, you're going to end up going backwards, in two years to get all your math requirements before you can go into grad school. But she did it anyway, and she did well. Her husband: high school sweetheart, is a landscape architect and planner. They live in Salem Ma. Both are doing well. They had a baby in August."

"Larry, she doesn't really wanna go back to work. She also wants to be closer to her sister, so her husband wasn't happy anyway about where he was at in life, so they ended up moving to Washington, DC to be close to sister and get a new opportunity for him. So now he has a job in DC with an extremely large architectural landscape firm. They live 3 1/2 miles from sister and everybody is happy; including us! So, now they're in one place. It'll be easier for us to travel there get to see them. We're going to be able to see them around Presidents Day."

"Jeff, here's a little Side Story that you might find interesting. I have another Otterbein connection with some dear friends that are a year younger than me. We've been friends ever since and Jean; the wife; had a cousin with a similar name to yours. Lamb, and Roger Lamb was a classmate of mine. Now he has an older brother named Bill Lamb, much like your brother. And brother Bill was in the Air Force and flew refueling planes, probably even at the same time Arnie was in Nam. He has told Roger who then told my friends, that he was in the air and heard some messages; airborne messages that were from your brother, shortly before he went down. Now that's not something I can confirm, but at least I can tell you that it came from a pretty good resource."

"Larry; Just a sidebar from what you were talking about. Otterbein has a room in the library that has a plate with Bill's name on it. That is; Arnie's name on it. So next time you're there why don't you go see that.? The placement of the plaque probably had a lot to do with Dubs Roush. They; my dad and Dubs were buddies and knew each other well. I believe Dub's wife was a Lamp, and therefore that's the connection between you and Wendy Roush."

"My brother was a good guy. When he was in Vietnam, he never liked to sit around; unlike me. Whenever he had spare time on weekends or whatever, he would go with one of the best doctors at Ton Son Nhut. They would end up giving medical attention to the local people in the nearby villages. He did that with a high degree of frequency. I hope you can get this CD it will give you the essence of my brother's life. He was a family guy, a good guy.

Larry, I have six months and 11 days before retirement. That'll be my 70th birthday that's why I chose that time. The Strait part of our business Strait and Lamp, happened this way. Mr. Strait and my dad started the business and then he; Mr. Strait, passed away early rather than late. I think he was 44, massive heart attack. Suddenly, the business part is up in the air. First, his wife decided she was going to take over his part, but she quickly learned that she did not like it. In fact, she hated it and just came in and announced,

"I'm out"

"How much do you want?" My dad asked. He paid her off and that was it? His son was two years older than Arnie. He had all the background and went to work for a wholesale lumber broker. He did that for about 15 years. I graduated from school. The assumption was, I take over the business. We decided to go to the bank get the money and everything would be good. At the time, honestly, I didn't have a pot to piss in, and even less of a place to throw it out. The bank said, "Hey, isn't your father supposed to give you the business?" but they didn't know my dad, and he wasn't about to give me the business. My dad wanted to retire. So, the Strait, the oldest son; went in and spoke.

"Arnold, I've done this long enough, are you interested in selling?" My dad said yes and was able to retire. At that point, I stayed on. We hit it off. He's 83 now and does all the commodity lumber buying. He's still active. He spends winters in Florida. He took really good care of me. He made me a stockholder in the company. About 6 years ago, his son in law and daughter decided they wanted to buy the company. Web, the dad comes to me and tells me of Steve's intentions. "Jeff, before Steve can buy your stock, he must buy all the outstanding stock. So, here's the price. Basically, it was a lotto hit for me, Larry. "So, what do you want to do now, Jeff?"

"Well, I want to stay on and keep doing what I have been. I've basically done everything.

Web Jr. had 4 daughters. One of them married a guy. He was made manager of the Hebron store. Didn't work out. 'We're getting a divorce.' Web slammed that right away. 'You're out of here!' This was in 2007. You know what happened in the economy in 2007-08, right?"

"Yep"

"So, Web comes to me and tells me about Brian and announces that "I'm now the manager."

Whoa…. I don't want to be the manager. You know how I am with people. That's not what I'm good at." So, I have no say?"

"Nope."

"So, he tells me. 'Sometimes for success, it's not what you do, skill wise, but more a matter of luck.'

Just before the business crash, we unconsciously did something that turned out very lucky!! We paid off all our debt. Paid for our buildings and land, and even our inventory. Had zero debt. We had a reasonable accounts receivable. So, the economic conditions took all the central Ohio lumber yards out of business except one and that was Fifth Ave lumber. And they were doing gangbusters. They just figured out a way to do business when nobody else could. Web told me; ' Hey son, you got to sell your way out of this.' Before I did that gig as the manager, I was the corporate sales manager, so I did know how to sell, Larry. I just didn't have a lot of confidence in myself. I spent a huge amount of time learning how to be a good salesperson.

Larry just to show you how the economy affected things. I had a young guy that was a terrific salesperson and in 05 he sold 70 homes (that is one of his customers did). In 06 that went down a little bit, but it was still high number. But in 07 he literally went down to; he did 7! I went home and told my wife 'I hate to have to do this but I›m going to have to become a salesperson, as well as a manager.' Next morning, I walked in, and my right-hand man was developing a relationship with a young man that came in. Didn›t know him from Adam, but he introduced me to him We hit it off. He became the production manager for Maronda Homes. They were big. They owned their own lumberyard. They owned their own truss plants. We did business with them because we could finish off their houses. I told him; 'we'll take care of that kind of thing and keep you guys closing homes and that would be great.' In 08 we did about 800 to 1200 a month with them. In the meantime, I started developing some heart issues. I went into Web and told him I›m going to have to do nothing but sales. I›m not going to be the manager anymore. So, he hired a manager, and I spent all my time with my Maronda connection. Now I›m the only salesperson, and they're my only customer. Last year with them alone, and me alone, we did 14 million! How about that.? So, my wife alerted me quickly.

"You're going in at 5:00 o'clock in the morning. You're coming home at 11:00 o'clock at night. You're going to die Jeff!"

"So, that's when I decided it was time. I told them; you'll need to get somebody to replace me because as of August 13th I'm gone. So, they hired a couple of really crack people. They're both females. The main one, wouldn't know a two by four from a floor system, but she gets behind a computer she is as good as it gets. Her estimates are always right on the money and nothing you must do to check her work, the perfect employee. She's going to take over my job and be the salesperson for the Maronda account. We hired another person to do the windows and doors and another to do the service. And then an executive assistant to the girl who replaced me. Took four people to replace me, Larry. I felt pretty good about that. If you can get closings done on time Larry, you'll own an account. Nobody argues about the pricing. They just want service. That's what we've gotten so good at.

"Great, for you, Jeff!"

"I've instilled in my people that 'close enough' isn't good enough. You've got to be striving to be perfect every single day.' I'm getting there, Larry. I've got six months to get it done, and in August, I'm done.

"Jeff, any idea of what you're going to do after you retire?"

", we're going to travel. In fact, my daughters bought us a ticket to Iceland. I've always wanted to go there, so we're going to do that. We also wanna take in, and make sure we do all the states, so we're going to finish that project."

"Great, that's perfect. My Barb and I did that and thought it was one of the best parts of our lifetime, getting that done."

"I did most states before I graduated from high school. My parents loved to travel, and they took us kids with them. Don't much like the idea of Florida. Too hot! Too many bugs. We have looked at a condo in Southern Pines. In the Pinehurst area."

"Jeff, I'm very familiar with Pinehurst. What a great place. Good climate most of the time and very laid back."

"Oh yeah." The other big advantage of Southern Pines is that it has an Amtrak that stops there. 4.5 hours door to door to our daughter's places. "

"I assume you are a golfer?"

"At one time I was a one handicap. During the time, when I had the most time, I would hit balls for hours. I got damn good at it. My dad grew up in Harbor Hills. His dad was a builder. They built barns, post, and beam barns. Have you ever spent time in Reynoldsburg? Right where Livingston and McNaughten roads cross was a huge barn that they built. My dad's dad owned the land that our company is now on. So, my grandad got involved with the development and building at Harbor Hills. When they started, the first thing they built was the golf course. My dad and his brothers would caddie.

Jack Nicklaus had a Pro-Am tournament every year. My dad played every year. He had two buddies, and they played every year. The three of them would draw a pro and they participated every time. They had a pro like Orville Moody, Gary Player, or even Jack himself. My dad had all the shots. One day at Scioto, they were at the second hole. Orville was their pro. He hit a drive that left them a tough shot around a dogleg. My dad hit around it and was just a few feet from the hole in two. Orville proclaimed.

"Arnie, that was simply the best golf shot I've ever seen." In his 70's and 80's he constantly shot his age and better. My brother was a great golfer as well."

"Wasn't he on the golf team at Otterbein?"

"He sure was. He lettered every year."

"Well, I'm going to let you go."

"Larry, I apologize. Me thinks I've given you way more than you came for."

Jeff, the privilege was mine. I got the story of your brother and more. Thanks so much!!

Debbie Lamp

I got a double bonus when Wendy Roush led me to Jeff Lamp. He asked if I knew that Arnie's daughters were in Dayton. We talked and he reached out to Debbie, the oldest. I was thrilled to get some words and thoughts from her. I was able to speak with her for about an hour. Jeff also told me about a "reel to reel" tape that existed. I asked her about it, and she was able to email me a copy. It left me speechless. The conversation was one sided only but contained Arnie's voice and his thoughts from over 50 years ago. By listening to it, I can confirm the type of man, husband, father, son, brother that my friend was. Listening to all three was a treasure. Arnie Lamp was a hero.

Here's some of my conversation with Debbie.

"Pat King and my dad were great friends. He was on the golf team. My mom and us girls have kept in touch over the years.

"I understand you have a sister, Laura?"

"That's correct. She has a nickname, 'Noughie' in case I call her that.

"Tell me what you do at Wright State. I understand that you're the VP of everything; right?"

"Oh, that's a good one !!" I'm the Associate Director of Student Involvement and Leadership. I have my hands in a lot of different areas, as you might imagine. I'm starting my ninth year here. I work with the student newspaper the radio station the programming board, student associations, and secret spirit society. I oversee the student workers in our office."

"Have you had to work remotely since the pandemic, or do you go into the office?"

"I love working remotely. I didn't think I would, but I really love it. Right, we worked Thursday and Friday remotely, because of the snowstorm."

"The pandemic has changed things, hasn't it?"

"Sure has. We used to need buildings for everything; to house offices and everything like that. But now with the idea of zoom meetings, not so much.""

I sort of saw that coming, especially in college. There's no such thing as the 'snow day' anymore. people have access to computers, and we can do just about anything remotely."

"Spent a couple of hours with your uncle Jeff in Granville the other day. I've never met him before, but we hit it off and I found him to be a very good person to interview about his brother. I could tell he loved his brother Arnie, for sure."

"You know, I frankly don't remember a lot about my dad because I was only two when he left and three when he died. I know this; that if I'd have been a boy, I would have been Arnold William Lamp III; sort of glad I'm a girl; hah hah."

"I believe it. You sure did get a better name. If you were a boy, you would have probably been called Trey."

"So, you were three and your sister would have been one. She probably doesn't have any memory at all about your dad; does she?"

"Sounds like you guys moved to New Jersey and lived with your mom's parents after this happened."

"I was born in New Jersey, at Dover General Hospital. My grandparents lived in Sacra Sauna New Jersey. You probably know this, but my grandparents lived next door to Arnie in harbor hills."

"So, your mom grew up next door to Arnie and met him there. At some point they started dating each other fell in love and got married, right?"

"Well, the story is that during spring break, my mom went down to Texas to visit dad while he was in flight training. During that trip and visit, I came around (hah, hah, hah); so, they got married because of that. So, it was a good thing!"

"So, a little bit of drama, but nevertheless."

"I understand that happens sometimes with first children."

"Debbie, when did your mom pass away?"

"2015. She was born on veteran's day and passed away on Pearl Harbor Day. Kind of easy to remember."

"Debbie I can relate. My wife passed away on my daughter's birthday, so neither one of us will ever forget that day. We choose to celebrate it instead of mourning it."

"My mom was a real trooper."

"Now Jeff tells me that all three of you lived in the same house in Dayton. Isn't that correct? That's where you still live, correct?"

"Yep."

"Did you consider that to be a good thing, living with your mom?"

"Oh yeah! When we moved here, I wanted to work on a P.H.D. So, buying this house, I didn't have any kind of a rent payment and we were all together. That was a good thing as well; especially after my mom got sick. You know I think sometimes that she probably had a premonition that she was failing and, in the house, together was a good thing for everybody. Turns out Laura and I've lived together for quite some time, and we get along famously. We love living together and that's never been a problem."

"Now tell me Debbie. Did you have a lot of interaction with the Jeff's family?"

"Oh yeah; we saw them at least once a year. We either went to Florida or we spent time in Ohio, at Harbor Hills. My mom was a teacher, so she had summers off, and we would often go to Ohio and spend quite a bit of time there. We were lucky because a lot of families like ours don't even know the dad's side of the family, but we did. We were so lucky because we did. They were so supportive of us and loved us and wanted to be around us. We were a connection to my dad for them. Sometimes when we were there, my grandma would hear something we said and breakdown in tears, just because it affected her so. Once she told me that after looking at me, she had to walk away because I had some mannerisms that my dad possessed. She noticed that and was very very emotional about it."

"I know just by talking to Jeff, that your grandparents were deeply affected by your father's passing. Never got over it. I'm sure that's not unusual but it worked certainly to make you guys wanna be close to them."

"How I got involved with the Jeff and with you guys; I›ll just refresh your memory. It was through Wendy Roush. Wendy and I met. I knew who she was, but we met more formally at the "O" Club golf outing at Otterbein this fall, on Columbus Day. She and I got to talking about my book and she said to me; 'Oh, you've got to interview Arnie Lamp's brother. So, she efforted to get me together with Jeff and of course Jeff then efforted to get me together with you and that›s how this is all happening today. Which I think is a 'God thing' that this is all coming together so well.

"Have you ever met Wendy?"

"Well, I know that she's a second cousin of mine or third cousin maybe. I know that her dad, Dubs, and my grandpa Lamp, were first cousins. We've been to their house and everything. When I was at Otterbein, I was a student trustee, and he was the chairman of the board. Turns out he in my grandpa look a lot alike, real piercing eyes and oversized ears. Sometimes I think there are only about 6000 people in the world, and it doesn't take us long to figure out a common thread that we can have with somebody. When I worked at Ohio Wesleyan. I found a girl there that was last named Roush and I asked her if she was related to the Roush family that I knew. She said Dubs Roush was her grandfather. There always seems to be a connection!"

"At any rate, I'm so happy that she led me to you and your uncle. Isn't Dubs Roush's wife named Lamp?"

"No, Dubs mom, and Grandpa Lamp's mom were sisters. So that makes my grandpa, Dubs Roush's first cousin. So, Dubs and Arnold Sr. were first cousins. The Roush's used to sponsor the family reunion at their house in Westerville."

"I understand that you; pardon me if this is not available to me, but I understand that you have a thumb drive that is taken from an old reel to reel tape of your father speaking while he was in Vietnam. Is that correct?"

"Yes, it is Larry. I'll try to get that for you. I know I have it somewhere, but I'm not exactly sure where. Laura and I only heard that after my mom died. We knew about it and had even seen the tape player. Apparently, we talked on tape to him as well. As kids, we didn't talk much about him. We knew that he had died. My mom and my grandparents were somewhat frustrated with me because I wanted to hear about that, but they didn't seem to wanna tell me. I understand that because it's hard to do. One time when I was at dinner with aunt Louise, who was Uncle Jeff's sister, I was efforting to talk about that. She just simply said; 'drop it, Debbie.' So, I know that they also found it hard to talk about, which was obvious when they stopped me from talking about it. Did you ever hear of how Uncle Jeff heard about it?"

"Yes, Jeff told me about that, and he also told me about how it affected his mom that day and in general, how it affected them over the rest of their life."

"From the reel-to-reel tapes we became aware that my dad was there twice. We never talked about that at all. Evidently, he volunteered to go the first time, and then was sent the second time. We didn't know that. We've requested his records, but there's like a three-year backup. I hope we get them sometime. I don't know if we'll ever see them. There's a guy over in Licking County that you might wanna talk to as well. His name is Doug Stout. He works on the history of Vietnam, and specifically the veterans from Lincoln County. Doug works at the Licking County library.

My dad sounds like a saint, from what everybody tells me. I always want somebody to tell me something about him that was more human, but I guess it's OK that I keep thinking of him as a Saint. Even listening to the tapes, I think to myself; 'is that what he really sounded like and is that what he was thinking at the time?' Seems to me like he ought to sound like my uncle Jeff, or my grandpa. He doesn't; though. He has a unique sound of His own."

"When you were growing up in New Jersey, you spent a lot of time with your mom's parents, right?"

"Yes, they lived close by."

"How far through school did you go in New Jersey?"

"I graduated in New Jersey."

I'm curious, Debbie; did you go to Otterbein to honor your dad's memory in any way?"

"Yeah, I think I really did. Yeah, I think that was a way that I could feel close to my dad. Also, maybe I could find out what he was like by being there. One time I was doing a report on Vietnam for an interpersonal communications class. I went to the library and the librarian looked at my ID as I was checking out some books. He asked me where I was from, and I told him New Jersey. He said sort of disappointingly; 'Oh, you wouldn›t probably know the Lamp that I knew then.' 'Hey, try me.' 'Ok; Arnie Lamp.' 'That was my dad!' He immediately started crying. He came around the desk and gave me a big hug. 'I was his golf coach here.' Sadly, he died that year in the crop walk. Lots of things have happened in our lives. Laura and I there›s just no way there›s any coincidence involved.

"I think I'm interpreting that to mean that God works through people that are placed in our lives at certain times for what become obvious reasons."

"Debbie those are called 'Godwinks'."

"Larry, as odd as it might sound, we think our mom came back as a stink bug. We'd always talked about how Laura would come back as a dragonfly and that I would come back as a butterfly. My mom never talked about what she was going to come back as. Well, she was kind of ornery. Real sweet all the time; but at the same time ornery. I think she either got up to the pearly gates and God said, 'the only thing we have left; Judy, is a stinkbug. Will you take that? And she probably said; 'Oh, that'll be fine. I can handle it, or he said…...'"

"Jeff described your mom as a Spitfire. Is that accurate?"

"Oh yeah!"

"So, she'd take anything you gave her and run with it; right?"

"Oh yeah, to everybody's chagrin. She would say to her dad; 'Hey dad. I've got this idea 'and dad rolled his eyes and there you go."

"One of the stories I know about my mom and dad. My mom went to a Singer store, and she was looking at a sewing machine. She went to the store talk to a lady. She showed her one of the refurbished ones and showed mom all about it. Mom decided she wanted it. She had a plan. Dad would come with her later that day and innocently end up at this sewing machine. She would then lure him into buying it. So, she told the salesperson she was going to bring her husband later."

"We're going to look around and we're going to happen to see it and hopefully we're going to buy it."

"Lady says OK. I'll be here later. So, my mom has a nice dinner with my dad. She brings him to the store and comes by the sewing machine and says, 'Oh, look at this one. I really like this one.' But when they walked in the saleslady says, 'Oh, Mrs. Lamp, I see you're back.' It completely blew her cover. My dad apparently grabbed his checkbook right away and just gasped. Hah, hah, hah. 'I've been had!'"

One thing you'll hear on the tape. Mom apparently had an accident in the car. The insurance company information got to him before it ever got to her, and he was scolding her. The whole bill as only $192; something like that. Laura and I howled because we spend more than that on groceries sometimes. Here he was having a cow about that. He also told her not to write checks towards the end of the month. I don't really have any concept of how much they've made or how much things were, but it struck me as funny. I also know that my mom went back to school at some point when we were in Texas. We don't know where or how she finished or how it was paid for. It was never anything she talked about."

"Was that to get her master's degree?"

"No, that was to finish her regular college. She actually finished up after he passed away. She went to summer school. Sometimes we would go to Grandpa Lamp's house, and she would do some classes while we were there. Then she also took some courses in New Jersey and ultimately got her degree from O.U."

"Sounds like you and your mom and your sister were a very close threesome. Does that sound accurate?"

"Yes, very much so. And I think she tried to get remarried a couple of times, but it didn't work out. You know right after the war she was still very young, and very attractive; but she had two girls and that was always a problem. She was a Vietnam widow. I don't know how popular that was with the guys then."

"Debbie, I can tell you it would have been a hard sell. Most young men aren't willing to take on the mantle of a widowed soldier's wife, with two little girls, here. That's sad; but it's reality. For

Judy, that must have been a tough thing; what do you do? Do you put yourself out there? How do you do that? They didn't have dating online then. So, do you go to a bar or try to get fixed up. I'm sure that she must have had a very tough time with that. She no doubt wanted to have a worthy replacement for your dad to help raise you guys; but finding that was a very uphill situation, I guess."

"We had a dentist in New Jersey. My mom was doing some just basic intake information with him, and he found out that dad was killed in Vietnam and so he asked about it; asking when he was there. She shared with him that her husband went out into what was called the 'hammocks' in Vietnam, with some doctor friends, and administered to sick Vietnamese adults and children. The guy: the dentist started sweating profusely. He looked at mom and said, 'I think I met your husband when I was in Vietnam.'"

"Wow!"

"That was one of the kinds of things that has happened our whole lives. There's no reason to think that it wasn't divine intervention. There's another group that I was a part of, a sharing group. One lady was there. As I talked about my dad, and she listened; her eyes got bigger and bigger. She ended up telling me that her husband did my dad's funeral. He left the ministry shortly thereafter because it was a lot for him to take. He ended up going into education. He was involved with the Newark schools. At the time, I was working at Capital, and I ended up going to this group. Otherwise, how else would I have ever met these people that had a connection with my dad? See what I mean?"

"You worked at Capital?"

"I never had ever been on campus before I interviewed there. I realized there was a big rivalry between Otterbein and Capital. After I worked there, I figured I could never lose again, because I could root for either team or be feeling good about it! I would always wear purple when I was working there and going to a game. If there were Otterbein people on the other side that I knew, I always felt like I could walk over there and meet with them and greet with them without getting pelted by beer cans."

"How many years did you work for capital?"

"I actually worked there for three years."

"Well, I know capital is a great school as well as Otterbein. It just happened to always be a rival of ours. My son played soccer for Ohio Northern. I got to visit Capital at least twice, to watch him play. I always got a kick out of the kids that were from the fraternities, who would come out and watch the soccer match. They would drag out some old beat-up sofas and sit on them, to cheer. We got a kick out of that."

"Well, I'm glad that we both went to Otterbein. It's a great school, and I think we both got a valuable education from there."

"I was at Otterbein and there was a guy. I think he was a Clubber. He was an insurance guy from New York. I can't think of his name, but he was doing a dedication at the time, and they were dedicating a plaque that was for all the fallen veterans from Otterbein. My dad, of course was on there. He found out that I was there, and he wanted to meet the Lamp daughter. Somebody tracked me down. Turns out he lived with my dad in the frat house for a summer and knew my dad. Larry: a once again instance of nothing happens that is happenstance. From that, I met another gentleman who flew a mission with my dad the day before my dad had his accident. He and my dad got to chatting. Later, he wrote a story. I think was called; They flew one for the Bein."

"How cool is that?"

"There's one story of him. This is an Otterbein story. He was one of the guys that had to do an all-night pledge walk with my dad. I don't know if he was the one who was picking him up or if he was the one that was dropping him off. He said to my dad; 'Hey, we got to get back! All kinds of fun stuff happening.' We did some fun stuff, but never anything like you guys did. By the time I was a Greek advisor, that would have been considered hazing. When I was at Capital there was a sorority that did some stuff like that. They got in big trouble for hazing. The idea of walking to a cemetery, which seems innocent; upset this one girl because she had a relative who was buried there. I ended up neutralizing her a bit by saying; 'yeah, my dad's buried there too.' It was the cemetery in Reynoldsburg right did it I told her; 'I get it.' I ended up dating a Rat (Zeta Pi) when I was in college. He lived in the house. My mom asked me what room was he in? I described the room to her, and it turns out it was the same room my dad stayed in. It was my dad's room when he was the house manager. They really liked when my dad was the house manager because my grandpa owned a lumber yard and helped him with some materials to fix the house up while he was there. Also, did you ever know my uncle Jerry? He was there up until 1960; Jerry Helfer. It was my Aunt Louise's husband. My grandpa Lamp was making it very tough on him. I guess he didn't like him very well at the time. He was at grandpa's house sometimes when I was there in high school, and I would have a date with a boy. My uncle Jerry would end up charging my boyfriend, saying; 'Hey, you ate a meal here and you used our telephone, so here's your bill. You had dinner; some drinks and a poolside chair.' My date would be saying, 'What the heck?' One other funny thing that happened was this. I was between my graduation from Otterbein and grad school. I was at their house, and I got a phone call from an old boyfriend that I was trying to rekindle my relationship with. My grandpa answered the phone and just hung up on the guy. I never did figure out who it was exactly until later. But they were characters; right? When my grandparents lived next door when my mom was growing up, Grandpa Lamp came to our house one day with a shotgun. It wasn't loaded. He came over and he came in the kitchen and got on my grandpa Armstrong, saying; 'men in Harbor Hills don't do the dishes! Why are you doing them?' So, it was a big joke because in later years grandpa did do the dishes, and he would have gotten razzed completely by my other grandfather because of that incident with the shotgun. Those were different times, though. Harbor Hills was a nice community to grow up in. The families there all had parties at each other's houses, and barbecues and things. One time my dad drove a mower into the lake. That was a funny story, for sure!"

"I know your grandpa was an avid boater, too. Jeff told me that he and his buddies would get up early; like 4:30 and take the boat out and do water skiing."

"Did you know Grandpa Lamp also had a plane? We went for a ride in it one time. Grandpa Lamp got his arm sleeve stuck in the in the door and my mom was convinced we were all going to go down in the plane that day. I think that plane might have sparked some interest from my dad to wanna fly, even when he was a young boy."

"Your uncle Jeff told me that when your dad first got to Vietnam, he was flying a bigger plane. A refueling type plane. He even remarked to Jeff when they were home one time that he didn't like flying those. He said had 'a need for speed,' and that's why he wanted to get into flying the F4's the second time he went over there."

"I know he flew an RF4, which was a jet reconnaissance plane. When we were visiting the Air Force Museum at Wright Patterson Air Force Base, we saw one of those. it looks so small compared to the one picture that Laura and I saw of the jet that he flew. In the tape, he talks about flying at night. He would remark that when the B52's would bomb, they made a lot of light; lit the sky up. He was always concerned that Vietnamese would see him and shoot at him, but they never did. They must not have seen him."

"It's kind of interesting that Jeff is the only living member of the Lamp family. I think maybe he was not quite appreciated as much because he was the youngest. I know he felt somewhat responsible for Laura and me when we had our house up in Delaware County, Ohio. He would call me and ask me if everything was going alright. I think he was fully expecting to have to jump in and help us at some point. It was reassuring, and I always knew that he had our backs. I know my mom would have probably stepped in ahead of time but at least we knew that Uncle Jeff was with us."

"When I spoke to your uncle Jeff, I truly thought of him as a great guy; a great supporter of you both. He always spoke well of you and Laura. To me, that's as it should be. That made me think highly of him; and of course, of your dad. He also remarked that even though they were ten years apart that they loved each other. I have a strong affinity for what was going on in each other's lives. I had never really met Jeff before that day."

"Interestingly, my mom was busier after she retired than she was when she was a teacher. She was in so much different stuff that my sister and I finally encouraged her to write things down and tell us where she was at, so we'd know. As it turns out we were becoming the parent for our mom. That's the dynamic that I wasn't exactly planning on, but it happened."

"Wow, I know exactly what you mean. I think my kids do the same thing with me sometimes."

"My sister and I never got married. I still hope to but who knows? Mom never had any grandchildren. So, anytime we were around kids, people called her 'Grandma Judy.' I think it was karma, but we had to do a little bit of raising our mom, as adults. I can remember this one time we came home to our house, and Mom was with a friend. I was with her daughter. We arrived to find her mom and Judy out by the pool. They were sitting in towels on our porch and giggling. We asked them what the heck was going on. So, her friend blurts out; 'We were skinny dipping in the pool!' She blurts out that and we look at each other and say' 'Well, hope you didn't put the lights on when you were doing that. At the time, my mom was probably 40. There was no reason for us to be too concerned but we were just because it was a little surprising."

"Well Debbie; I appreciate everything you've given me. I believe that between what I learned from Uncle Jeff and what I learned from, plus what I will learn from this thumb drive, will present a story that will rightfully show your dad as a wonderful father, a wonderful husband, brother, and son. A guy "who served with honor and a true hero."

"I guess I just think this way about my family. We're very patriotic. Some people would wonder why, because of what happened to my dad. We still believe in everything he was doing. I know that the Vietnam War was deemed as somewhat senseless, by many. I appreciate that you called a conflict rather than a war, because it was never really determined that it was a war. I became a member of the "Sons and Daughters in Touch." They've had some video meetings and things. We were supposed to have a big shindig in Washington DC on Father's Day. It was all ready to go then COVID hit. By being part of that group, they submitted names to be on ornaments on the Christmas tree in the White House. Our dad got picked and so my dad is on those one of those ornaments. Supposedly, they're going to send us this ornament. I hope they do!"

" Debbie, I can tell that by hook or by crook, you and Laura grew up well; even though you never got to formally meet your dad. Any memory that I can honor through this epilogue should surely help do that."

"Uncle Jeff may have told you this, but his youngest daughter just had a son. They named him William, in honor of my dad. They call him Liam though, but they did name him after my dad. It's even uncanny how little William and my dad look alike. They both have a little cleft in the chin, which my dad had, and their other two children don't have."

Reel to reel tape of conversations of Arnie; sent to Judy

Next, I listened to a recording made by Arnie while he was in Vietnam. It was approximately 30 minutes of his voice. In most ways it was nothing awe inspiring. It was a one voiced tape, as he would send it to his bride Judy, back home. She would record over it and keep it going back and forth. I found it to be fascinating and inspiring. It ultimately showed me some things about the young man; Arnie, and his relationship with Judy, his two daughters, and his fellow airmen.

He was concerned about Judy and the girls. He said "hi" to Debbie, his oldest daughter and wished her a Happy Birthday. It was so clear that he missed her and missed not being there for her party." Have you been a good girl for Mommy? Have you been treating your little sister Laura good? I heard you've been going to Sunday School. She says you are getting to know all the kids' names."

"Hi, Laura. How are you doing. Being a good girl, I hope. Mommy says you are walking all over the place. She said you take a few fast steps and then kerplunk, you plop down and just start laughing. Daddy was sure glad to hear that. Everybody was so worried about this and now you're walking up a storm and you're not even a year old. Everybody thought you were going to be just a little tyke. Wow, you showed em.' By the way, Judy; how's she doing with the braces on her feet? ¿Do they hurt her? Laura, say "Da, Da, Da. Laura, say Da, Da, Da."

"Judy, now that I've talked to the girls. We need to talk about the money situation. You asked if you could use some of my money; a hundred from January and another from February. Well, the January money is already spoken for. I had to buy some things for my apartment here and don't have any left over. You can take a hundred now, if you tell me, so that I can keep track of it in my checkbook. If you need any other money, just let me know. Dash me off a postcard, so that I can keep track of it. Don't write them for more than $100. Also, don't write any checks in the last week of the month, so we don't ever get overdrawn."

"Well, I'm all alone, Charlie moved downstairs. I got a locker and put it together; only took about 6 hours; hah, hah. I'll walk you around the room, so you can visualize my redecorating. Now as soon as I get the girls pictures hung up, this place will look great! Oh yeah, about that bedspread you said you'd make me. You know, the one with the woman on it. Well go ahead and see if you can get one from your mom and make it. Should be a great conversation piece around here! I'm already a topic of conversation anyway.

I bought a hotplate for my room and fixed me a fancy lunch today. Pretty proud of myself. One of my buddies made us a roast with mushrooms, gravy, creamed corn, and a good old bottle of Rose Mateus wine. So, you see, we're living like kings over here. As we all say as we sit in our plush air-conditioned buildings; "War is hell." But we'll likely get a taste of reality if we get an attack.

You said you've been watching "Laugh In." Boy, I wish we could get that. We don't get much of anything, like Johnny Carson and other good stuff. We get stuff that's about two years old like, Ironsides and Bonanza. We do get specials, and sports shows, even if they are a few months old. We guys get together and yell and scream like they were live!!

I got to go to a movie and saw "Valley of the Dolls." Boy it sure was different than the book. Hey, one of our old friends came to visit. We had dinner at the O.C. and then came back to the room and had a few drinks and talked the night away. He talked about their son and wife back home. They're all doing fine. We talked about how we've got it and we all agreed we were better off than the guys sitting in a ditch over here.

Remember that guy I told you that I had a talk with a while back? Well, it apparently did some good. We talked about his sex life and all. It got to the point where no one of the guys could stand him talking about his comings and goings with the women. He's got a wife and kids and he was surely on a path that was going to ruin all that for their future. There are lots of guys over here are like that. They can't resist.

A lot of my buddies back home are turning in their papers to get out. Lot of stuff going on with the war that makes us want to get out ASAP.

I hope you are not too disappointed that your girlfriend is getting to come and be with her husband. Honey, to be clear, it's not great and you should be glad and not disappointed. Living over here is no bargain. Don't worry, I'm soon done and back home with you.

Boy, flying at nights is no bargain. It sure is dark around here. When I'm up there, it's like my head is on a swivel. Mountains to watch out for, plus people shooting at me. The closest that I've come to getting hit was during a B-52 raid. We started into our area for the day, when we heard that there was potentially going to be a B-52 raid. My navigator fired up; "What do you mean, potentially.!!" That's something we need to know! Soon enough it was confirmed. We were on our last line, so we pressed through and made a left turn. I looked behind us and all hell had broken loose. That strike just lit up the world around us. Even if people call them

"Monkey killers." They must do a lot of good and wreck the world of those on the ground.

Other than that, being on the night shift is actually pretty good. We get up at one, back in by four. Sleep four or five hours. Get up around Noon, get lunch, get some sun, go watch a movie, read, or write a letter. Go back to bed and get up around one again. They try to fly us about 6 nights a month. That way they balance us out.

Looks like I might get to fly in the northern part of South Vietnam. It's mountainous there. Seems like you are pushing down on the stick all the time and heading up a mile a minute. Oh well, certainly better than ending up on the side of a mountain! Even if that did happen, I doubt they'd name a mountain after me.

Guess I'm finally going to get to fly with Charlie next week. People found out about it and have been razzing us; "How will the plane get you two off the ground?" I guess that's why we're in the F-4. Plenty of power to get anyone airborne. I'm a little worried about Charlie. He came in one night here and was all drunked up and weaving back and forth. So, he comes over to me with that 'shit eating' grin and promptly starts kicking my new locker out in the hall and making all kinds of noise. This got the troops mad in a hurry, as it was after midnight. So, he comes back into the room and declares, 'Well they wouldn't let me sleep one night when I was trying.' Next thing, he goes back in the hall and starts screaming. 'Get your ass back in here, Charlie.' So, he comes back in and reiterates his plea again. Next, he has a baloney sandwich and a Dr. Pepper. Anyhow, he proceeds to go in the John and visit with 'Ralph O'Rourke.' Know who that is? That's what the guys scream when they puke.'RRRalph Ohh Rourke' Anyhow, he finally goes to bed, as he was due to fly early in the morning. I sure hope he doesn't make a habit of this.

Well sweetie, your ideas about improving this place worked out well. Starting a library was great, but we already have one. We have something like a bulletin board, you suggested. Suggesting that the guys put pictures of their families up there should catch on. Your idea of putting 'girlie' pictures up will surely be a big hit! Then you said to put up a 'frustrations/suggestions' section. I think I'll do that and then give a prize at the end of each month for the most creative.

You were mentioning that Nixon is going to be giving a speech tomorrow. I hope he says something encouraging. I also hope that the peace talks will resume. Sure, would be nice if that could happen in the next week or so, as the TET is happening. If it's anything like it was last year, I don't want to be anywhere near this place.

Well, how's everyone up in Michigan? I hope good.

Well honey, I wrote down a bunch of things I wanted to say. I thought it would take about an hour, but it only took half that time. Only One thing more. I would like to encourage you to sign us up for Hawaii. I know we might be a little short on money, but if we save as much as we can, we should be able to swing it. Sure, would be nice to see you over there. Even though it would only be a month or so till I got done, it would still be great for both of us. I'd get to see you. You'd get a break from the girls, and you would get a break from your studies.

So, till the next time, when I can think of more things to say; so, I'll just say; 'goodbye now.'"

JACK ERNEST

AGE WHEN ENTERED MILITARY: 19

DATE OF ENTRY TO MILITARY: 07/21/1965

VIETNAM TOUR DATES: 10/26/1966-10/31/1967

YEARS OF DUTY/RESERVES: 4

JACK ERNEST

I met Jack when I had my insurance office. His daughter Cindy and her husband Scott were long time clients. During our time together, they had a large housefire. I visited them the night it happened and always considered that as one of the most meaningful moments in my career.

Jack got a chance to meet me the week of the fire. He remembered me when I called to ask if I could interview him. I knew something of Jack's Vietnam experience and knew that he was well known by many veterans, as he has for many years spoken, advocated, and dealt with his fellow soldiers ever since. He has also gone back to Vietnam over 40 times, where he has served in missions to the natives there; building schools, churches, and any other need he and his group could do to serve.

"Jack; how did you get involved? Did you get drafted?"

"No, Larry, during the time I was growing up, I was expected to serve my country. All my brothers, cousins, and uncles before me served and so I just fell in line. I graduated from High School in 1964. A good friend of mine and I went to town and tried to get jobs in the steel mills. They wouldn't hire us because they (fully understandable) felt for sure we were getting drafted and didn't want such a short-term commitment. So, we got fed up and bored. We decided to sign up. We decided to join the Marines. We wanted to stay together. We were able to do that through basic training and then we each went our own direction. When it came up, I volunteered to go to Vietnam. So, in July of 1965, I was shipped to

Nam. I knew that being a Marine and specifically a sharpshooter and infantry that it would only be a matter of time till I ended up there. If I volunteer maybe, I'll save some guy who has a family from going. So, in October of 1966, I was sent over and became a "Grunt". Soon after, I was in a tent there and someone told us the "Old Man" (a term for our C/O) wants to see you at his tent. I was a little shocked, as I wondered if I had done anything wrong. At the time I was a 'Lance Corporal.' I got there and he says, 'Pack your bags Lance Corporal; you'll be leaving in the morning."

"Is it okay of I ask what I'm to be doing and where?"

Not at all; you'll be flying to Okinawa; Japan and you will be in a Vietnamese Language school. By that time, I'd been in about 4-5 months. Now I'm one of two chosen for this training. So, I catch a helicopter in the morning, to Da Nang, where I get on a plane to Okinawa. There I stay for 35 days and receive intensified language training. Eight hours a day, 5 days a week. We were taught by Vietnamese natives. Then I was returned to my original outfit. I was promoted to E-4, which was a Corporal. Then I was transferred into a Scout team, where I worked with an actual North Vietnamese soldier who for various reasons chose to become part of our side. He was worth his weight in gold, Larry. Then I was made "Head Scout" and put in charge of 12 scout teams, which were comprised of at least one Marine that could speak the language. Most of the other guys were similarly trained, but in California. I was also put in charge of the P.O.W. camp for our company. I thought I'd got it made. I thought I was safe from harm for the most part. I quickly found that was wrong, as I was wounded by shrapnel while try to save a fellow Marine who was shot. He was yelling for help. I was hit and lived. My buddy was killed. I was wounded but recovered and served out my tour of duty. So, I got to come home. Larry, that was the time when all the protesting was going in at home. We were treated and called rapists, murderers, baby killers and worse. With that kind of reception, I couldn't stand it. I wanted to get back as soon as I could. I had about a year and a half left. So, I did and was promoted again to Sergeant. The officers there were trying hard to get me/us) to re-up. To reenlist for another 4 years. I asked the First Sergeant; "Man to man sir, if I decide to reenlist; with the qualifications I have as a language specialist, interrogator, and scout, where would you send me?"

"Son, you'd go back to the exact place and group you were with before."

"How long would that take.?"

"You'll be back there in less than 6 months."

"Sir, with all due respect, I was wounded once. I don't want to press the envelope. I'll just spend the rest of my time. I'll serve it out and go home.

So, I did that and was able to get out. Back home, I could get a job on the steel mills. I got married and began my life again. We had Cindy and things were great."

"Jack, respectfully you are leaving out a chapter. How did you meet your bride?"

"Oh my, that's a good story, Larry."

I figured. Let's hear it."

"Okay, well she worked in a Howard Johnson's restaurant in Fredericksburg, Virginia, which is right off Rte. 95. So, a bunch of us Marines were on a trip and were traveling back to the base in North Carolina. We decided to stop at his place. I saw her and was smitten. She was the cutest thing I'd ever seen. Her uniform was at least a size to large. So, I write her a note on a napkin.

"What's your name, address and phone number?" She smiled at me and turned around. She wrote on the napkin, and I thought; 'This is the greatest thing, Larry. It said, No name, no address, no phone number." Boy that changed my tune in a hurry. But it just made me that much more eager to get to know her. Anyhow one of the other girls at the restaurant said, "Patsy's parents are very strict. She's my friend and if you write here to the restaurant, I'll make sure she gets them. So, we started to communicate. We "dated" through letters for a year. We got engaged and eventually got married."

My uncle was a supervisor in one of the mills. So, I got started and all.

***As Jack began to tell this part, I could tell he was getting emotional. ***

"Larry, I was just kind of bear with me, if you will. Here I was, trying to come back into a society that doesn't want you; it was tough. Unbeknownst to me, I was suffering from P.T.S.D. Things that you see in war stay with you the rest of your life. You can hit the delete button all you want but you can never eliminate the things you saw and did. I started doing drugs. I was drinking. I had a motorcycle. I was a bad person! Fortunately, the steel company I was working with was trying to get me help through the V.A., and on and on. I did not know that I was also developing Cancer and Heart problems. This was all a result of the exposure to Agent Orange. I'm still dealing with those conditions."

I ask.

"By the way, when did these conditions start? Were they after you were married and had Cindy?"

"Yes. At first, I thought all this was just life. Being a tough Marine and a man thing. Here I was getting in bar fights and knocking people around. I didn't really understand. There wasn't much talk about that kind of stuff in then. I was a mess. I tried to hide from it through drugs and booze.

In about our eighth year of marriage, Patsy had had enough. Cindy was 4. She left. Larry, at thirty years of age, I lucked out. I became a "born again" Christian. I went to church with my dad. A guy there was giving his testimony. He was a John Wayne type, Larry. Everything he went through was exactly what I had. At the end he said.

"Whosoever will; may come. This alter is open. God is no respecter of your past sins. His door is always open."

"I gave my life to the Lord. Patsy came back and we recently celebrated 53 years together."

"Wow, Jack. What a wonderful story."

"Then I end up going back to Vietnam 44 times on Mission trips."

"Were you with an organization when you did that?"

"I founded a ministry called; "Welcome Home." It was mainly for veterans. It was designed to help them integrate their lives back into society. I met a guy up in Cleveland. I was at a convention of sorts. He had a booth set up and an organization called "Point Man" ministries. I helped him set up and do stuff while I was there. Don't know why, for sure. Just felt God leading me. It was brief, and we never met again. But he basically prophesied over me and told me what my ministry was to be. At first, he could have been speaking Japanese. I didn't understand him or believe him. I still have the words he spoke over me that day. It's right here on my desk. I was helping him tear down and pack up. He looked at me and spoke. 'I really believe God wants me to speak these words into your life.' Larry, I thought he was a wacko when he said this. I was so skeptical, I asked him to write it down and sign it and date it. He did and I still have it right here in front of me. That was October. In just a few months I was on a plane to Vietnam with Morley Safer."

"Wow!"

"That was in 1989. I the next eighteen years, I went back 43 more times. Another thing, Larry. God restored my ability to speak the language. It had been 24 years since I left and ever spoke the language. Research says a person loses the ability to speak their native language after not using it for 6 years."

I respond.

"Sounds like a God Thing" to me, Jack!"

"He was going to use me and that was part of the deal. We would become involved in humanitarian work, work with the underground churches. Smuggling Bibles and other Christian items. It was amazing!"

"Jack, you speak of 'we.' Who are you speaking if?"

"Well, when we went back on the first trip, there was a total of 11 of us. We were all veterans, from across several states. One was a doctor, One a lawyer, one a pastor, plus many other walks of life. We were there a total of 21 days. We went all over South Vietnam. After that, I went back by taking my vacation time every year. My family supported me as well and it became my mission and my passion, as time went by, I was speaking in churches and service clubs and people began to support us financially. After a while, the was enough to support the travel for our group and much of the work projects we did there."

"Does the ministry still exist?"

"No, I retired from it in 2005. Instead of 'Welcome Home' ministries, it's now called 'We Believe Ministries.' We don't have a website right now. I still go around the U.S., speaking and advocating for veterans. In May, I'll be speaking in Louisiana to a worldwide conference. In October, I'll be doing a revival service in Virginia. So, I'm still busy with stuff."

"So, in the meantime, your daily dealing with the ravages of Agent Orange. Am I correct?"

"Absolutely. I have some skin cancer and have a deep removal of a cancerous mole. I go up to Pittsburgh for a C.A.T. Scan for my heart condition. I had cancer in my tonsils. I had to have several treatments for that. I've also had kidney problems. I also have a thing called "tremors" My hands will shake. They say it's not Parkinson's, but similar. Larry, with all this stuff, I still get up every morning with a positive outlook, and praise God and live my life. I'm 75 and still able to do stuff."

"What about the flashbacks and other P.T.S.D. stuff. Do you still have?"

"They call what I have as "triggers." One of my worst would be a helicopter. As you know, in Vietnam, they were used for Med Evac. That noise is one that just drove me crazy. I handle it well. Our house now is now on the flight path for our nearby hospital. I just pray my way through it now, Larry.

One time after coming home, my brothers and I went deer hunting on West Virginia. They didn't know how bad I was. My brother thought it would be funny to fire off a few rounds with his 30-0-6 rifle. I immediately hit the ground; turned over and assumed the position to return fire, I was aiming right at my brother's chest. I was lucky I didn't shoot him. I said to him; 'You cannot do that!' He replied, 'Jack, I am so sorry. I had no idea!' I went home and took all the ammo from my rifle. Larry, there is so much difference between a veteran" and a "combat veteran." I now serve as a Commissioner with the State of Ohio. Every day, I'm called on. Just the other day I was called to the hospital at Weirton to calm a guy that was getting out of hand. I'm also a Chaplin. I'm on staff over there and have a badge that gives me instant access if needed. "

"Are you connected through the V.A., or with a local hospital, or several?"

"I'm on The Veteran's Service Commission for the State of Ohio. I've been a commissioner for about 8 years now. I had to be appointed by a judge. Anyway, I've been Ohio's Veteran of the year.

I'm in the Veteran's Hall of Fame in Columbus. Larry, I'm not telling you this to brag. I was in the Legion of Honor in Philadelphia, Pa. All of this is because of service. You know, God calls us to serve. To serve humanity. As a servant, if you're humble and go about your business of serving and not looking for any glory, people will see it and you will be rewarded. You weren't seeking it, but it finds you. The Lord says, "Let you light shine." So here I am, 75 years old and still getting to serve every single day!"

"How wonderful; Jack!" Now if you don't mind, I'd like to go back and ask you about some things that we haven't yet talked about. When you were in the thick of it, in Viet Nam. I know you said you had a buddy that got killed in your presence. How about on the flip side of that, did you knowingly kill someone?"

"Yes; yes. Most people are reluctant to ask that question. You know the adage; 'kill or be killed.' I never, ever wanted to kill another human being. There was one incident where we were being shot at from a village. There were water buffalos and chickens running around. We were getting fired upon from those grass hooches (huts). We had to return fire or face death. Larry, that's called a "firefight."

After the N.V.A. that were firing on us ran away, this old lady comes out of one of the huts, holding this little boy in her arms. The little boy is dead, of course. Now we don't know who of us fired the shot that killed the child because we were all shooting in that direction. The poor little boy's head is hanging over because he was dead. She was crying and saying, "Dai Show? Dai Show?" which means "Why? Why? You see, I could understand her, being trained as an interpreter."

I add.

"Hard to know whether that was a blessing or a curse; Jack."

"And then on the other hand, yes, I did knowingly take a life. I remember a time where we were getting hit (fired upon). There was a Vietnamese running away. I remember putting my sights between his shoulder blades and he went down. I killed that human being. Notice, Larry; I called him what he deserved to be called; a human being/ Not a Gook, or a Slant Eye, but a human being. I have one more story. If you want me to tell you, I will. It's part of my P.T.S.D. issues and I will never outlive it. So, now I'm a translator, interpreter, and interrogator. We're out and marching along and suddenly, we got hit with enemy fire. We fired back. My Lieutenant calls to me. I go up to where he is. There was a wounded Vietcong soldier. He was lying on the ground and could have survived. Eventually his buddies would have found him and rescued him. So, my Lieutenant said to me; "Get as much information from him, then catch up with the unit. On his way, he turned to me and said, "Corporal Ernest, we're not taking any prisoners today. So, what was he saying to me, Larry?"

I understood and responded.

"He was telling you that you had to kill him after interrogating him."

"Yep. So, here's me. I'm getting as much as I can from this guy. He's alive, but he knows he's going to die. He's a soldier. He's the one I'll never get out of my mind. He's the reason for my P.T.S.D. So, I began to question him. Of course, he' not going to give me much. But they tell us; 'Do not get off course. Stay on task.' So, he says to me.

"Oum Kai Con?"

He was saying.

"Do you have a family in America?" Larry, I knew better but because I; I'm a humane person I said.

"Choir Ka;" "No I don't have." I shouldn't have, but I asked him.

"Um Ka?" Do you?"

He answers.

"No com Jai; No com Jai" One son, one daughter."

Then he says.

(More Vietnamese) "Would you like to see their photos?" You see, when the Vietcong went into battle, they always carried their family photos with them. In their Buddhism belief, they believe that's going to protect them. Larry, I should have never done it; but I did. I looked at the picture of his beautiful young family. Then I realized my orders. I had to kill this man. So, I pulled out my 45, pulled the hammer back and I shot him in the temple. He was partially sitting up when I shot him. It blew him to the ground. When he slammed to the ground, then sat up a bit and the blood from his wound hit me on the face, Larry. I literally tasted his blood. I left there wanting to go forward and shoot my Lieutenant. But you're a Marine. You must take orders. You do what you're told. It's war. People don't understand. And you can't expect them to. I told my psychiatrist once.

"I'll never be able to have a baby, so I'm never know what it's like."

He kept telling me.

"Mr. Ernest, you were at war, and you had to do what you did. I asked him.

"Do you see this index finger here?" This finger pulled the trigger that day. I could cut it off right now, but I'd still have that memory. Those are the kinds of things combat veterans live with. Of course, God has forgiven me. With Him, I'm clean. But my mind won't let it go. Larry, lots of guys come up to me when I'm speaking, and maybe they went to Germany instead of Nam. Often, they tell me they feel guilty that they didn't have to endure the same fate that so many did in Nam. I would tell them;" You didn't have to go through what I did. Please don't feel guilty. We all served on one way or another. That always surprised guys. Many hugged me and expressed that I've lifted a heavy load from them. I don't even know if my daughter Cindy knows that. I don't think I've ever told her that. I wouldn't be afraid to tell her. She doesn't really need to know. But I get along now. My relationship to Jesus Christ protects me. He has saved me. If it weren't for my relationship to Him, I'd be a definite mess!"

I add.

"The Marine I met from Westerville, who I worked with for several years also went to language school, like you. He said his was in Northern California, while yours was in Okinawa. Like you, he was in a select group and became a scout and led scout teams as well. So, he had many similar things happen to him that you experienced. He also talked about having Montagnard's join his teams."

"Oh yeah, "Mountain People"

I speak.

"He told me they helped him on patrols and were instrumental in many captures he made. He told me about his experiences, and many were just like yours.""

Right now, Larry, I want others to benefit from my experiences."

Jack, in my estimation you are a hero."

"I never feel that way sir."

"Well, you should. If anyone chooses to call you that, tell them; "guilty as charged." Thanks, so much. I got far more than I bargained for.

FRED SEESE

AGE WHEN ENTERED MILITARY: 19

DATE OF ENTRY TO MILITARY: 11/11/1965

VIETNAM TOUR DATES: 02/1968-07/1970

YEARS OF DUTY/RESERVES: 24

FRED SEESE

Fred is my first cousin. He's 3 years younger than me. We grew up on the same street and were close till our college years. After that, he joined the service and our paths diverged. He and my brother Bob are very close. When I talked to Bob about the Epilogue, he said; "You must interview Fred. I'm pretty sure I wouldn't have if that conversation hadn't taken place. Not that I would purposely leave his story out, I had most of my subjects near me in Ohio and had 2 Army guys already. After talking with Fred, he; at first; was reluctant, as his duties were of a nature that he felt was a hard subject to hear about. Even though I agreed with him, I assured Fred that I was the author and I wanted to write his story. With that we agreed and here is his story.

"Fred; I always start by asking how you got in the service to begin with?"

"Larry, I got drafted. I was a student at the University of Indiana-Pennsylvania. I wasn't doing that well. I get in and was given the opportunity to go to officer candidate school. So, I was aware that I would have to give at least two years of service if I did that, and that was doable for me. I went in and was commissioned as a second Lieutenant. I went to my training in Texas and was a battalion leader there."

I interject.

"Now back up on step. Had you gone to college at this point?"

"Yes, and at the time I wasn't doing well, and I just wasn't mature enough at that point. I knew I could do college. but I wasn't getting along with it well at the time I was there. My counselor advised me that I had just ruined my life forever. Just from other actions and things. He was also my math teacher. We ended up having the same book I had in high school. I was frustrated with the way he taught; or didn't teach, I would say. In high school I did well with the same book and same class, but this guy taught it totally different. I barely got through it."

"And you had met Sherry by that time, had you?"

"Sherry and I met on Valentine's Day. On Fridays at school, we had something called family style dinners. They would take 10 people in line and put the 10 on a round table. The dress requirements were to look decent so we both showed up looking decent. Sherry says that when she saw me, she said.

"I'm gonna sit by that guy. I like his looks."

So, she chose me and not me choosing her? Worked out well. I walked her home that night. She was in a dorm off campus, so we had a nice long talk on our walk home. When I got home, I called her right back up and asked her out. Rest is history."

"Where was Sherry from? I don't think she was from Connellsville?"

"She's from Gibsonia, Pennsylvania which is north of Pittsburgh; off of route 8."

"I know eventually she was in the Army as well; right?"

"Yep, she did join up with me later, but not right away. I'll elaborate on that later."

"So, were you married at this point?"

"Sherry and I knew each other for approximately 5 years before we got married. I was at Fort Lee Virginia when I went through officer candidate school. After O.C.S. I went to Vietnam for one trip and then when I came home after that tour, I ask Sherry to marry me."

"So, you were in Vietnam once or twice."

'Twice."

"And each tour was how long?"

"One year each. That was quite enough, Larry."

"So, you volunteered to go to Vietnam, right?"

"Yes."

"So, as an officer when you got to Vietnam what exactly did you do?"

"Well, I was assigned to the U.S. Army Mortuary in Saigon. This is the specialty school that I went through. After O.C.S. I went through a three-week school on memorial activities, which included graves registrations. It taught us how to identify human remains by different methods.

"Was that a choice that you made or was it thrust upon you?"

"It was a choice, Larry. The first eleven weeks of O.C.S. training was basically leadership training; how to be an officer. The second 11 weeks we were taught different specialties that a Quartermaster officer candidate would learn. That's the specialty that I wanted, so we had some additional training in certain areas. I thought my best bet was to go to another school after O.C.S., so that I would have more than one specialty. At that point I chose the graves registration area. I felt it was an area that was very important. Some of the kids chose commissary officer and I said whoop Dee do to that. I just knew that would not be something that would be of particular interest to me. I just decided on something I felt was greatly needed. And after I got into it, I found out I was right about that. Lots of the young men went into the schooling that I did and then ended up saying that's not for me."

"I know that when you do something like this you have to be careful what you choose. Sounds like you went into it eyes open."

"Yeah, I would agree, Larry. After I got into it, I realized how important it was. I did begin to enjoy it. It greatly sorrowed me to see the bodies. In the evening, as it turns out, most of us drank a lot to get the images out of our minds. But that never worked, really."

"Now I'm in Saigon."

"Saigon was a big city. Right?"

"Yes, for sure. It's now called Ho Chi Minh city."

I ask.

"Now, were you on a base there?

"Yes, we were on a section of the Ton Son Nhut air base."

. "Yes, I've heard of that. Were you staying in a barracks or a dormitory?"

", the officer's barracks were back in town. We were put up in motels and hotels. I seldom got there, though. It was right after the T.E.T. offensive when I got to Saigon, so we had over 400 bodies on hand to process at the Mortuary the moment I got there. We needed to make sure that they were who we said they were, so we could send their remains back to California or over to Dover Air Force Base in Delaware, depending on where their home of record was and what service they were in."

"And then you're Army but sounds like you were processing bodies from all other service areas as well. Is that correct?"

"The Army had the detail, so we processed bodies from all service areas. We were even in charge of all allied bodies not just Americans."

"Allies, meaning like Australia or Canada, such as that?"

"We got very few allied soldiers in. It seemed to me very quickly that the other nations had duties that didn't require them to face the enemy that much, so there weren't that many allied casualties. I can only remember two or three that I processed that weren't American soldiers. By the way, not everyone wants to be called a soldier that's an Army term for sure."

"Fred, I agree. I found this out in interviewing John Keir, who was a Marine. He stressed to me that he didn't wanna be called a soldier he wanted to be called a Marine. I respected that and certainly addressed him as that. Looks like you were well protected from battle. Is that right?"

"Yes, we were, during the TET of 68. We would get attacks of rocket fire at night. As it turns out we weren't even allowed to travel on the roads after dark because of the threat of being fired upon. That means that I seldom got to the motel. It was so busy that we worked up until after dark. When we got tired, we just went to sleep right there where we were in the Mortuary. We just sort of slept wherever we could. I chose to sleep in the commander's office. When the attacks started, we all would get really close to the heavy desks."

. "At the point of all those attacks going on, was there any time that you were close to getting wounded or killed?"

"Yes, a couple of times. Right outside the Mortuary we had a large bunker. One night, a couple of us young and foolish officers decided to go outside. You can set your watch by when the attacks would start; usually happen about 1:00 A.M. So, my buddies and I decided we wanted to go up and sit on the top of the bunker and watch the attacks happen, cause so far none of the Rockets had even come close to us."

I speak.

"Like watching fireworks, right?"

"Yeah, that is right. I hate to say it, but it was like that. We were tired; we had a couple drinks in us so there we were. We were watching rockets come in we could see three of them coming in. They were mortars. Coming through the air they look like rockets, though. We saw where the first two hit and decided quickly that the third one might hit us. So, we scurried down and got in the bunker. Luckily, it landed short. We went out the next morning to see where they hit and figured very quickly that there were only three. A fourth one would have probably hit the Mortuary. Oh, by the way, we never did that again!"

"Can't blame you!"

"It was a learning experience. We decided we would not watch those suckers again. Then a second time, a mortar landed right beside our supply section. Right beside there was our church. Unfortunately, Larry this is a little tough to talk to and I've talked to my psychiatrist about this. The rocket landed right next to our supply section and severely damaged the church. Unfortunately, in the church was our chaplain. He was supposed to fly out and go home the very next day. He was supposed to go out of Benoit, but he pulled some strings and got himself heading out of town. Sadly, it proved to be the wrong move because he died that night, Larry. We were all battling the fire in our supply section. We lost more than half of that supply section that night. Nobody in the Mortuary was injured but our chaplain, who we loved dearly, was killed. It was tough to process his remains as you might imagine."

I ask.

"Now this is still on your first tour, Fred?"

"Yes; Later, I was sent out to the personal property depot. It was off base, and I served my rest of my tour at the personal property section of the Mortuary. Instead of handling their remains, we handled their personal property. It had to be processed as well and sent back to the next of kin. It was interesting, from time to time, to identify the real next of kin. I remember one case where we were processing this guy. They brought some letters to me. All the letters that any soldier received had to be reviewed. I was one of the people that had to review all these letters. Then they got sent back to the people that sent them to him. In this instance, they really weren't sure whether this guy was married to a girl in Texas or a girl in New

York. As soon as I saw the name, I realized that he was a guy I knew from Texas, when I was in training there. Now Texas has a weird law. If you introduce a lady as your wife in Texas, she is legally that person's wife if they are deceased. The letters that he had from the girl in New York were what I would call love letters and the wording in that showed that he thought of her as his wife. I determined that his real wife was the one in New York, so the personal property was sent there. The lady in Texas got her letters back, but no other personal effects. See Larry; this is why the letters must be reviewed; because occasionally, you would find something that looked unfavorably upon the soldier and that if so, they were not sent to the next of kin. If he were writing to a person and the letters were too explicit, they were never sent back. Even getting them back to the parents; they were never going to need to know what exactly those letters said. Also, occasionally, we would get explicit pictures and those were never sent back, as well."

"Now you're at the personal property depot. Did you consider that a good move? Seems to me like that would be a lot easier to deal with than processing remains; right?"

"Yes, exactly. I didn't have to see bodies all day. Unfortunately, I had to deal with another man I knew from Texas who was my Intel Sergeant I was in a battalion S-2 in Texas, and I had a very sharp Sergeant first class there. This guy did nothing on his off time except read military manuals he was like a bevy of information. If you wanted to know something he very likely he had read the manual and knew about it. I would say you must have had a photographic memory. He could quote regulations word for word. When we were not doing anything, we would get together and he would tell me stuff that was just amazing, Larry. Just a very interesting guy. In our duties one of the things, we had to do; was run gas chambers that soldiers must run through. Tear gas chambers and chlorine gas chambers. We would be teaching the soldiers how to use their masks effectively; how to trust them. It required them to go into the chamber with their mask on, then take it off. Then say their Social Security number or their service number or their rifle number; one of the three. Then exit. During that class, the soldiers were taught the tests are masked before they went through. Once we started running them through, I was in the chamber, and he was outside This was at least eight times; about a half hour each time. He gave me a mask one time. I went to the chamber. Sure enough, I hadn't tested it properly when he gave it to me. So, I went in with this mask on and suddenly, I'm coughing like crazy. So, I'm out there and he's looking at me and laughing his ass off. He was a Sergeant, and I was a young Lieutenant and if we know better, we listen to the sergeants, even though they're noncoms and we're officers. So, I threw my mask off chased him around and we finally just laughed our butts off about the whole incident. Anyhow, we got done with this duty and we're going back to our barracks in a Jeep. Most of the dust that came from the gas ended up blowing back in my face. My uniform was almost white from the powder; crazy. We laughed about that too. He became quite a friend of me, Larry. When we were in the Jeep, I kept saying.

'Pull over; pull over; pull over!' He wouldn't do it. He just got a good laugh out of it. What saved me from a lot more harassment, was that on Saturday we had to wear our dress uniforms. I'm there in my dress uniform. So, I ended up having a Good Conduct badge on my uniform that saved me a lot of criticism, because I was respected for having been a Noncom enlisted man before actually becoming an officer."

I ask.

"Were you there in Vietnam one year without any break, or did you have any R&R or other time off?"

"According to regulations, we were allowed one R&R during the time we were there. I chose to go to a place in the southern part of Vietnam it's called Vung Tau. That area was very interesting. It was run by the 5th. Mech. When you got there, you had to turn over all your weapons, including any pistols. You could have a knife, but that was it. The interesting part about that place was that the Vietnamese enemy used it as their R&R center, as well. Hey, you might be sitting in a bar; there'd be Vietnamese in there and American soldiers. You really didn't know whether that guy next to you was a civilian, or a soldier on his R&R. It was rather interesting. They had a very nice beach there and that's where we went during the day. Might play some volleyball or swim or just lay on the beach and get some sun get your let your mind get away from the war at hand."

"When you were there at that beach area did you find guys there with you that had been in battle or were most of them back up people?"

"Oh yes. There were plenty of guys who were in combat. When we got together, we didn't talk about the war though. Tried to separate yourself from that as much as possible."

I add.

"Well, that's why they called R&R, I guess."

"Yes, that stood for Rest and Relaxation. Also, in jest, some called it I and I. Intoxication and Intercourse. Vung Tau it's how you spell it. It's a very beautiful beach resort. You can probably find on the map."

"So, that first year you spent part of the time in the Mortuary and part in the personal property area; right?"

"Yes, that's right. Three months in the Mortuary and the other nine months was in the personal property depot. Which I thought; 'Hey this will be a nice memory."

I ask.

"Now the Mortuary area; was it the only one in Vietnam?"

"No. One was in Saigon; the other was in Da Nang. Vietnam was split into four Corp areas; first, second, third and fourth. The first section was called I-corp. Saigon handled I-Corp, while DaNang handled the rest. DaNang was bigger and handled more volume.""

Fred, from a few guys I talked to, I was told that bodies and body parts were sometimes collected; literally in big nets and put on helicopters and shipped probably to your Mortuary. Does that sound right?"

"I don't understand what they meant by cargo Nets. That really wasn't the way I understood bodies were collected in the field."

"That was just something that was described to me by a Marine I talked to. Otherwise, I can't verify it."

"Well, that was one of the problems we had in Vietnam with identifications. Before I go on, Larry, I will tell you that I have the highest regard for all my service friends, especially the Marines. What I will tell you is not a criticism, as they in no way deserve any. It's just a protocol/procedure that I found frustrating in my position at the time. The Marines initially, and for a while did their own identification, which was unfortunate. Then they sent them to us at the Army Mortuary. This practice was later stopped. The Marines had a processing center; supposedly using the same regulations; but they were not as careful as we were with the identifications. When we got a body that was processed by the Marines, we marked it as an X body. A few times we had occasions where a body was misidentified and that was not a good thing for all intents and purposes. The main headquarters for this whole operation was called USARV (U.S. Army Republic of Vietnam) all identifications ended up in that headquarters. Sometimes it was the wrong person, so it created some terrible situations because that information ended up going to the wrong parents and that was certainly not our goal. While I was there in that first tour, I was promoted to First Lieutenant. When we ended up correcting something like that; all our paperwork showed without a doubt that this was John Jones instead of Billy Smith. So, this misidentification was a big problem."

I ask.

"So, the end of the first tour happens, and you go home for a while?"

"Yes, I had a two week leave at home which was a freebie, so to speak. We had 30 days leave a year. During Vietnam however, we never got to use our 30 days. So, you got home; had those 30 days of leave and then you went on to your next assignment."

I add.

"So, you went back to Connellsville for that event, correct?"

"Yes, I did."

"Was your dad still alive then?"

"Yes, he was. In fact, he and I went out and shopped for a new car for me. It was my first new car, and I was excited about it. I was all hyped up on getting a Camaro. We looked at one and I was all set to buy one till I opened the trunk found out that it was so small. I couldn't even think of getting my military gear in there. So, I changed my mind and ended up buying a Chevelle. I did a little bit of a trip to get this. I went first to Greensburg; found out they didn't have the car I wanted. Next, I was sent to Donegal where I got the car. quite an adventure for just a car!"

"When you came home; is this when you got engaged or married?"

"Well actually, I got engaged that time. Sherry and I had been writing back and forth from Vietnam all the time I was there. In fact, Larry; she wrote me every single day. She would write a letter that was 10 or 11 pages long. It was very encouraging to get such letters from this girl that I've been dating. That's probably when I really fell in love with her. I liked her very much and thought that I loved her but as the year in Vietnam went on her letters and exchange of words in those letters were quite wonderful. I was thinking I met her in Hawaii when I was on my R&R but actually; now as I remember it was Cousin Craig that I stayed with when I went there. He was married and lived there and he and his (then) wife; I think her name was Sandy, housed me and showed me around like a wonderful tourist guide. I stayed at his house and not on the military base, which was allowed. Interestingly, they knew I was coming, so they invited a friend from the United States that they knew, and she was my constant date while I was there. That was neat to have somebody at my side that I could do things with them, and not feel like a loner. It was all very proper, Larry! It was nice to be walking around with a 'round eye' which is something I hadn't seen many of since leaving for Vietnam."

"So, anything left to report on this first tour, or do you wanna move on to the second?"

" When I got home, I was assigned to Fort Lee Virginia again. When that happened, I asked Sherry to marry me, and we planned for a wedding in June. We got married at Fort Lee, Virginia in June. lots of my friends and family from Pennsylvania came down for the wedding which made me feel quite good. Tom Boland who was a good friend from Ohio; went to Kent State, was my best man. He's always been a dear friend." a dear friend."

"So, Fred you got married before you went back to Vietnam?"

"Yeah, I was in the states for 15 months before I went back to Vietnam the second time. That was a quick turn around by all accounts. They needed Mortuary officers. They were hard to find. And I had done well enough in my first tour and as my work as the commander of the 16th Mortuary division. Also, during this. I was promoted again this time to Captain. Finally, that accomplished, I was getting some decent pay as well, Larry."

Curious, I ask.

"Now was most of that pay needed or could you send some of it home and save it?"

"Well during Vietnam, I sent most of it home. Even though we weren't paid that much; how much could you spend in Vietnam?"

I ask.

"In Vietnam you had a commissary, right? If I'm correct, you have a P.X. (Post Exchange) where you can get groceries and household stuff, and a B.X. (Base Exchange) where you can get about anything else; right? I also heard that you got very reasonable prices there."

"Oh yeah. Even to this day if you went to the commissary and bought all your groceries; as opposed to buying them in a civilian economy, you'd save at least 30%, Larry."

"Now, I know when I went over to Korea, I went to an Air Force Base. It wasn't war time but still on high alert. Those two places were quite nice in Korea. They were almost like a department store or a super grocery store instead of anything looking very military.

Oh yeah; they were and still are as nice as they could be. Plus, you can get most anything you wanted there."

I ask.

"Now did you cook, or did you eat at a mess hall?"

"In Vietnam we ate at the mess hall three times a day. Stuff you bought at the B.X. or the commissary was for your evenings or pleasure eating."

"Now tell me more about your second tour."

"In July of 69 was when I got to Vietnam the second time.

When I got off the plane, I called up the Mortuary division there and said I needed a ride. When they heard my name, they said; 'Who are you?'

'Well, I'm your new commander.' That was followed by a real long pause. We will send a Jeep for you. Well, I got to the Mortuary, and I met the commander, and that poor guy had no idea that I was coming to replace him; very uncomfortable, Larry. He was being relieved and that was not a good thing. So, he and I went to the headquarters of the 88th general support group which was responsible for the Mortuary. He waited outside while I talked to the executive officer. Through a discussion, I agreed that I would allow this Captain to still command the Mortuary for at least one month so that he would have six months in command. If that didn't happen, he would look bad because the six-month mark was used as a measuring stick for whether you were successful or not in your job. Also, it would look bad on your record if you were relieved of your command. This guy was a good commander, but he didn't have enough schooling in the Mortuary affairs and unfortunately, he didn't allow his N.C.O.'s to do their job. In the army an officer commands, he doesn't really run anything. The N.C. O's run things. If you don't have the knowledge of what the difference is between running and commanding, then you're gonna have a real problem; and this guy really did. When an officer tries to run something it's gonna get screwed up, because we were not taught to run things. That was a problem at the Mortuary. He thought he ran the unit, and he didn't understand the difference. So, I worked as the Mortuary officer of the 88th support group. I could go out to the Mortuary anytime I wanted and recommend changes. But I couldn't tell him or order him to do such and such. He was told by his commander however that if Captain Seese comes out there and asks you to change something you will change it. That's how we worked. I spent about six weeks in that mode. I was positioned as the S-3 Worthy unit. The executive officer's name was R.A. Herts. He was very particular. In fact, most of the people in the group hated his butt. They usually ended up ignoring him when he gave them orders. Turns out the officer corps of the U.S. Army was not well thought of. Larry, I grew up quick in the Army. I learned fast about the term, responsibility. Back in college; as I mentioned, I wasn't mature enough to handle responsibility. but I learned both of those things quick in the Army. That's why I was such a good officer and such a good commander. I turned around my unit in Fort Lee from one of the worst into one of the best in the first Army. It's one of the reasons that I got sent directly as a commander. So, for six weeks I did whatever was necessary. Unfortunately, it was to go down and check on the battalions. We had two main ones. One was in Chu Lai and one in Fu Bai. Their C/O told the people in those battalions that when I came down there what I spoke was what would happen. So, with that in mind when I did make those visits it was tense for sure. I think you can see that, Larry. Here I am a second Lieutenant, telling a Colonel or a Major what they're supposed to do. That didn't go over very well. So, I didn't make many friends in those encounters, Larry."

"So, after those six weeks was up, you took over; right?"

"Yes, I did."

"The guy I replaced, did some sort of duties because he had six months to go. Anyway, I never saw him again. During the six weeks I had made some changes with the Mortuary and the staff there. Couple of the N.C.O.'S that were there, I knew from my assignment in Fort Lee Va. Two of them were dead heads. They had gone to personnel at the Mortuary officers and suggested changes that were in place when I got there. Larry, they were not good changes. It was good for them, but not for the Mortuary. These changes were good for them, because they knew that they would likely be court-martialed then demoted. I had some experience and those guys both got demoted and reassigned out of my unit. when I got to the Mortuary, we had a full assignment of N.C.O.'s, which was 50 enlisted and supposedly, five officers. But what we really had were two officers. I had a great first Sergeant happen to be one of our instructors in the school I was in back at Fort Lee. Sargent Hackleberry. You know; he and I got along well, because he understood that he ran the unit and that I wouldn't step on his toes as the head enlisted man and that he would never step on my toes as the commanding officer. So, we got along well. My success at the Mortuary was very much in part due to his success and cooperation with me. When I needed to do something, I went directly through him."

"Now when you were there, what kind of volume did you process through your area? As I remember, in the whole conflict there were 57,314 who died."

"I can't really tell you how many men we processed, Larry. Never kept track of numbers."

"It was obviously a fairly high-volume; right Fred?"

"Yes."

He adds.

"One of the first things I did was that I wanted a flagpole out in front of the Mortuary. We didn't have one; and I thought that was wrong. So, I got some guys to come in and work up a nice little drawing and design. I approved it. A couple of days later they had it installed. We had a flagpole with approaches. We raised the American flag, Larry. Now I told them that that flag is not gonna be brought down. It would fly 24 hours a day until we have no bodies in this Mortuary. If we have one body, it will be flying. It was flying every day I was there except one, so that will give you an idea that we always had bodies to process. We ran the Mortuary

24 hours a day. We didn't have any officers on the night shift, but we had N.C.O.'S and enlisted men on the night shift. There were two shifts: 7 A.M. through 7:00 P.M. and then 7:00 P.M. through 7:00 A.M. I always had to tell the Sergeant in charge where I was gonna be, so I really was there in reality all the time. Sometimes I was at the officer's club and a few times I went to play cards with my buddies in the Marines. Our barracks was on a Navy compound. It was also a Marine Air Group M.A.G. group. I was on call 24 hours a day."

"Fred; in this second tour when you were the commander did you; I'm guessing not get as involved with actual processing of bodies?"

"During the day; yes, I did get involved in the handling. I didn't really have to do the (quote unquote) dirty work handling the bodies; but. Most of them came in with names identified but the X bodies, as I mentioned to you were the toughest ones. We had to go through a lot of material records. We took fingerprints if we could. That's another gory subject. We also used dental records from those, and other information about where the guy was what was going on in the unit. As well, we tried to find out what happened after the deaths occurred, so that we could identify him as is correct identification. I got involved in that way. Once a person was identified by my soldiers then the records of what they developed went to Civilian Identification Officers. They would put a stamp of approval on it then they would send that to me, and I would put my stamp of approval on it as the commanding officer. Most of the time they were correct but occasionally I would find a mistake and I would disagree with them. When that happened, they really got sticky because I would point out the I.D. officers; 'Oh my here's where the problem is.' The biggest problem was the United States Marines. You could identify a body three ways; by the I.D. tag he was wearing. Fingerprints:

everybody was fingerprinted when they got to Vietnam. Everybody got a dental inspection when they got there. It was supposedly a requirement that we would receive the dental records and the fingerprints. Sometimes we got them sometimes we didn't; but most of the times we did. The Marines liked to identify people quickly. The third way you could identify a person was called 'facial recognition.' Two signed statements of facial recognition from two members of the unit. Marines often used this because it was very quick. But it came to a head one day when they sent the body down with the name of so and so on it. I looked at the chart showing where the wounds were on the body and how he was killed. Here was a young man who died as a result of a gunshot wound to the head. I went out and looked at this body and there was no face, Larry. Yet we had two statements of facial recognition of this guy. I said, 'This has got to stop.,' Larry, I immediately made an appointment to talk to the two-star general the Marines I went over and discussed the problem with him, and he agreed. USARV put a little pressure on him as well and after that, stronger protocols were installed. Up until that point from my first tour till then that practice was being used. After that, thankfully it wasn't. Luckily, that was ended. One of the things that disturbed me most both tours as when a Colonel or a General would come into the Mortuary and want to see their men. I would say to them; 'Sir; they're not your men, they're mine. When we heard that a Colonel or General was coming and we had some very bad remains on a table we would put them in the backroom and that kept those guys on a short leash. They didn't like what they saw. Now down in Saigon, the area between the backroom and the processing room had a door that swung both ways. My commander down there painted it green. We let those senior officers come in. Our Major would brief them. He would call me Junior. Would you escort the officer into the processing area? Many times, the officer would follow me into the processing area and many times; before I could turn around, he was back in the other area, because he didn't wanna face what I was looking at or what I was going to show him. So, and on my second tour, I continued that same practice. When somebody wanted to see their men. It was the same result; they didn't stay long. I liked it that way because I was left to my own, I was allowed to command my area; process my bodies and not offend anybody. As it turns out Larry, nobody wanted to hear or see what my unit did. A lot of times I'd go to the club and start talking to somebody and they'd ask me what exit section I was in, and I would tell them and that would be the end of that. They would say 'Oh; okay and let's go on to something else.' If we had war correspondents in the area, we didn't want them in the Mortuary anyway; and especially we didn't want them taking pictures that would be a misinterpretation of everything that we were trying to accomplish; Larry. No pictures were allowed of any of the bodies. That was a regulation; it wasn't my rule."

"Alright, so that took another year and basically you stayed in the Army quite a while after that; right?"

"Yes, as an Army reservist."

"So, you were in a reserve role after that; right?"

"Yes, I served in many units. Everywhere from the 433rd. support group, which was at Oakdale Pa. to commanding psychological operations company. I had a detachment up and Butler Pennsylvania it was a personnel Administration Battalion. Many many duties; many many jobs. I enjoyed them all, Larry."

"Being back in the United States; those roles you were in were more like a job, right.?"

"Oh, right. Yeah, it was a daily job. Well, it wasn't daily. It was one weekend a month plus an administration meeting every week. The advertisement says, 'one week a month,' but that's not correct. As an officer or senior N.C.O., you went once a week in the evening for four hours which was unpaid in most cases; plus, two days on a weekend in the month, when you were paid. Four days for two days work. Every drill you did was a day's pay. I did 5 1/2 years active duty, and the rest of the time was as a reservist. During that time, I also worked for the Army reserve. I was at the 99th. R Corp."

"At some point you were recruiter, weren't you?"

"Yes, you're right. I was a recruiter. I was a civilian recruiter working for the Army. We had our own office for that purpose. We had our office in with officers that we shared with the other services. When I was in Butler. Pa. I was working with active duty as well. When we went out to schools and so on, the active-duty people would do their spiel and then I would do mine. I would take a thick magazine with me I would hold it up between my hands say this is the United States Army. Full time soldiers working full time. Soldiers working 24 hours a day. Then I would take a book putting back at that I would show them that that was the Army Reserve the Army Guard together. This is the backup to The United States Army. There were more people in the reserves than there were in active duty. So, we were a bigger back up. That's why I showed the book; to show that if you hit the magazine, it'll bend if I put that book behind it, you hit it doesn't bend; cause of the strength of the book represents the strength of the Army Reserve. The Army Reserve backs up the active Army; so, if somebody didn't want to serve in the active Army then they would certainly have a place in the Army reserves."

"Fred, what a great illustration!"

I add.

"So, when did Sherry become involved?"

"We were in Butler Pa. I was in the 300th transportation group. I would be going to an admin. Meeting. Once, when I came home, Sherry said to me.

"What the world do you do there all the time?"

"Why don't you join and find out?"

"She looked at me and speaks.

"Okay, I'm going to. I'm going to join!"

"We had a program at the time in the Army Reserves that took the expertise of a civilian and converted it to military expertise. She could go to a two-week basic training; come back to the unit that agreed to take them. Then they would finish the basic training. They already had a skill, so they really didn't have to go to individual training. They would use that skill that they had, as a bridge. Sherry's skill was in administration. So, she started out as the clerk typist. Came in as a Pfc.; not as an E-1; but as an E-3; because she already had a skill. The normal soldier would make Pfc. in about 8 to 10 months. It was called a civilian acquired skill program. I gave her the oath of office in the commander's office with Greg sitting on the desk, with Sherry standing beside it, in front of the American flag, with her hand raised. I got a nice picture of that with her and Greg together; special. Greg was probably only about three years old. Couple of weeks later, she went to her two weeks training. Mom came up and watched Greg during the day. Sherry would come home and then she would start coming to our unit. She did quite well. She decided that she wanted to become an officer. Shortly after she got in, she was in a meeting, and was told that; because she had college experience she could have enlisted as an officer. Sherry then was told by her officer that she could have become one. He then asked her why she wasn't enrolled.

She responded.

"Well, it's because my husband didn't tell me I could be enrolled as an officer."

"So, I told her; You'll become an officer when I tell you. I wasn't trying to be difficult. I just didn't want her to take any shortcuts. I made her take three command courses and learn certain things before I'd let her apply to become an officer. Because of her experience and college time, she was commissioned as a Captain in U. S. Army. She was made a First Lieutenant. That's when we couldn't always be in the same unit. The military tried to keep couples in the same unit even when they joined the active Army, they were guaranteed their first assignment would at least be together. In the reserves, they tried to keep them together as much as possible. Most of the time we had such different skills that we would be in different units. Every time she was interviewed, she held her own for sure and was easily given new positions. She did well for 22 years, Larry."

"I'm sure you were very proud of her."

I add.

"Now did you also have a civilian job during this time?"

"All during this time I work for the 99th ARCAM. Right towards the end, I opened my computer store and got out of the military job. That was the time when I already had my 20 years in. About a year after that I got completely out of the Army Reserves, and retired. That was 1989; I was in from 1965 to 1989."

I ask.

"When you were getting Army pay towards the end of your career, would you consider that 'good money?'"

"Larry, I retired as a Lieutenant Colonel and the decent money started coming when I made Major. Yes, I would say I did make decent pay. As a civilian, I went from a GS-7 to a GS-9 in my civilian job. Yeah, it was decent. We got decent raises also. By the time I got out I was a GS-9 step 7, which set me up comfortably."

"Would you say it was comparable to an experienced teacher, or better?"

"I would say certainly equivalent to if not a little bit better."

I add.

"Also, wouldn't benefits be very good?"

"Yes. When you reached age 60, you could draw your military retirement. So, we didn't have to necessarily save into individual accounts like IRA's and things like that. The money we had saved up in various ways we decided to take it in one lump sum when we got out. Because the number of years and the ranks we attained, our retirements were very good."

"You guys deserved it!"

"Larry; sometimes I think that the benefits should have been even better. One of the things that the U.S. Army; or the military, says if you serve 20 years and retire honorably you have medical the rest of your life. Well, what they meant was you have basic medical. We're not covered under vision or dental. That was a misunderstanding of young soldiers joining. In fact, that was a big one. Being a combat veteran, I was able to get vision coverage. Sherry is not a combat veteran, so she doesn't get vision. Also, Sherry is not eligible for V.A. because she wasn't a 20 year plus combat veteran."

"Fred; here's a question about something that I talked to all the other guys about. Did you get Agent Orange when you were in Vietnam?""

"Everybody in Vietnam was exposed to Agent Orange. Yeah, all bases were sprayed around perimeters. Each base had to have an area where no enemy could come into with short range weapons and attack. At the base where I was, the field of fire was about 1/2 a mile. That was where they had to clear all that vegetation. They used Agent Orange. So, if you were in or about an Air Force Base you got the effects of Agent Orange. Both of my tours in Vietnam were in and about Air Force bases, so I was exposed, Larry. Also, I was exposed when I did a sortie into the Asho Valley. That was a mission I haven't told you about; but I will. That was a mission to recover bodies. All the vegetation was destroyed in that area, and everything had dust on them. If you brushed any of the vegetation, everything was blown up into the air. So, unless you were the first man through the vegetation you were gonna breathe it."

"Fred; would you want to elaborate on that mission, or not?"

"Larry, after I got P.T.S.D., I could hardly talk about anything like that. Still once a month I talk to a psychiatrist. Anyway, at the U.S. Army Mortuary, the second trip, we had to go out on 'search and recovery' missions. It required an officer and the C/O and a couple of other soldiers. With only having two officers underneath me instead of four, if we had recovery missions, every other time one of those officers had to go. I felt that that wasn't quite fair, so we set up a schedule where they would go out twice; alternating normally and then I would go out. Then they would go out twice, and I would go out. So, I went on quite a few recovery missions. We probably had a half a dozen a month of those."

"What were they like, Fred? Were you going into an area that was totally unknown to you finding bodies haphazardly or did you already know where they were?"

"We already knew where they were; roughly. This one mission was to recover the bodies of two pilots who had been in a cobra helicopter. They had gone down in the jungle. They were shot down in their Cobra helicopter. It was shot down in 1966 and never found until this small unit of Vietnamese soldiers came across it. They marked it on their maps where it was and reported it through channels. It eventually came down to us that we would have to go into the Asho valley and recover these bodies and return them. Asho Valley was not a place to be, no matter where or when. It was totally controlled by the Vietcong, and North Vietnam regulars. So, we were sent out in a helicopter. Right before we got there a ground unit of security was flown in to set up security for us when we landed. Then after we landed another group of engineers were brought out. They had to set explosives on the Cobra to destroy it so it couldn't be used by the enemy. We got there and were led by the Vietnamese that found the place. We had to hike up this mountain. We were in a 'triple canopy jungle,' which most of Vietnam was. So, we trekked up to this mountain site. We didn't have to search too much because the location the Vietnamese soldiers found, was close to where it was. The Cobra helicopter that had crashed upside down, on its head. So, it was laying on its top; belly up. We had to break through the belly to get to the Cockpit and bring out the remains. But as you can imagine Larry, by this time the remains were all bones and nothing else. Now when you go out on a search and recovery, you must make a map of the search and recovery area. While the N.C.O. and the soldiers we're getting through the belly I was getting making drawings of the area; making markings where the helicopter lay and where we had to break through it and bring the bones up. That's what I was doing. the N.C.O. and the two soldiers retrieved all the bones. We placed them in sandbag sacks. That's how we recovered them. Now when you handle any remains you handle them gently and with 'reverence,' because; believe me, it might sound crude that we put them in sandbag sacks but that was just the way it was."

I couldn't add much.

"What else could you do?"

"Right; each pilot was put into two sacks. One sack couldn't hold one body. After this was done the engineers set explosives in order to destroy the helicopter. This Cobra helicopter still had two pods of active rockets on each side of it, so we couldn't allow those to be left in place. That was one of the main things that had to be exploded. Once the charges were set, we had to run like hell down that mountainside, so we didn't get blown up. There's only much time that you can put on those charges, so we did not have a leisurely walk down. We got ourselves down; jumped behind some fallen trees and we just managed to do that before the explosion went off. Boy; bits and pieces of that craft went flying everywhere. Debris was landing all around us. That was a day that I didn't like at all, Larry. We got it done. The security team had their own choppers. Half the security team was sitting there at the mouth of the Asho Valley, with Light Infantry security and no helicopter. We needed two helicopters to really handle the amount of people we had. It wasn't one of those big Chinook helicopters. It was just a small chopper. One Huey (a smaller and popular helicopter used by the military) showed up. We all got in barely and we were overloading it. So, when we left, it was just turning dark. We're in an overloaded helicopter; flying barely over the tops of the trees. That was an anxious time for me and all the guys that were with me. As we were riding out of the valley, I happened to look at the soldier handling the door gun. I noticed that he had a second Lieutenant bar on his shoulder. So, I said to myself; 'Oh shit, that tells me that the door gunner is flying the helicopter.' Turns out the helicopter pilots like to handle the guns and here we are being flown out and we really have a Sergeant flying us on the Huey. The other light moment was when we landed at Phu Bai. We had to get on a plane to take us down to Saigon. We were always the first on board when we were handling military remains. Our flight was called We headed out to the aircraft. We're loading out. The pilot in charge said to us.

"Wait a minute. You guys were supposed to be taking out human remains. Where are the stretchers? Where are the remains? The two soldiers handling the sandbags held them up and said, 'Here they are.' The pilot says, 'Oh crap; get on the plane!"

Fred adds.

"That was definitely the worst mission I ever went on."

"I totally understand. Now, Fred; if you will, tell me the effects of Agent Orange on your body. What has it done to you over the years?"

"Give me a moment, Larry. I'm trying to get it together. That's a reality that I've rarely liked to talk about."

"Fred, I think it's important."

"I do too, Larry. I don't normally discuss this with nonmilitary personnel."

"Sure."

"That's why I'm hesitating. I'll be 76 in June. Right before I turned 70; maybe 68 or 69; well actually I can go back to when I first got out. That's when I had some bad dreams. I had nightmares every night. When I would go on my reserve weekends, which were two weeks, I would get bad dreams; thinking I was back in Vietnam. I found out that what I was dreaming about was very common. I dreamed that I was captured; being held captive, tortured cruelly. Even though I was in a position where I hadn't experienced true combat, but I was in positions where it was uncomfortable, I saw things that no one would want to see; Larry. I didn't tell you exactly some of the things that happened to me on my first tour, where I was shot at. But right now, that's inconsequential. Those first dreams were about being captured. They were awful and so real! After a while they went away, but it took a couple of years. I would have them especially during the weekends, and sometimes afterwards. a lot of those times we weren't even out in the field. We were in the reserve centers. Mostly, these dreams happened when I was out on bivouacs. We; in fact, did that routine more and more as time went on, because they wanted us to get more involved with outdoor activities, which was outdoor training of course, or bivouacs. Then training was more extensive. We did that in mock gear, but that gear was very uncomfortable and heavy. During the most intense periods, you might not eat for eight hours. You'd only have water. When I retired in 89 that dream stopped after a while. Then when I was around 68, they started back again. My psychiatrist and I agreed that when they weren't happening, was mostly because I wasn't put in any kind of position where I would be remembering anything about Vietnam. Nevertheless, I cannot watch many movies about Vietnam. So, I just stayed away from them. Even some episodes of MASH would trigger stuff for me. Twice a month I go to group meetings with other folks that have P.T.S.D. With those people, you find out what's common and what's not. For sure what I had was very common. My dreams really got worse at this time. I would see mangled; almost zombielike soldiers chasing me. That would wake me up in the middle of the night screaming. Especially when I first got out; these dreams would drive Sherry up the wall as you can imagine."

"I can; Fred."

"So, those came about again. My other dream was about all the bloody uniforms that we had to burn in the personal property depot. I would dream about the limbs of the soldiers that we would have to burn because at the Mortuary we had incinerator. We would get bodies that were in pieces. They came in on stretchers and in body bags in most cases. We would take the human remains out of the body bags put them on a table; and as I say there were lots of times arms and legs that were separated. They would be removed and put into separate bags and mark with the same number that we had for that soldier that we were processing. Once we got enough of those and 'parts' as they were called, we would have to incinerate them. When the hospitals would amputate limbs, they would be put in coolers and we would put them in bags and we would; in lighthearted way on something that shouldn't have been treated that way, call them 'spare parts.' Once we had a commander come in and we were counting bags. The bags would have numbers on them; X- 5, X-27, etc. He was counting the names on the board, and he kept coming up with one extra. First, I couldn't figure out the difference. Finally, it dawned on me what it was, and I said; 'Oh; this is the bag of 'spare parts.' The commander about fainted. He said what do you mean 'spare parts?' 'My apologies Sir but that's what we call them. They are spare limbs that come from the hospital when amputations are made. So, I'd have dreams about that. It got to the point where I couldn't hardly do anything during the days because of those dreams I was having at night.

I became very upset; very offensive. Brian was down visiting one day he and I took a walk, just to keep me calm. Just one street off Virginia street; where I live, this lady came out of the house, and she asked what we were doing. I think she thought we were casing her area. My reaction was this. I read her up one side down the other and scared the crap out of her."

"Wow!"

"After we got back to the house, we were in the back sitting on the patio. I said to Brian; and I'm shaking like hell and feeling bad. Mostly, I'm feeling bad because of what I said to that woman. It really hit me and really upset me. I told Brian; 'I'm gonna go back up and talk to that Lady; explain who I am and what was happening.' Brian says.

'No, no, no! let's not do that. Let's not go back there.' I told him we must. So, we went back up by; knocked on her door; I introduced myself properly and apologized. I showed her my U.S. Army I.D. card I told her that I was so sorry what I had done. I also tried to school her on what she had done wrong. I told her; 'The sad thing is; if I were armed, I probably would have shot you.' That's certainly not what I would want to have happened.' I added.

'If you ever find somebody that you can't identify in your yard, please just call the police. Let them handle it.'

She accepted my apologies. I felt so much better after that."

"Well, she should have. It was a wonderful gesture; and it also should have made Brian more understanding of what was going on with both you and her."

"As it turned out Brian did understand. Shortly after that, Greg came up and visited. I think he came because Brian called him. when Greg came up, I told him; 'Greg, I want you to take my pistol.' Greg said, 'Dad, you shouldn't necessarily have to do that. I said, 'No, you take it. I'm telling you right now you take it.' I was in such a bad state that I felt I might injure myself. I was afraid I was gonna kill myself, Larry. I wasn't planning on hurting anybody else, but I sure could have hurt myself. So, he took my pistol. I went to my V.A. right after that and told them I needed help. That's when they started treating me for P.T.S.D. and anxiety. They wouldn't just call it P.T.S.D. They had to add the anxiety part on as well. The V.A. doesn't still truly understand P.T.S.D.; even though they wouldn't probably admit that."

"Fred; now that you've been officially treated for P.T.S.D. and anxiety, do you think it's been helping you?"

"Oh, most definitely; most definitely! Besides that, I've gotten into a group that's called "Healing Waters." They first started by teaching us to tie flies. When you're sitting there doing that, your mind just goes blank. You don't think about anything except tying that fly. They take us on trips on the weekends, fishing trips. We fish. It's very very calming; very healing, very great. They've done as much as the group therapy and the psychiatry have done put together. It calms me down very much. I'm at the point right now, when I can get together with other soldiers that have had P.T.S.D. and with my fly-tying buddies; that's all I need."

"Great; Fred! In fact, very great."

"I started taking medication. It took me about a year before I could really tell my psychiatrist about all the things that happened to me. In our discussion today, I probably haven't talked to you about a third of what really happened to me. I'll admit to you that I have still one thing that I haven't discussed with my psychiatrist. I'm not gonna tell you, for which I apologize. Greg doesn't even know. Funny thing about it is that I talked to Greg; about some of these things before I even talked to the psychiatrist about them. He's another military man, so we can get together. The psychiatrist I have never served in the military, so he really can't be fully qualified. However, he's worked a lot with soldiers with P.T.S.D. so he's gonna help as much as anybody can. He served for 20 years. He has also talked to soldiers that have come back from Afghanistan. One of the first things he did with me was to apologize for never serving in the service. Larry, I told him immediately; 'Don't ever apologize. You have no reason to. You're doing more help the soldiers now then you could have if you did serve in active military."

I add.

"Absolutely great point, Fred."

"Most of the V.A. people are prior military. But I've told anybody that'll listen, that they don't need to apologize for never serving."

I ask.

"What has the Agent Orange done to your body?"

"Well, I have Diabetes. It has also given me neuropathy. I have tingling in my legs and my feet all the time; constantly. When I got the neuropathy, it was very difficult to drive. I had to learn quick. 'Okay, my foot's on the accelerator. And we're going at certain speed. Honestly Larry, I can't feel my foot on the accelerator. I had to learn quick when to push my foot forward, even though I couldn't feel myself under it. I also had to learn when to switch from the accelerator to the brake. So, I drive much differently than I used to when I was younger. I try to know where I'm at and what I'm always doing. Funny thing about it; this happened to my friend the Sergeant major who I meet with in Connellsville. He even stopped driving for a while. I didn't understand that until I got neuropathy also. It was down for a while but it's getting intense, more recently. Monday, I have an appointment with my dietitian. I've got my Diabetes medicine increased temporarily until I can get this neuropathy down to a manageable level. It's not dangerous but it's too high. I take two medicines a day for my sugar the Diabetes and I don't have to take insulin; thankfully."

"What about cancer, Fred?"

"I had a test last year and they found no cancer in me, Larry. There was really no reason to give me the test, but I felt it was necessary. They thought it was the proper thing to do as well. I took the test and I'm very relieved to tell you that I'm cancer free. I felt very good about that. I still very feel very good about it every time I think about it great that's one thing I don't wanna get. I've got many friends that do have it. I'm of the opinion; as well as most of my friends, that if it ever got that bad, and even though they can give you drugs to prolong your life for another year and a half or so, I would not take the medicine."

"Fred; I understand. I agree with you that if I have that fate myself that I wanna do the same thing that you're doing."

"I consider you 100% a hero, Fred. I respect that I got a chance to talk to you. I'm glad I did."

"I hope in this Epilogue, that you're able to interject some of the good times. because in Vietnam there were some good times. Those good times really kept us soldiers going. The good things that we did. I feel very good about the service that I performed.

Getting the soldiers to their correct next of kin was so important. I can tell you a few instances where it's possible that we were going to make a mistake and I send notes ahead that I would not be satisfied completely until the F.B.I. could make an identification: through prints. Anytime that happened and a mistake was made the "news" would get ahold of it and they would certainly use it to create ill will between the public and the service sector. Certainly, I did not want that. The one time I can so remember, when I got a note back from California. The name it was believed to be was not correct. Then a week or so later we got in the guy we thought we had and realized the mistake. It was terrible mistake. However, Larry, we got it corrected before it ever got back to the next of kin. I felt very good that I made sure every time. I'm happy to say that no one left Vietnam under my command that were misidentified. I feel very good that everyone that got buried by their next of kin was the correct person."

SHERMAN MOSLEY

AGE WHEN ENTERED MILITARY: 18

DATE OF ENTRY TO MILITARY: 08/23/1971

VIETNAM TOUR DATES: 1972-1973

YEARS OF DUTY/RESERVES: 6

SHERMAN MOSLEY

I met Sherman through my friend Bill Cooper. I felt the need to have at least two interviews from each branch of the service. I had this covered except for the Navy. I went to Bill once, and he could offer no help. After efforting with some local organizations, I went back to Bill and added a way to have a wider scope. I told him this person did not need to be local, as I was comfortable with a phone interview as opposed to a face to face. Soon he offered Sherman. Turns out they were shipmates on the U.S.S. Strauss. Interestingly, they never met personally till long after Vietnam. The Strauss crew often had reunions and that is where they met. Now they are close friends and have traveled together with their wives. Bill was on a 2/4 path and Sherman was 4/2. Each Navy commitment was for 6 years. Bill served two years active and 4 years as a reservist. Sherman did the opposite. Bill's position on the ship had him out on the deck, where he could see things that were happening on the shore. Sherman was down 2-3 levels inside the ship. The ship was a destroyer and had over 300 crewmates on board at any time. As Sherman put it; it would be like working in a large building. It would be easy to know only those in your immediate area.

Sherman was born and raised in Nashville and now lives in a small-town south of there. He's lived there for about 15 years. Sheman and his wife retired last year. His career was in the area of being a diesel mechanic. His longest job being with Firestone, lasting 45 years.

"Sherman, how did you get into the Navy?"

"Larry, my father was in the Navy in W.W. II. After high school, Vietnam was still going on. They had the lottery system happening. My number was around 137. It appeared that 150ish was the number, that if you were under that, you would probably be getting drafted. I decided to avoid that. I wanted to be in the Navy, and knew if I were drafted, I would not have a choice. So, in 1971, I enlisted. I didn't join with the notion of going to Vietnam, but knew it was a possibility. I was probably hoping to go to the Mediterranean or someplace else nice like that.

Lots of guys in that time had cars and liked working on them. I did too. When I got to boot camp, I took a "battery exam" to see what my aptitude was. They test every aspect of your head, such as foreign language, math, mechanical and some others. Of course, I tested out very high in the mechanical area. So, after boot camp, I was sent to diesel school and spent a few months in Chicago. Then I got my orders to report to The Strauss. It was then stationed in Pearl Harbor, Hawaii. But when I got there, it had already left on a WestPac cruise. So, they put me on a 23-hour flight and another long flight that took me to the Philippines. Once there, I got on a ship and was transported to DaNang Harbor, Vietnam, where the Strauss was at."

"So, Sherman; when you finally got to Vietnam and the Strauss, how active was the war around you. What was happening?"

"I became an engineman. The Strauss was a steam driven ship. I was put in the R division (Repair) division. I basically worked all over the ship, but my main job was the "boat engineer." If the Captain or the Commodore needed to go ashore for any reason, I would be on that boat, as the mechanic. That size boat required a minimum of three enlisted men. On was a coxswain, a bow hook, who handled the lines, and a mechanic."

"So, this is 1972?"

"Yes, I met the Strauss in February of 72."

"As such, you probably spent most of your time down in the ship, right?"

"Yes, when we were at sea, I would stand throttle watch. The captain would set the dials the way he wanted them, and someone (me) had to physically open the valves to comply. At sea, mostly I was assigned to the engine room. Anytime we were at port, I was assigned to the boats. We were in DaNang. When we went ashore it was usually to pick up mail or other supplies. Once I made a beer run. That time it was a South Vietnamese M.I.C. boat. Our C/O borrowed it from their Army. We made two runs. The first day we brought on 150 cases of beer. The second day we picked up 200 cases. Each guy on the ship could go down for an hour and drink as much as he wanted. That was considered a Liberty Call in DaNang Harbor."

"" So, when you were in that Harbor, what was going on in that area? Could you see or hear actual fighting?"

No, we were outside the base. Anytime a ship stops at sea, there is constant maintenance going on. The theory is that once you stop working on the ship, it will sink."

"So, how long were you on The Strauss?"

"I was there from February 2nd of 1972, through June 15th of 1975."

I speak.

"Of 75?"

"Yes; most sailors count the days."

"So, what rank were you when you went in?"

"Everyone starts as a recruit. I was an E-1 in boot camp. Once you leave, you are an E-2. After that you must earn any further promotions."

"By 1975, what rank were you?"

"I was an E-4. Third Class. I was offered a promotion at the end, but I chose to get out."

"Most of the people I've talked to, somehow ended up with effects from Agent Orange. Did you?"

"Yes, I'm on the Agent Orange Registry. I receive a 30 % medical disability now. I'll probably make another claim for Neuropathy. By being there and traveling to port on the M.I.C. boat, I did get exposed."

"Sherman, what exactly is a M.I.C. boat? Sorry, I should have asked that earlier."

"Most people spell it MICK but that's not correct. It's a Mechanical Amphibious Boat."

"You were on the Strauss a little more than 3 years. Is that what you signed up for?"

"All enlistments are 6 years. Now, Bill was a 2/4 and I signed up for a 4/2."

"When you got out, you went back to Tennessee, is that right?"

"I had a girlfriend in Ohio at the time, so I went to see her. Then I came home. I didn't do anything for a while. I collected unemployment for a while. I really didn't want to go to work right away."

"I know you said that you're married now. Did that happen right after you got home?"

"I came home after travelling the world. I married a country girl. That lasted just under 3 years. We had one daughter. We got a divorce and after three years, at age 29 I married again. We're still married."

"That's great. Any children with her?"

"Yes, we have one boy."

"Sherman, when you got home, did you experience any of the awful stuff that many returning servicemen endured; spit on, sworn at, accused of awful stuff?"

"I was never spat on, but I had people up in my face a time or two."

I speak.

"I still haven't resolved why that terrible treatment happened."

"Larry, my opinion of why, is that W.W.II was a spectacular win for the U.S. Everyone was proud and happy and came home to a hero's welcome. The economy boomed and all was good. Korea came along and we didn't win. That only lasted about two years. There were casualties, but not as many. Vietnam dragged on. The government funding: in my way of thinking was always making it so that nothing was clearcut. We were set up to fail. Television was big and it was on the news every night. It became an embarrassment that we could not be the clear winner. You said your book character was a draft dodger. There were many others who did not take that radical step, but who were truly opposed to the war. The media gave them a voice and a platform. My brother was a conscientious objector. He would not go."

"Did your brother ever get in your face after you joined?"

"No, but if we were ever in a discussion, he would get upset. He was very tender about the subject. He would probably get upset if I ever quoted him on the subject."

"After you came home, did you ever get to use your G.I. Bill opportunities?"

"No, I started to school a couple of times but never really got going. I really felt like I was behind everyone who didn't go to Vietnam. I wanted to get a job, get married, get a house, and catch up. To me, college slowed me in that pursuit. I felt like I missed a lot. That's pretty much why my first marriage didn't work, out."

"I'm so sorry that happened to you, sir. As far as any health maladies that came along with your service, when did those materialize?"

"Well, I first just thought my maladies were part of the aging process. Then, probably in my 40's I noticed things that I thought were caused by my service. I was in my 60's when I first decided to go to the V.A."

"How old are you now?"

"I'm 68. I'll be 69 in June. "

I ask.

"Now the Neuropathy. I know you said you now have it. How about anything else. Are you Diabetic? Do you have Cancer; heart problems?"

Yes, I have Diabetes. Of course, just about everyone who was in the service has Tinnitus. My ears always have a ring. I plan to make a claim for the Neuropathy but haven't yet. You eventually learn things about the V.A. I found that if you "front-load" all your info for a claim, the outcome will be better. If you try to load info piecemeal, things don't turn out as well."

"What about P.T.S.D. Many of the men I talked to have bouts, flashbacks, and awful stuff. Do you?"

"I believe I do."

"When you were on the Strauss, did you ever have a time where you feared for your life?"

"Yes, a couple of times. We hit a mine. In my case, when we were at "General Quarters" (battle preparedness), I was in the forward generator. Below decks is where this equipment was. When a mine or a torpedo ever hit, my likelihood of getting out was not good. Especially when I was with the generator, which was three decks down. The night we hit those mines I was in the forward generator. So, I was up front, below the water line. When it hit, the ship took a 43-degree roll. We were always told that if/when a 46 degree it would just keep rolling and the ship would sink. When you're down below you don't know exactly what's happening. It was very frightening!"

"Now P.T.S.D. has people having bad dreams and flashbacks. That ever happen to you?"

"Lots of nights I have dreams. I'm on the ship. Those nights you go through stuff again and again."

"What else can you tell me about your experience?"

"Well, you make a lifetime of friends. Everywhere I go, I could easily find friends to visit. The bonds a strong, Larry. Hard to ever break. You talk to guys and find out things. Private stuff. They go through substance abuse, divorce, drinking."

"Now, according to your friend, Bill, you guys have gotten togethers, right?"

"Yep, we do."

"How often do you get together?"

"Well, we are supposed to get together once a year. Covid put a crimp in that.! The 2020 one was cancelled. The next year, many of our group were still nervous about getting together. We had a "non-reunion" that year. There were about 20 of us there. This coming year it's supposed to be back in Myrtle Beach. The one after that is the one, I'm really looking forward to, will be in Mt. Rushmore."

"Wow, I really hope that happens!"

"And beyond that, the plan is for all of us to meet back in Pearl Harbor where we were stationed."

"I really love hearing about this. The bonds you have and the get togethers are so great. You and Bill were on the Strauss together, for 2 years, right?"

"Yes; part of that time we were on a "war cruise," of course. I was on the ship when the armistice was announced."

"Sherman, while you were in the conflict did you ever have a close buddy that either was killed or injured?"

"Not while on the ship. However, just last year, I lost a close friend who had several diseases related to agent Orange.

"While in Vietnam, did you know anyone injured or killed?"

"I did, but he was on a different ship."

"How did that happen?"

A shell came down through the ships deck. Everybody was in General Quarters; ready to fight. A shell came through the deck and travelled about 30 feet down a passageway. It killed a sailor who was sleeping."

"Wow."

"Have you been to the Vietnam Wall Memorial?"

"I have; yes."

"Have you seen a "travelling wall?"

"Yes, as well."

"I have also. I found my classmate from Otterbein, and a cousin from my hometown. Very emotional!"

"When you came back, you seem proud of what you accomplished. Would that be accurate?"

"It sure is!"

"Now, even though public perception of Viet Vets was not great, most who I've talked to have said; bullshit on that. I'm a hero and I'll always be one."

"Larry, when I'm in a restaurant and see a guy with a ball cap on, or a pin of recognition, I always try to strike up a conversation. I've probably picked up a dozen meal tickets for guys and couples I've met around. It's happened to me, as well. It's a brotherhood."

"Today, do you think there's more respect given for what you guys did back then?"

" Not really. I think for the veterans of other conflicts, yes. For us, I don't think we'll ever get the true recognition we deserve. When a conversation comes up and talk begins, most want to change the subject and let you know that they really don't want to hear it. No one's ever truly been proud of it."

"Well, you should be proud of your own efforts. Everyone I've talked to has made me see that the efforts you all went to are worthy of praise."

"I think the best of our entire generation has been lost over this conflict."

"Can you think of anything else?"

"No, I just came home and tried to resume my life; best I could. It took a while. It took away my first marriage. I eventually do feel I got back in a groove. I'm as proud as I ever was of what we did over there. "

"What did your wife do, Sherman?"

"She worked at Vanderbilt University for over 48 years. We probably wouldn't have retired when we did. Covid had her working from home for 6 months. Then they offered her a nice buyout package to leave, so she took it. I was still working and had a good job. After 4 months of watching her be at home, I decided I'd call it quits, too!"

"Now that you're both retired, have you been doing anything special? Any travels, trips?"

"We did a 26-day road trip out west. We went to Montana, Idaho, Wyoming, all that area. We were with Bill and Paula! We drove to Westerville, Ohio. We spent the night with them. Packed up and did all those things together. Then we came back to their house, then went home."

I add.

"I lived in Westerville for over 50 years. I moved up to where I'm at now, which is called Apple Valley, about 3 years ago. Bill and Paula became great friends over the years. I was an insurance agent and besides our church affiliation, they were my clients. They're good people."

"Yes, they are. They've been down and stayed with us a few

times. They would stay over with us, then travel an hour or so to visit their son who was a coach at a college near here. We've become good friends in the last few years."

"Now, have you ever read Bill's book?"

"Bill Cooper?"

"Yep."

"What book? I didn't know he wrote a book. What's it about?"

"It's about witnessing to people. You should ask him about it. It's small but mighty."

"For sure, I'll do that. I just talked to him this past week."

"Thanks for helping me with this project. You are on my list of heroes; for sure!!"

TIM YOUNG

AGE WHEN ENTERED MILITARY: 22

DATE OF ENTRY TO MILITARY: 09/1968

VIETNAM TOUR DATES: 05/1969-05/1970

YEARS OF DUTY/RESERVES: 2

TIM YOUNG

This next story was written by Tim Young. He's my trusted financial advisor. He and I did have an extensive interview. He then chose to do his own story in his own words. I agreed, and here it is.

SHOES

PROLOGUE:

My sense is that it is nearly impossible to understand where a person is coming from because we have not been standing in their shoes. I recall reading once that the Department of Defense calculated that between a million and 4 million troops had actually been on the ground in Vietnam during the war period. If that number is correct, then there may be that number of different perspectives.

I believe that our perspectives are a function of our experiences and upbringing. To put what follows into some perspective, here is my background relative to role models related to the military and my life in general.

Because of what was happening in Europe in 1940-1941, there was a draft. My father graduated from college in 1941 and was drafted. He was a mechanical engineer and he loved taking things apart and putting them together. The Army noticed this and his perfect eyesight, and said, "You're gonna be a pilot, my man." Thus, the Army Air Corps; after his training, flying mainly A-20's.

Then, Pearl Harbor happened. Dad grabbed Mom, his college sweetheart, and they married. Then he spent 1942, 1943, and 1944 in Africa (including the severe events at Kasserine Pass) and Italy.

My father never talked about, or even mentioned, his experiences. I learned about what he did when his Army buddies would stop by the house when they were in the Columbus area to see Dad. I heard many times; "the only pilot they would want to pilot their plane when it had been shot up, was Dave," my father. One time I found a box of medals in a drawer with some onionskin paper write-ups. Included was a Distinguished Flying Cross given when he flew a battered plane (that should not have still been in the air) with wounded crew back to the base. In spite of what "the book" said, he would not ditch a damaged plane in the Mediterranean with wounded crew members unable to swim. (Reason: "You don't leave your buddies behind.")

In Dad's Family Tree is General Eisenhower. Dad truly respected D.D.E. I learned so as well. I also was enamored with space growing up. The Mercury 7, including Ohioan John H. Glenn, were and remain heroes to me.

My early years were spent in a suburban community. From my young age, it seemed most in the community had a direct link to W.W.II. On one side was a man who had been in the Finance Corps. On the other side, a Purple Heart recipient. Two houses down lived a woman with a young son, whose husband had been killed in the war. Another soldier came home from the war and married her, because you just take care of your own. A band of brothers.

Politically then and now, I view myself as being in the middle. That is my background.

Why was the United States in Vietnam.

There are many who provide answers to that. Many of these

answers seem to be taken from the view of looking back after several years. Those making the decisions had to do so in real time, including:

- Russia was dramatically ahead in the space race. (Sputnik)
- We were not the only ones with the nuclear bomb. (Our schools had nuclear attack drills.)
- The Berlin Wall came into being in 1961. Eastern Europe had recently fallen.
- Khrushchev was at the U.N. slamming his shoe on the podium while saying, "We will bury you."
- We had just suffered humiliation in the Bay of Pigs.
- There was the 1963 Cuban missile crisis, stopped just short of a nuclear war.

The people making the decisions were adults during W.W.II, Korea, and the Berlin air lift. General MacArthur's advice to not get involved in a land war in Asia was several years before 1960. It may be that in the early 1960's, the government saw Vietnam as not at the top of the list of priorities given the other areas demanding attention.

One of the leading political scientists followed in Washington in the late 1950's and early 1960's was George F. Kennan, who espoused the "Domino Theory." Vietnam falls, Cambodia falls, Thailand falls, India falls, then the Communists are at the land of oil (the ultimate prize). At the time Thailand was suffering internal pressures. India was still splitting from Pakistan. The Domino Theory certainly appeared a likelihood.

How did I get there.

I graduated from college in 1968. Anti-war activities abounded. Individuals burned draft cards, protests in several cities and riots at the Chicago Democratic convention. There was extreme unrest arising from the assassinations of Dr. King, Robert Kennedy, and others.

The class of 1968 assumed that we would go on to Graduate School, continuing our student deferments. I would go to law school and, if the war continued when I graduated, go in as a Captain. In January 1968, the Tet Offensive happened. President Johnson announced that all graduate school deferments were ended, and the military ranks were being expanded materially. So, everybody scrambled.

I called my local Ohio draft board and asked about my situation. I was told that since I was to graduate June 10, I would be drafted in July. So, I enlisted. By doing that we would get a 120 day drop and I didn't have to go to basic training in the summer. I entered in September 1968 and went through basic training and advanced training (in artillery).

I shortly had orders to Vietnam. My advanced training was predominantly on a 105mm howitzer. I was to be in an artillery unit attached to an infantry unit. When I arrived at my unit, instead of being on a 105 in one of the fire support bases surrounding a base camp, I was assigned to the base camp commo (communications) section of the headquarters unit of an artillery unit (H.H.B.) When I asked why, one of my officers told me that some Congressman had stood up and said that the government should make better use of college graduates. They did not know what to do with me so assigned me to the commo section.

Background Note: A few basics for the reader without a military background. The military breaks skills down to a few very simple tasks. Now I was with a section for which I had no training. However, learning the basics of the equipment took a few days only. In any event my role was to be a utility player. (I had no particular place on the unit org chart.)

Because of the draft, the Army at this time was a mixture of the entire society. There were college graduates, 18-year-olds who had never been away from home, "Lifers" (career military enlisted men). I believe that pulling from all parts of the U.S. made the Army better.

Where in Vietnam was I deployed.

I was in a Field Artillery unit attached to the 25th Infantry Division. We were on the Cambodian border; III Corps. The Miliary divided South Vietnam into 4 areas. I Corps, or "Eye" Corps was the area immediately south of the D.M.Z. II Corps was to the south of that. III Corps was Saigon and to its northwest. IV Corps was the southern portion of S.V.N. (the Delta).

If you look at a map of Vietnam--go to Saigon; go 65 miles northwest of Saigon, you›ll see a formation in which S.V.N. forms a little peninsula, surrounded by portions of Cambodian. The bottom part of Cambodia surrounding us was called the" Fishhook." The top part was known as the "Parrot's beak." Tay Ninh province (where I was most of the time), is the peninsula in the middle. The Ho Chi Minh trail (the long supply channel from N.V.N. through Laos and Cambodia) ended on the west side of Tay Ninh Province. Our mission was to block the trail and keep the Viet Cong (V.C.) from getting to Saigon.

We were in a rice paddy and jungle area. It was very flat except for one mountain. It was the sacred mountain—Nui Bah Din. There's a lot of vegetation due to considerable rain. Lot of bamboo. That stuff grows like a weed, as you know. We occasionally went into the next province over. We ran some operations there. There was an enormous Michelin rubber plantation there. Rubber trees were all in rows.

   a. Like any operation, for every person on the front line, there are many behind him/her supporting and getting them

there. Same here. While most readers may think that every soldier had a role like that of Forrest Gump or John Wayne, the roles would overlap. The percentages that follow are merely my guesses. Those in direct combat frequently with the enemy, in the field looking to engage – less than 10%.
b. Those in direct support of a. – e.g., artillery, direct supply, etc., maybe 15+ %.
c. All others going back to the those off-loading the supply boats at Cam Ranh Bay and the other ports, the major airports (such as Tan Son Nhut – more daily traffic at the time than O'Hare.)

Because of where we were and the nature of the conflict, there was no defined front line. The V.C. did not wear N.V.N. military uniforms. In essence there was the infantry which was out searching for the V.C. Then there were those in the camps who were a stationary target. Our base camp had the infantry when they were standing down, the direct support and supply people, a small air strip for choppers and Caribou with Short Takeoff and Landing capability.)

Because of my position on the org chart (i.e., not there), I ended up doing a variety of things—some mundane, some interesting. I went out with our radio man and set up a commo station in advance of sweeps by the infantry. We would organize loading 105's on barges down the river to cover infantry sweeps. I also did some communication codes (I had a top-secret crypto clearance, but that was not probably necessary). Sometimes I would be in a helicopter. We had sensors scattered in the area. (Locals were told not to be out of their villages or they may set off a sensor.) If a sensor went off overnight, we would throw ordinance on the spot and then go out in the morning to see what was there.

The People:

While any generalization of a group is unfair, I will do this anyhow. The Vietnamese people are a mixture. Some from the mountains. Some rural. Some from the cities. From what I have read about Saigon (I was never there), the people there had been under the influence of French colonialism for some time. Not the case in the rural area in which I was stationed.

In a sense, the people were tribal. While Saigon was the capital, the people of Tay Ninh province (although not far from Saigon) did not appear to look to Saigon. They were farmers and shopkeepers; Industrious.

The farmers went daily to their rice paddies. Several generations lived together in relatively small spaces. If the rice crop was good and everyone healthy, life was good.

There was an interesting mix in Tay Ninh. It was the seat of the Cao Dai religion. Supposedly there were a million plus adherents worldwide. Their belief is founded on the basis that there is no one prophet that has the complete way. Thus, they read the Old and New Testament, the Koran, Buddhism, writings of Victor Hugo and Sun Yat-sen, etc. The symbol on their places of worship was an all-seeing eye; interesting.

Also in Tay Ninh were a large number of Catholics that has migrated south from North Vietnam when the French Garrison Dien Bien Phu fell in 1954 (resulting in the D.M.Z. line being drawn forming the North and the South). Several priests had gathered their parishes and moved them south to Tay Ninh.

Many times, local residents of these religions commented to me that they were glad the G.I.'s were here. Otherwise, they would not have been able to live their lives (including to practice their chosen religion).

Daily life

Six months of hot and dry and the other six months were hot and wet. Basically, I was there a year, counted to 365 and went home; unlike World War II.

80-90+% boredom/routine. The remainder, over-excitement.

The Routine/the boredom:

I am not sure what most people think of as what a day was like. I suppose that many think that every day for every soldier was like the scenes from Forrest Gump and Lt Dan. The forces had several different roles and styles. There were the combat infantry units. That is, those of the Forrest Gump and Lt. Dan's. We were direct support—involved directly but not crawling into tunnels.

The routine/boredom was getting ready for something unknown. The remainder involved taking fire, which we did several days a week.

As I said, we were not the infantry, but rather the support. Thus, we were not out crawling in the jungle like Forrest Gump in the movie. We spent the majority of our time within the base camp, going beyond for supply missions to the fire support bases (each with 6 105mm howitzers) and other excursions. However, we were on the front line. Because the front line was all around. Unlike W.W.I when the front line was specific and moved from time to time. Because the base camp was always in the same place, we were a common target.

The effective range of a 105 was 7 miles. [155's and 175's had more range.] The idea was that the infantry would generally be within the range of artillery or other fire support. The 105's were towed, meaning that they could be hooked up to a truck and moved. There was also mobile armor.

At night we slept in bunkers (to protect from mortars and rockets). There were a few small bunkers. Most were large. Inside

2 by 4 slat construction, each had sleeping spaces like a mausoleum. There was no natural air circulation (no windows in a bunker). Sleeping was on an air mattress. When the person above you moved, the sand (which was everywhere) would fall. There was one large fan at the end. We hoped that the generator would work all night. Our main bunker was next to a pit that housed 8-inch artillery pieces. When they fired over us, the bunker would shake.

There were showers. We had a raised pontoon painted back to warm the water by the sun. Turn the spigot on. We had a choice. Shower at night (waking up in the A.M. on the air mattress in a sandy pool of your sweat and grit) or shower in the A.M. when the water would be cold (or non-existent since the pontoon would not be filled until morning. Third frequent option—put water in your helmet and use a rag to sponge off.

There was a mess tent. Food was plentiful. At times when we were under fire, there were C- rations. Everyone had a P-38, a small device that hung on your dog tags to open the tins.

Beer was available at night. 10 cents (M.P.C. –Military Payment Currency) a can. The high-end beer did not make it past the coast. Since we were at the end of the supply chain, we had what no one wanted. Still, a bad beer was better than no beer.

Sunday afternoon was generally a "stand down," unless there was an operation going on. A large block of ice would appear so that you could roll your cans to cool them. After a few minutes there would be a depression in the middle of the block which would speed the cooling (by allowing more sides of the can to contact the ice.)

We had movies, probably two or so a month. They were projected onto a sheet. Again, we were at the end of the supply chain so not much choice. I saw "The Graduate" so many times that I memorized the lines.

There was Armed Forces V.N. radio (e.g., Adrian Cronauer "Good Morning Vietnam" and the "Chicken Man" series) which helped keep me up with what was going on outside of my A.O. (area of operations). I learned about the Moon Walk a few days after it occurred.

Recently my son (an environmental studies major) asked a question that I had never been asked. "Did you have trash?" Of course. Outside the wire, the dozers dug a large hole in the ground pushing the dirt to form a barrier around into which the trash was dumped. Birds loved it. Also, the V.C. found it a welcome place to set up their mortars, since the mounds around the hole offered some protection from our return fire.

Human waste disposal was important. Outhouses (generally 2 seaters) had a lid at the back. Lift, pull out the 55-gal drum that had the top half sawed off; add a generous helping of fuel oil, light and move away from the foul-smelling black smoke. That was our sanitation.

There were opportunities for amusement. As the newest member of the commo unit, I was charged with maintaining the Commo Lieutenant's jeep. With the responsibility came the opportunity to name it. [Historically vehicles had names painted on them. Example: Dad's plane in W.W.II was "Queenie."] Most of our vehicles had artillery related names. E.g., "On Time; On Target." I got with our supply clerk (a U. of Washington marine biologist) to come up with a name. We chose "Rocinante" (Don Quixote's swayback horse). Upon seeing this painted on the Jeep, the Sergeant Major came over and said, "What is that?"

"Sergeant Major; that is the name of a noble steed from Spanish literature."

"Well, that's OK, I guess." The Lieutenant understood and was amused and fine with it.

We had a basketball hoop nailed to the side of a building. One time a soldier from another unit walked by and asked to play. He began draining buckets. I astutely commented, "You've played before." Response, "I was the backup to Elvin Hayes at Houston last year." (The "Big E")

Often when I had to go to one of the Fire Support Bases, I would go in a L.O.H. (Light Observation Helicopter). This helicopter moves by tilting in the chosen direction. I would be sitting in the front with the glass folded underneath my feet. Tree-topping in the front seat was a hoot.

Mail call was always a big deal although delivery was very sporadic. My Mother was good about sending things. She got me a subscription to the Wall Street Journal, so that I could read the columns (when it got there) on the front page to know what was going on in the world. One time she decided that I should get some food that I would not otherwise get at the mess tent. Given the mail, spoilage was a concern. So, one day I received a tin of clams. Really, Mom. My mates were amazed.

I did two R & R's. The first was to Sydney. The Opera House was almost finished. I was there with the supply clerk. Since he was a marine biologist and I was a college swimmer, we went to the Great Barrier Reef and strapped on rented scuba gear. He said, "I will point out things. When we get back up, I will tell you what you have just seen." It was marvelous.

The second R&R was to Japan. We took the bullet train out of Tokyo past Mt. Fuji, to Osaka where there was Expo 1970. Our next stop was Kyoto (which was amazing) before returning to Tokyo to see the coy in the ponds surrounding the Palace. What a Treat.

The rest of the time:

I was 22-23 years old while there. In a sense I was "older" than many of those non-lifers in my unit. I had been away from home in college. Had traveled the U.S. and in Europe by myself. Had worked in Europe for a summer. I was fit, having done two varsity sports in college. For a strange, (and looking back) non-rational reason, I viewed myself as invincible. Actually, I never even thought about it. This was the case even when two in my unit 10 yards from me "bought the farm", when the shrapnel splash went their way and not mine.

We took fire (according to someone in the unit who kept track) on average 3 days a week: small arms, mortars, and rockets. The first thing to do when that happened was to kiss the dirt.

Example: one late afternoon, mortars began hitting our area. We hit the dirt. As we were all on the ground, there came the cry that we all feared; "Medic!" Someone was hurt. Suddenly, this big blond soldier, in fatigue pants, no shirt, came racing by; his medical satchel flapping behind him. It was Swede, our medic. (I will never forget that image.) Not sure his real name. He was big and blond, so he was "Swede." The V.C. were walking mortars. (Mortars are tubes on a plate. There is a calibrated fixture on the tube. After a shot, turn the fixture down one notch and reload. The result is mortars hitting the target in a line.) With shrapnel still coming, Swede was on his way.

Some things you plan for and when it is over you say, "I did it." Other times, something occurs that you do not appreciate at the time. Sometime after it is over, you look back and say, "Really?" One such example was when the base camp began to come under constant, extended fire--small arms, mortars, rockets, and attempts to come through our concertina wire and claymore defenses. It was sustained. I did not realize it at the time, but it turned out that I would be awake for more than 5 and a half days straight. (Right, no drugs/no sleep.) Adrenaline is quite something.

There were a couple of short lulls during the time. At those times, the order was too rotate taking time to catch a few Z's. About 3 days in the X.O. came by and said, "When did you last stand down?
" "Not yet, Sir."
"Stand down, that's an order."
"No, Sir. I've got things to do." At this point, the standard enlisted man thought was "What are they going to do, send me to Nam?" He tried to stare me down. Failing that, he swore and stomped off. A week later, he wrote me up for a Bronze Star.

There may be some truth to the words of Winston Churchill: "There is nothing more exhilarating than to be shot at with no result."

Coming Home.

I came home in early May 1970. I packed my unit up to go into Cambodia and headed home to take my jungle boots off. (The V.C. had camps within Cambodia just out of reach of our artillery.) The decision was made to attack those camps, obviously across a border. That caused a stir in the U.S.

As I was getting on the plane (a "Freedom Bird") flying out of Tan Son Nhut, I picked up an Army newspaper called the Stars and Stripes. There were a couple of things that caught my attention. Nicklaus had just battled Palmer in the most recent golf tournament. Second, was on the Backpage. There was a picture of a young lady leaning over a body. You know the photo, Kent State.

The" Freedom Bird" flew me to New Jersey, where I got on a bus to Ohio. The military gave everybody leaving, a new uniform. I had been scheduled to fly to San Francisco. My sister lived outside of S.F. at the time and had been sent civilian clothes for me. My Family was not expecting New Jersey (No cell phones.) So, I took a Greyhound home from New Jersey to Ohio.

I was warned that I would run into people in those bus stations that will not like you. I did run into those people. Looking back, it was just a week or so after Kent State. Nevertheless…

What did it mean.

When the U.S. involvement ended, S.V.N. eventually fell. Shortly thereafter, the "Killing Fields" in Cambodia began. There, the Kymer Rouge slaughtered several million people while the world stood by and did nothing.

Maybe George F. Kennan had some insight. The U.S. involvement in Vietnam delayed the westward sweep of the Communists long enough for Thailand and India to stabilize so that the Chinese sweep to the oil lands did not occur. Maybe we somehow won.

I will let others debate and do the cost/benefit analysis.

Then What.

I seldom talk about it. Probably because few would understand. Occasionally, I would talk with a long-time friend who was in an armor division in my A.O. ("Area of Operations") over a glass or two of scotch. We are godparents to each other's youngest son.

It strikes me that the press reported mainly on what was happening in Saigon. (They probably preferred the living accommodations there, which would have been much better than in the rural areas.) They focused on the Vietnam ruling party (which was universally viewed as corrupt).

I suspect that it would be difficult to convey to someone who was not there what it was like. (I also suspect that Dad felt the same.) What do you say to someone who did not walk in the shoes of someone there. Words sometimes are poor substitutes. I have encountered few who have asked. When I say I was there, it is just a "Thank you for your service" and let's move on. That is fine. My words would be less than helpful; their experiences would not be sufficient to understand.

Maybe the movies might help. My long-time friend said we should go see "Good Morning Vietnam." (There was a real Adrian Cronauer. At 6:00 am someone would blast their radio so that the camp heard loud and clear, "Good Morning Vietnam.") Although it was supposedly Saigon, the movie struck me as authentic.

There was a movie about the 25th that won the Academy award for Best Picture in 1986. It was directed by a person who started college with me; dropped out and ended up in the 25th. Supposedly they had the Brat Pack as actors. One of these days I may watch it.

Ken Burns did a series on Vietnam. I watched the first several sessions which I thought set forth a good background. At some point I put it down and did not finish it. Struck me as Burns was building the V.C. as freedom fighters. (Not the picture that my local Tay Ninh's would have agreed with.)

I visit Washington DC from time to time. I visit the Wall and put my hand on names of those whom I knew. (It was designed by Maya Linn when she was a senior at Yale College, to focus on those U.S. soldiers and nurses whose lives were lost, rather than the reasoning/politics.) In 2003 when I was at the Wall a D.C. TV station came and asked if I had seen Bob Hope in Nam. (The day was Bob Hope's 100th birthday.) I said yes, in Chu Chi and told them the story.

There are 58,281 names on the Wall. (39,996 were 22 or younger.) This year the Vietnam Veterans Memorial Fund completed a project to collect a photograph of each person whose name is inscribed on the Wall.

I am now blessed with a wonderful spouse and wonderful children and grandchildren. I have been fortunate and happy like my Dad.

There is my pair of jungle boots with the protective metal plate in the sole in my closet. The treads on the bottom are worn and not as deep as when I first got them.

EPILOGUE:

In 1973 I graduated from law school. The job that I had taken did not start for a few months. I had a former roommate who had also served in Nam and was in the same situation, so we decided to travel to Europe. We looked into traveling to Russia. At that time, you needed to be on a tour to enter Russia (so they could keep track of you). We signed up with a Scandinavian student tour. As chance would have it, one of the stops/events was an evening watching a company of the Bolshoi Ballet at a theater inside of the Kremlin.

We were in our seats awaiting the opening of the curtain. The 3 seats in front of us were still vacant. A minute before curtain time, 3 soldiers came in and sat in the seats – one was a high-ranking Russian officer who was flanked by two North Vietnamese officers. So, there we were sitting in the Kremlin, watching a Bolshoi Ballet Company with two N.V.A. officers in front of us while at the same time several thousand miles away, life was different. Maybe take some time to think about it.

STEVE MORRIS

AGE WHEN ENTERED MILITARY: 18

DATE OF ENTRY TO MILITARY: 04/30/1962

VIETNAM TOUR DATES: 01/1965-06/1966, 02/1968-02/1969

YEARS OF DUTY/RESERVES: 22

STEVE MORRIS; SPECIAL FORCES

Just when I thought I was finished with my interviews, I run into Steve Morris. I'm shopping at Kroger's in my new hometown, Mt. Vernon, Ohio. I'm walking down an aisle looking for protein bars. Steve is in the same aisle. I noticed him because he was wearing a Vietnam era ball cap. He impressed me immediately. He had a leg brace on, plus a black arm sling. He still looked like he could take about anyone in the store. I spent some time thinking before I approached him. I finally decided it would be the proper thing to do.

"I noticed your ball cap; what branch were you in?"

"Army-Special Forces."

We made small talk and I let him pass. I went about my shopping and waked out of the store. Then I guess I felt the urge, as I returned and talked to him. I told him what I was doing, and he agreed to be interviewed. Turns out he lives in my neighborhood only 6 minutes away. Here's what he had to say.

"Steve, tell me how you got into the service."

"I went to Kent State University. I was there on a football scholarship. One of the football players contacted me and said, 'Hey you need to get in this fraternity. We have all the football players in it. Our fraternity is cool for football players. We have all the tests, and all the professors' notes, and we can get you through Kent State with ease, for sure.' My opinion of this was that I was going to college on my mom and dad's nickel, and I wasn't about to slough off and get through that way. If I did that, I would come out about the way I went in, which would be stupid. As well, it would be just because I was good at football. So, I left. I knew my mom and dad would be upset with me. I went over to the Army recruiter office and signed up. I signed up; came home and told my mom and dad that I was going to officially go into the military. My mom said, 'please don't ever darken my door again.' My dad had a little different view of it. He told me; 'If you go in and decide to make a career out of it, get in a unit where you're likely to get killed.' This was a strange sort of a perspective but that's the way things go faster if you're in. I took that to heart. I went to Fort Knox for basic training. Then I went to a base in Maryland and went through 'imagery interpretation.' You look at things different ways and determine what they are. I was good at that. Then I went to Fort Benning Georgia for jump school. I was shocked when I got there. It was a grow up and get sober' episode for me. I found out that, for the most part people didn't expect much of you unless you perform for them. Otherwise, they could care less who you were. You're penalized if you didn't do it. I made it through jump school and was assigned to the 82nd airborne, in an infantry division. Pretty quickly, I met this guy. He's a little short guy parading out in front of us, and he had a green beret on. He walked up and down and looked at each one of us and what he said was; 'I didn't send for you sons of bitches, and it's my job to make sure that you wash out of here. I'm going to mess with you day and night. I'm going to make you quit! That's my job. If you have any doubts in your mind, get back on that bus and go down to that air division. Three of the guys left right then; but I stayed on with the others. The guy wasn't kidding. He messed with us 24/7 all the time. We had all kinds of drills. He would wake everybody up at 2:00 o'clock in the morning; tell us to fall out with nothing on but our shorts and a baseball cap. We would think; 'what the Hell?' Then he would say, 'OK you did that. Now fall out and go back. This time I want you to come out with your boots, shorts, and jacket. He went off on one guy because he came out with his socks on. 'You idiot. That's not what I told you to do. Did I say socks?' So, what he's doing is messing with your heads. He wanted to see if we were able to listen to exactly what we were to do. Within the first week, several guys quit. We went through the training in the infantry. Then we were sent to Camp McCall. We went to a base camp out in the middle of a woods, near Southern Pines, North Carolina. Out there, we went through more Special Forces training. Being able to determine who was good at what, is what they were up to. We had eight weeks out there. Another couple of guys quit. We come back in. We do some individual training with weapons, and other stuff. So, I went through the weapons training which was 12 weeks. Then we were formed up in teams. We parachuted into Pisgah National Forest. Each one of us took the lead and was the compass guy. We didn't have G.P.S. in those days, so we used a compass. At some point, each of us was to lead us towards our target; one at a time. We would have to formulate a way to get to the target. Based on that we got a grade. It was pass or fail; nothing in between. Our team passed. Larry, the only way we would have gotten through is if we all passed. Otherwise, we would have all failed. That made us aware that it was not an individual effort, but a team effort. It was very good training. So, that was the first time we met up with the officers. Once we got done, I was assigned to the 7th Special Forces group. I was there six months, and they formed a new group called the Third Special Forces group. They called our names and took all the new guys first. Each of the groups were assigned an area of the world. Our group; The Third, was assigned to Africa. While we were there, we were in Ethiopia. We were there to train the Ethiopian army for six months. Then we came back in. My next orders came down, to place called Vietnam. At the time I'd never heard of it. Most of us hadn't. 'Where the hell is this place?' I got a call at 2:00 o'clock in the morning to get my bags packed and prepare to go on a mission. At that time nobody was told anything. All I knew was we're going to Vietnam, wherever that is. They also didn't tell us what we were supposed to be doing there. The first time we were there, we were there as advisors only. We were not supposed to be in combat. We were to teach the locals how to fight; the South Vietnamese and the Montagnard's. It was a one-year assignment. We found out very quickly that the North Vietnamese recognized that this support was from the Americans. They got on megaphones and yelled out to the South Vietnamese to leave. The idea here was that that would only leave the Americans and they could quickly kill us because they didn't have any opposition. From that point forward, things progressed; became more proactive for Special Forces. Then we became a force of our own and we started building camps, which were manned by Special Forces in teams. We had 12 men teams. A team always consisted pairs of like skills. I was a weapons guy. I had an assistant. There was a demo guy and an assistant. What happens now is, you can split the team in two and have two six-man teams. They can do the same thing that a 12-man team can do. Everybody's got a duplicate. So, they moved me from weapons to operations intelligence. I became the next in line for the operations Sergeant. If we split, I was the operations guy for the second team. My first assignment was Khe Sanh. That was bad news. Everybody that came down through there had to make a probe. We had many probes and made a lot of contact with the North Vietnamese."

"A probe would be like a firefight or a mini battle?"

"Yes, a probe would be like four or five soldiers coming in and trying to get through our wire (a weak point) and attack us. That went on for about a year. At Khe Sanh, while I was there, they sent some A.S.A. (Army Security Agency) guys to put up an antenna on top of Dong Tre Mountain. So, they sent me and Sergeant Osborne. He is my buddy, and a demo guy. Ozzy and I went up to set up a perimeter with Claymores and booby traps, to protect these guys when they were going up there put up the antenna? While I was coming back in the chopper, we came under fire. That was my first Purple Heart. I got shot through the bottom of the helicopter. Funny story about it was this. I got hit right here in the temple. Came up through the temple. It knocked me out, for sure. As you might know, the temple bleeds a lot. So, I fell backwards and was right near a door in the helicopter. I saw what was going on and I turned to tell the gunner that we were being fired on. He got shot and was killed. Two A.S.A. guys that were in there had never been in combat that great. Those guys were sent in to set up these antennas so that our guys could communicate back and forth when things were happening, and battles were going on. Anyhow, the chopper auto rotated in and lost its ability to fly. It crashed right by Khe Sanh. The team Sergeant comes out. He wants to know; 'Where's Morris; where's Osborne?' Well, Osborne was still up on the mountain, and they said Morris is dead. He was shot in the head and he's lying in there dead. Another chopper came in and took me (or supposedly me, as actually they thought it was my body), to Dong Hah airport. They had a hospital. Well, I wasn't dead! While I was there, the General came through and pinned me with a Purple Heart and a Bronze Star. After two weeks I was released. They asked me if I wanted to go home or go back to my camp. I told them I wanted to go back to my camp. I got out; one of the guys saw me and turns white, saying; 'shit, I thought you were dead.' He said to me; 'You know we need to get you home fast, Morris!"

"Why?"

"Because we are sending word home that you are dead. That's not going to work very well now, because you're not dead. We sent notification to DaNang that you were K.I.A. They sent it on through to USARPAC (United States Army Pacific Command). They would be sending a notification through to the United States, and finally a team would go to your house and report this to your parents.'

"Wow!"

"They flew me back to the main camp, then down to Than Son Nhut. Then I took a flight straight to the East Coast, where they put me on another plane. I got home two days before the notification. I decided to have a little fun. So, I met them at the door when they came. They asked if my mother and father were there. I told him they weren't home. They said, who are you?' I told them; 'I'm Steve Morris.' They said, 'No, you're dead!' So, they had the whole notification paperwork that I was K.I. A., and there I was standing in front of them. Quite a scene. So, I went back and finished up my tour. I came back to the States and stayed about a year. Then I got orders again to go back to Vietnam. I got to go back to Khe Sanh. It was at that point that the Third Marine Division decided they were going to take over. So, they moved us to a place called long Bay. There we set up in an old A.R.V.N. camp. A.R.V.N. was another name for the South Vietnamese forces. So, we rebuilt the camp. We were assigned three companies of Montagnard's. We trained them to fight. The advantage to that is that they know the area, they know the language they know the ins and outs of all the territory there. We used them to assist us in hunting down Charlie (the enemy). During that time, we got hit several times. One time we got hit by two Mig 21's. The Migs came in and our commo guy Gerald Chambers; he was the only one left on the team other than me. The Migs came so low that they bent our antennas. They banked. He looked up and said, 'Hey looks like the Air Force sent some guys to take care of us. I just laughed and said, You're full of shit.' Once again, they banked up and looked like a fan as they shot off some rockets. We're scared as crap, so we all dive into the medical bunker that's right beside us. Took out our whole west wall and half of our Montagnard's. Then they came back down through and dropped some 250 pounder bombs. It just blew everything out of the West wall. They bank the third time. They came back around again. This time they dropped napalm all over the place. So, for the next 48 hours, me and Gerald Chambers and one other guy; we spent that time crawling around the village and trying to get people out of their bunkers. We were also dodging gunfire, constant small arms fire. Couldn't tell what direction it was coming from, a lot of confusion. All I knew was we needed to get those people out of there that were still living, right? So, we got them out best we could."

"Where did you take them?"

"We took them up to a helipad. We had aircraft helicopters come in and pick them up best they could; take them to the A.R.V.N. hospital. The village chief's daughter: she was somebody I was working with to teach her English. She came walking up to me with the top of her head gone. she was asking for our medic. "Buk she, Buk she, she said. I could not believe she could even walk. Her brain was showing, Larry. Sadly, she died soon after that."

"Steve, most of the people I talked to said that the enemy didn't have aircraft. but you said they did."

"Yes, they had Migs; those were from Chinese Communists."

"Were those prevalent?"

"Well, most of Vietnam was politics, Larry. I will tell you that until the day I die. Big business was making too damn much money off Vietnam. Otherwise, we could have won that war anytime we wanted to. We could kick their asses. Could have finished it up in six months. They decided to put restrictions on us. We couldn't go across the border, and back across. 'Don't shoot unless shot at first.' Hey, I'm not going to let somebody shoot at me if I see them first! For that action there, I got the Soldiers Medal. I prize it the most. The military says that you get an extra 10% added to your retirement if you have that medal. Never saw a penny of that; not one damn person that ever got that medal that I knew of, got any money that was associated with it. That was another part of the 'big lie.' At one time Larry, I felt more attached and felt more home in Vietnam than I did back home. When I came back here, I was called all kinds of dirty names and not respected. Never congratulated, other than by the military community. At one time I can honestly say that I hated Americans. I really did. They didn't care about anything except themselves, and they called us murderers. Larry, there was a magazine article at some point that said; 'Special Forces team murders innocent women and children in a church.' True, we did kill. But what they didn't tell you was that there was a 50-caliber machine gun in there and that they were using the women and children as human shields too keep us from shooting at them. So, we're pinned down and have no options. I called in Air Force reinforcements. So, they take out the church; but obviously there's collateral damage. But the news media; they were telling the truth; but only half the truth. It would be like if I saw you go out and hit somebody with a baseball bat. But the truth of the matter is that somebody was throwing bricks at you, and you go out with a baseball bat to defend yourself. That's the truth, but that's the way a lot of stuff happened in Vietnam, Larry. I lost a lot of friends over there; comrades' guys that I knew. I still have trouble with it at times. I spend a lot of time to myself. I like to stay away from people' cause there's always somebody who's going to say something, and I'm going to come unglued. The truth is the law protects them in that situation and not me. I still I love to hunt; that's what I do for recreation."

"Steve looks like you›re good at it by looking around this room and seeing all the mounts that you have."

"You're right. I am good at it. It's something I love. I don't say I'm the greatest, but I'm good at it. The military does two things for people, which makes me wish they still had the draft. It teaches respect and it teaches if you start something you finish it. You have a problem you solve the problem. You don't push it off on somebody else. We're in a society right now where if it feels good; do it. If it doesn't feel good don't do it. But there's a lot of things that don't feel good and you still must do them. That's the facts. That's one of the things I really miss.

Anyway, after my time with the Special Forces, where I spent 16 years, I came down with orders from the department of the Army and a promotion from Master Sergeant to First Sergeant. Along with that, which I couldn't figure out came an order for me to report to the 27th. combat engineers airborne. I called Mrs. Alexander, who oversaw Special Forces. I said, 'Hey Billy; why am I being transferred to a non-Special Forces unit?' 'Turns out you've been requested, Steve.' 'Requested by who?' 'Do you know Sergeant Major John Heilemann?' 'Heck yes, I know him. I spent time with him in Special Forces. 'Well, he has requested you, Sir.' So, I went over and reported in. He said, 'Stephen how are you doing?' I said, 'John, I'm doing fine. Now, what are we doing here?' 'There's one thing to get straight really quick, is that when we're together like this we're Steve and John; but when we're with anybody else we're going to be First Sergeant and Sergeant Major; get it?' Okay, that's fine. He takes me in his office and says, 'Here's my problem. I have a company. It's called Charlie company. They're full of bad people. They're not doing what they're supposed to do. 90% of my headaches come from Charlie company. I know how you operate. I know how you are. I want you to first go home for a 60-day leave. I want you to not shave. Don't cut your hair. Then I want you to go in and do your thing. I want you to find out what you can find out and correct it. 'Hey, I can do that!' So, about 45 days in, I walk into the day room with a 6 pack of beer. I sat down. Guys are playing ping pong, shooting pool, and generally screwing off. One of them comes over to me (who I later found out was the company clerk) He says, 'Who are you?' I said, 'Oh, I'm nobody. I just thought I'd come in see how you guys are doing. Anybody want a beer? 'Heck yeah!' Then he said, 'Hey, we're not allowed to have beer in here.' "Yeah, well I can get it for you anytime you want it.' So, he invites a couple of other guys over and we're chit chatting about the company and who's, who and what's, what. Who does what? Two weeks later beard comes off; all shaved up, I come into the supply room with my uniform on. The company clerk stops and looks at me, and does a double take and says holy shit; you're a First Sergeant?' I said, 'Son, don't you ever say that again!' 'I want you to show me to my office. So, I go into my office, and I call him in there. 'So, I want you to get ahold of every swinging Sergeant in this company and I want them out here in formation in three hours.' I said to him; 'You wanna remain a Spec Four? If you do, then get er done! He managed to do it. Only one person was missing. I got them all out there and I said, 'You know I'd like to introduce myself. I'm First Sergeant Morris. Larry, I had this brace on my leg here even then. 'So, we're going to have P.T. from now on. 5:30 every morning we're going to do a daily run. Then we're going to come back; get cleaned up; then we're going to take the troops out for P.T. Couple of them put up their hands and said, 'Hey First Sergeant; are we going to do P.T. twice a day? Is that what you're saying? I said, 'shit, you can count. I guess that's why you're a Sergeant. There's twenty-four 96's in there on the desk. If you want to, you can go in there and transfer. Anybody else that stays here's going to go with the program. If you don't, I'm going to ruin your fucking careers. That's the way it's going to be. Too much crap going on down here. The second platoon Sergeant was taking one of his privates and they would sign out the motor pool, pick him up at his B.E.Q. take him by the N.C.O. club, so he could have breakfast. Then, he would take him from the N.C.O. club to formation. After formation, they'd go back to the N.C.O. club and sit there drinking all damn day. Then he'd pick him up at five or six o'clock at the end of the day; back to formation, then back to his B.E.Q. In return, he didn't have to pull any extra duties. Well, that was one of them."

"Steve; what are B.E. Q's?"

"Well, they're really called bachelor quarters. There's also O.C. Q's (officers' quarters). Anyhow the L.E. platoon (stands for light equipment); their Sergeant was a drug dealer. I found out that he was dealing drugs and he was doing this during P.T. We'd be in doing P. T and I'd see five or six guys peeling off near the back of the line. They'd go behind the barracks. I called up the Lieutenant, who was the company commander. I said, 'Sir I think tonight we need to play Batman and Robin.' He said, 'Well what are we going to do, First Sergeant?' I said, we're going to have fun with the troops.' He said, 'Okay, what are we going to do?' I said, Come on in. I'm going to let you know. So, here's what we do. There's this special knock that the guys use to gain entry. Just stick with me. I'm going to show you what's going on in your company. So, we went out did the special knock on the door. It opens. Here stands one of the guys in the L.E. platoon. He's standing there with a pipe full of marijuana. Then we see five joints laying right across his bunk bed. He goes to turn around and I said to him quick; 'Don't touch them!' 'So, what am I going to do?' 'You're going to close the door. You're going to sit here. Don't you say one damn word when another person comes in.' Within 5 minutes, we heard the special knock again open in walks another Sergeant. He closes the door sees us and says, 'Oh shit!' Told him to go into the latrine and close the door. So, we did this and eventually about five of them came in. Lieutenant says, 'Hey; we're going to put them all in jail?' I laughed and said, no, we're not going to put them in jail. We can't do that. In fact, we don't wanna do that. We might take a stripe off them, though. But we're not going to put them in jail.' He says to me; 'How come?' I said back; Because there's no evidence.' 'What you mean there won't be any evidence?' I called them and told each one of them to pick up a joint. Then I said to them; 'Guys, if we don't have any evidence, we can't put you in the stockade, right? So, what are we going to do? They all look at each other. 'Smoke em? Flush them down the toilet? No.' So, they look at each other and say, 'Well, how the hell are we going to get rid of these things? I said, 'You're going to eat em, boys!' My Lieutenant says, 'We can't make them eat, can we?' It was funny as hell watching them chew on those things and gag. Lieutenant says to me; 'First Sergeant, I've never seen anything like that before.' 'Hey, you got to play the game play it the way they wanna play it. Anyhow I got them squared away and they became the best platoon in the entire battalion. It was basically because the other First Sergeants were afraid of their troops. You shouldn't be a First Sergeant if that's your attitude. I told the Sergeant Major that Brady said, 'Yeah, I know.' So, after that word filtered down and soon, I got a call from the Post Sergeant Major. He wanted me to come up there and talk to him. "So, what we've decided is that we're going to have the first noncommissioned officer run the Recondo school at Fort Bragg. A lot of words have been said about you, Morris, and we want you to do that job. So, they put me in charge. I ran two classes. I guess I didn't like it, so I decided to retire. I was on the Sergeant Major's list. I was number 5 on the list. They told me they wanted me to go to Fort Bliss to go to the Sergeant Majors Academy. And then I would go on to the second infantry division in Korea. I basically said; 'No way in hell am I going to do that!' They asked why and I simply told them; 'I've been in these 16 years, overseas. So, I come back and every time I do I see the same guy with the same M.O.S. sitting at the desk. He's never been anywhere. Why in the hell is he always ahead of me?' 'Well, if you don't like it First Sergeant; there's papers over there. You can sign them if you want. He hit me just right, so I signed, and I retired."

"Let me get one thing straight about your past, Steve. When you went to Kent State, what years were that? "

"I was there in 1961 and 1962."

"So, it sounds like you are 78, same as me. So, you'd have been a freshman in 61. Then you enlisted and then you were in Vietnam for six years."

"Yes, I was in Okinawa first, and did something called "snake bite" which was a T.D.Y. (Temporary Duty Assignment) That took six months from Okinawa into Vietnam."

"The incident where you encountered the young girl with her head blown off. What year was that?

"That was 1967."

"So, that was toward the end."

"No, I came back a second time after that. I was assigned to Khe Sanh and into Long Bay in the B-36 guerilla force."

"But during that time, you were in combat mode most of the time; and kill or be killed sorts of things happen to you? You spent a total of about 16 years; correct?"

"I had a total of 16 years overseas, and I had six years of combat duty. I was in the service a total of 22 years; 16 of those were overseas in Special Forces. Six of those 16 years overseas I was in combat mode."

"Steve I've been noticing this picture ever since we sat down.

Tell me about it. It looks like you and two other buddies I assume that's accurate?"

"It sure is. We were called the "three amigos." This guy is Armando Canalys. He was the brother of Moe Canalys. Moe was on my team and was the only guy I ever knew that made a jump in a parachute that didn't open, and still survived. This is Dallas Longstreth. Dallas was with S.O.G. (special operations group.) He used to fly curvy. They are Tiger Hound Air. They were light aircraft. They flew just above the ground; gave us observations that helped us either locate the enemy or stay out of the way of the enemy. Tiger Hound was the organization. He protected me on several different operations."

"Okay then, what about this picture?"

"When I was in Vietnam, I had an interpreter. I ended up in Chicago one time: of all places. I was seeing my mom and dad. They lived in Edgewater, which was a big apartment building there. They had a restaurant in the bottom floor of the building. Mom and dad said, 'Hey; you ought to go down there. They have a Vietnamese guy who's a chef there. I went down, son of a gun, it was my interpreter right there in the middle of Chicago. What were the chances of even meeting him there, let alone in the same apartment complex that my mom and dad lived in?"

"Did he recognize you?"

"Oh yeah, right away!"

"Great story, Steve!"

"Alright, here's another picture. Tell me about it."

"Okay; these are some brood Montagnard kids that I used to play games will with."

"Now I was told those Montagnard guys were used as scouts is that accurate?"

"Yeah, that's right. They would be scouting leaders for us."

"Now is this a picture of one of their homes?"

"Yes; this is a typical home that they would live in. Not very plush for sure."

"Now this landscaping that's pictured with the kids. I assume is the result of Agent Orange be being sprayed over it to defoliate it. Is that accurate?"

"Yes, that is exactly what happened there."

"What's this plane?"

"I was on the first team to test parachuting out of a C-141 aircraft."

"This was a picture with my first wife when I was a Staff Sergeant."

"So, the 16 years; six of which were in Vietnam; where did you spend the other years?"

"Of the other years; I was in Ethiopia first. I was also in Okinawa for four years. There we did those snakebite trips I talked about. We would go to different places in Vietnam and support someone that had a camp there already. The final one was a trip to South America and there we were pursuing the drug cartels. Quite an experience."

"I know you said you have one Purple Heart. How many do you really have?"

"Sorry; I have three of those."

"I've got all my stuff hanging in a nice frame upstairs. I'll show you when we're finished."

"So, if I remember right, after all those years you were given an opportunity to take another overseas mission and you basically said screw it, I'm getting out. So, what happened then?"

"I retired in 1984."

"Then you came home; and not to a hero's welcome; right? I take it that even in 1984, people were still hard on you for being a Vietnam vet.

"You know Larry; even today some of the stigma is still there. People used to come up to my wife and say, 'you're married to a Special Forces guy; aren't you afraid?" She would say, 'What the hell are you talking about?' 'Well; they kill people!' "The truth is Larry, that's what all soldiers do (did) in all wars. They either kill or be killed. That's the name of the game."

"You actually got in near the beginning of Vietnam, is that right?"

"No, it's not right. That's one of the fallacy's of the whole conflict in Vietnam. It started under Eisenhower in the 1950s. We started in Laos. That's where the first casualty was. It was a Captain Moon, who was from Fort Bragg. There's a building at Fort Bragg that's named for him, still today. He didn't die from his wounds but from an infection that was caused by the wounds. Sargent Ballinger was the one who survived and came back. But that was in 1952, Larry. So, it started then. At that time, they were not called the Vietcong or the north Vietnamese they were called Vietminh. Or some were for referred to as C.T. (Communist Terrorists.) When they sent us over, we were the first American troops. There was a lot of professional jealousy I guess you'd say, among the services. We were there and we had the 4th Infantry Division support the Air Force. The rest of the services said that the Special Forces' guys were getting all the combat training and all the combat experience. The other branches complained that all their guys are basically World War Two veterans who are leaving, and we don't have anybody with combat experience to step in. So, that was the argument. Now here comes the 82nd in, The 4th infantry Division. All different types of units came. Then the Marines came in. The Marines position in war history was typically for storming beaches and beachheads; not jungle fighting. Yet they sent the Third Marine Division over. So, you had a conglomeration, so that things got built up. With that building up, there was a general lack of communication between service branches. We had a lot of Americans that were killed by Americans! We were winning the battles, as Special Forces, and we›re training the people to protect themselves. We were training the A.R.V.N. We had; yeah, I mean as Special Forces alone, we were training them well and we had them well on the road, with the right tactics and support; but not yet being involved by the military. Then the north Vietnamese started singling us out' because we were the ones on the phone, calling for an airstrike. We hadn›t yet gotten to them trained well enough to let them take over the phone and make a radio call. So, everybody thinks the Vietnam conflict started with that Tet offenses. Those were in the 60s and so everybody thinks that›s when Vietnam started but it really started in the 50s with Eisenhower, as I told you."

"Thanks Steve. That helps me a lot!" I believe that timeline misconception would be widely held; don't you?"

"For sure."

"Steve, I know this might strike a nerve. Have you been to The Wall?"

"I have not gone to the wall yet. I simply can't face it, Larry. I still have lots of problems. I have flashbacks and nightmares. I can't watch combat movies. If I do, I have bad nights. So, I basically kind of stay away from them. I loved the service. I miss it. I miss a lot of the camaraderie. I miss doing what I did. I considered myself just about like anybody else that was out there. Most would agree that we considered ourselves good at what we did."

"As you should!"

"Yeah, I give a lot of credit to the guys who trained me. They trained me right and they trained me well. The right way always wins. It might take a lot more time to do that, but it works. The fact is that we could have won over there within six months. anytime we wanted. Too much politics; not wanting to create international incidents. We had teams who went into Haiphong Harbor and took pictures. They constantly saw ships from China and Russia delivering weapons and supplies to the North Vietnamese. So, everybody was afraid if we did something, those two would get more involved. They were just using Vietnam as a puppet. China and Russia were sitting there with magnifying glasses on, watching all of this. Of course, realizing that our government might eventually escalate things and wanna move into their areas as well. This wasn't the case, but it was what those entities thought. Part of that stint when I was in Okinawa, was in Thailand. We were training 'third country' people. We took them into the Plain of Jars. North Vietnamese soldiers were in Laos as well. Part of the Ho Chi Minh trail came through Laos. We were not allowed to go there. We were sterile. In other words, if we were ever to be identified, we were not Americans. That's the way we operated it in many cases, and that disconnected us from being directly attached to the United States. In other words, you were on your own if ever captured."

"So, let me get this straight. If you were ever captured, Steve; then what am I to understand? You wouldn't identify yourself as a soldier of the U.S.A.?"

"Yeah, we knew that going in. I am who I am. I'm just over here helping them. I would give them my name, rank, and serial number only. That was just the rule. Today they've changed the rules and if you're captured you can tell him anything you want. With today's technology, they'd find out quickly anyway."

"After your service when you got into civilian life. What did you do then, Steve?"

"I dabbled around doing several things. I decided I wanted to do some things along the lines of what I was used to doing. I found myself getting into some things that dealt with 'The dirty' side of life. I got involved with the San Antonio TX. Police Department I did work with the homicide division, doing some cold case files. I opened my own company of armed guards. At one time I had 200 employees. I did that for about four years. I finally got fed up with it. Larry, the general populous has no idea of dedication necessary. I couldn›t stand that. What dependability is; what being on time is; seemed lost on most of the people I had working for me. if you›re going to be late, you›re supposed to call in. Even common courtesies like that were lost. Employees just weren't very dependable. Larry, it was like a revolving door. I caught people doing stupid things all the time. I once got a call 1:00 o›clock in the morning from a store manager I had guards at. 'Commander Morris, I got a question. Do your guards usually show up to work with a pillow and a blanket?' 'No, of course not. Where are you now?' 'Well, I›m at home now, but I saw your guys when they came in.' 'I said, 'Don›t worry about it. I›ll take care of it.' I go out to this place. I›ve got a passcode to get in. I walk around the store and see nobody. I go back in the stockroom. Over in the corners is a little office. Here is my guard; pillow behind him, laying back; feet up on the desk and blanket over him; sleeping like a baby. I took the gun out of his holster. I went outside and locked the door. Next day at formation I asked for everybody to come in for a weapons inspection. When I got to him, he said; 'Oh, I forgot. My gun's back at the house.' 'Where's your weapon?' Well, I think it's at the house.' 'What do you mean you think it's at the house? Don't you know where it is?' 'Yeah, it's at the house.' 'Are you sure?' 'Yeah, I'm sure.' 'Would you bet money on it?' 'Would you bet your paycheck on it?' 'Yes, I would.' 'Okay, I'm going to give you one hour. Go get your gun.' He comes back in an hour and doesn't have the gun and says, 'I just don't know where it is Sir, I think somebody must have stolen it.' Well, I know what happened to it.' 'How do you know what happened to it?' 'Well, it's in my desk.' 'It's in your desk? How did it get in your desk?' I came in the store; took it out of your holster while you were sleeping.'

"That's both funny and pathetic. Did you do this privately or in front of your guys?"

"Oh, I did it in front of everybody! His reply was 'What are you going to do? Are you going to fire me?' I said, 'No, I'm not going to fire you. What I want you to do is for you to turn your uniforms and all your equipment, and I'll call you when I need you.' 'Why won't you fire me?' Cause I might need you.' The truth of the matter is that if I fired him, he would be eligible for unemployment. That affected my bottom line, and he didn't deserve it. I didn't wanna do that. If I put him on hold, he can't draw unemployment and I don't have to pay him that."

'Well done, Sir."

"So, I did that for 15 or 16 years. My ex-wife wanted me to move up here. But, as soon as we got up here, she decided she didn't wanna be with me anymore and so we got a divorce. I stayed single for four years then I met Jo. We've been married for two years. It's been wonderful. I finally found the right woman!"

"Good for you."

"When you came up here to Ohio did you come directly here to Apple Valley?"

"I went online looking for houses in Ashland, which is where I was born and raised; Mansfield; Apple Valley, and all over the place. I found this house. It appealed to me, so I bought it online. I put it in the hands of the realtor to make sure he looked out for me. I did a little dickering with the seller, and it made an agreement and bought it. Six months later, I'm single. The house was more than I needed, as you can imagine. So, I decided to try an Airbnb here. I started doing that, and it turned out to be very successful, Larry."

"Very good!"

"Now we're at a crossroads and we basically decided that we want to move up north. By up north, I mean to the Upper Peninsula of Michigan. So, we put this place up for sale. We're going to sell it and we're going to move up north. We're going to be in an area where; if I don't wanna see anybody, I don't have to!"

"I remember you telling me that before when we met at the store. I think that's great."

"It'40 acres, and it's right next to several thousand acres of Ottawa National Forest."

"So, you go basically across the Mackinaw Bridge and turn left; right?"

" That's right. You go about an hour West and then an hour north. We will be about 15 miles from Ishpeming and 30 miles from Escanaba."

"So, the nearest town to you is how far?"

"15 miles; that's right down my alley, Larry!"

"You're close to Lake Superior, I bet. So, on your 40 acres you can hunt?"

"Yes, I can also hunt the 9000 acres."

"How about fishing?"

"Yep, they got a couple of nice trout streams nearby. There's lots of lakes, and one stream where they have a salmon run every year. Yeah, I'll have just about everything I ever wanted. Jo wants to raise goats, so we're going to do that. She's going to have goats and chickens."

"Now let's back up a little bit. You said you had your leg injury, which was a purple Heart incident. How did that happen?"

"I was in an operation with the 36th. mobile guerrilla force, in III Corps. The guy in front of me got hit with a rocket. It blew him back into me. At the same token, I was under fire. Then I got hit in the knee with my A.K. Blew the knee and the leg off so that the only thing holding it was the hamstrings and a flap of skin. I didn't even realize it was me. I was in shock, and it really didn't hurt at the time. I like kept trying to get up and run over to the dike. I kept saying to myself what the hell is the matter with me? So, I'm looking down and I see what I thought was somebody's ankle. I said to myself; 'shit, somebody lost their leg. Then I realized it was my own. So, I rolled over did what I could to keep it together and crawled over to the dike. a gunship came in; cleared the area pretty much, and a Slick came in and picked me and another guy named Williams up."

"Steve, what does Slick mean?"

"Slick was a non-combat type helicopter, used for transporting people who needed to be moved. They usually have one gunner on them. The gunner jumped off, grabbed me like a sack of potatoes and threw me on. We went to the 27th field evac. It took me through there; through the process and sent me down to Than Son Nhut to O.G. Japan. That's where the 10- seventh field hospital was. They did amputations. They were going to do an amputation. I said a I don't want aa amputation. So, they ended up sending me to Walter Reed Hospital where they had a new type of surgery called laser surgery. It's very common today. They put the leg back together. I spent about six months there and they sent me to Womack Army Hospital at Fort Bragg. That's where I finished up my healing process. I met Sergeant Major Leo there. He came in and said, 'Hey, I got a good deal for you. You were Special Forces; right?' 'I said yeah.' 'Come and see me when you get out. So, I did. They put me in G1 procurement. I was with Drew Dix and Fred Zapotosky, both Medal of Honor winners. We traveled around the country together. They did their dog and pony shows and I went behind the scenes and recruited guys for Special Forces. They even kept me on jump status, even though I had my leg situation. We did water jumps at White Lake. Once I got healed up, I went back to Vietnam. I got hit again. This time it was rough. I got hit right here in the sternum. It went over into my heart area. Had it gone all the way through my heart, I would have died right there. I was very fortunate; very lucky. So, between the leg, the head, and the heart I got three purple hearts. Some people dwell on them. I don't. Like this cast here, Larry. I got my shoulder replaced. My wife gets very mad at me. I hate this thing!"

"So that sling is not a war related thing. It's a new thing, right?"

"Right; yeah, it's related to age and all the things that I did in my previous life that put wear and tear on my shoulder.

"Now what about Agent Orange. Did you know that you had it?"

"Larry, in 1986 I got a black bordered letter from V.A., saying congratulations. You're certified Agent Orange. Along with it a check for $365. At that point I didn't even know what Agent Orange was. They gave me a report time to report to the V.A. So, I reported to the V.A. office that was at Audie Murphy V.A. Hospital in San Antonio TX. I went there; they drew blood verified the fact that I was Agent Orange. They put me on the registry. I never have gotten a damn dime since. But I am certified. When I was there, we only knew it as 'defoliant.' "

"So basically, Agent Orange hasn't really done anything to you physically; right?"

"So far. However, the rest of my team has all died of cancer, so I might still have something in my future. So far, I've been lucky! I count my blessings every time I wake up."

"How about Diabetes?"

"I don't have that either, Larry."

"I don't see any skin cancer on you either, Steve." So, you are blessed, I'd say."

"Yeah, I'm lucky. I know I'm lucky."

"And obviously you get around. You still go hunting."

"Not sure how that will work after this surgery. I might just have to use only a bow."

"Then Jo, your wife. Where did you meet her?"

"It's kind of a funny story. They have a news thing here; called 'Next Door,' online. I happened to go on one day, just looking at that comments and requests I came across a request from a woman, who happen to be Jo, wanting to know if there was anybody down there who could put in a mailbox for her. She had everything ready. The post, the mailbox, and cement. It was all just laying on her front porch. All the person would have to do would be to dig the hole and put it in. I saw that a lot of guys were coming online and saying, 'I'll do it for two hundred, $250, $300. I said to myself that they're taking advantage of her. So, I got ahold of her and told her; 'I'll do it for nothing.' She said, 'Great!' I went up there and did it. Her cement was already hard, so I ended up going down buying a new bag. I came back and installed it for her. She was happy and said, 'Hey how about I'll make you a pie.' I said, 'Well I appreciate that. I like custard pie.' She said, 'Well, I've never made a custard pie.' 'Well, that's what I like.' So, she said; 'I'll give it a try, Steve.' So, I got tied up doing other things and sort of forgot about it. Larry, I always try to do things for people. That's just how I am. I realized about three months later that I never got my pie. So, I called her up and said, 'Hey, I never got my pie, this is Steve.' She said, where do I know you from?' 'I'm the guy that put in your mailbox; remember? She says, 'Oh my goodness.' 'you told me you'd make me a pie. I got a hankering for some pie and so I'm calling you back.' She showed up at my door the next day with a pie! Anyhow I eventually called and asked her if she would like to go out to dinner sometime. She said yeah. That's how we met, and the rest is history. Two years later we decided to tie the knot."

"So, she lived here right in Apple Valley; correct?"

"Yep, she only lived about a mile and a half from me."

"I like it, great story! I'm happy for you both."

"We got married on the 7th of December."

"Does she have any kids?"

"Yes, she has a son that lives in Minnesota. I have a son that lives north of Chicago. She has two granddaughters and I've got two granddaughters. So, this place we're moving to; it's 4 1/2 hours from her son's house in five hours from my son's house. It's right about in the middle. If she goes to see her son from here it takes 15 hours! It's a big difference."

"And you've already bought that house; right? And this house is on the market?"

'Yes; we bought the other house with the condition that we can sell our house first. They agreed to that. They didn't have a big timeline problem, so we're just waiting till we sell. Neither of us is in a great rush. It's a very stress-free deal."

"Very cool, Steve. It's hard to find such a workable arrangement."

"I'd like very much to see your stuff upstairs, if that's okay, Steve. I certainly can acknowledge to myself and to anybody that would ask, that you are a hero. I hope you see yourself in that light. Thanks again for taking the time to be interviewed and I'll make sure that I get back to you with results of our day."

As a postscript to Steve's interview, I called to tell him things were progressing. I asked if he had moved. He told me that he had experienced some serious health issues and that the move to the U.P. was on hold. He and Jo now reside in town in a lovely community with both independent living and assisted care. They are still very hopeful to move north.

DOUG HAMMOND

AGE WHEN ENTERED MILITARY: 24

DATE OF ENTRY TO MILITARY: 01/10/1967-12/27/1970

VIETNAM TOUR DATES: 10/1967

YEARS OF DUTY/RESERVES: 4

DOUG HAMMOND

Doug was a classmate of mine at Otterbein College. We pledged the same fraternity and should have known each other well. However, we ran in different circles and only crossed at times that were not exactly noteworthy for me.

Doug was a football star. I was the janitor of the Freshman dorms when we were both freshmen. He was aptly called "The Animal." It fit him well at the time. My first recollection of Doug was when he started against our archrival Capital. My memory tells me he played left defensive end. He wore a black sleeve on his left arm. He swung it while sizing up each play. I personally was intimidated just sitting in the stands. At the time, the visitors bench was on the opposite side of the field and the stands were across the running track behind the bench. Doug made a tackle near the bench. To make his impression felt, He carried the opposing chap over their bench, across the track and dumped him a few rows up in the stands. He calmly walked back to the field with no opposition. The referees however, and quicky dismissed him from the field and the game. Our fans cheered. Theirs booed. A legend was born. Later in the year the two basketball teams met in our rather old and small gym. Once again, Doug made an impact. The seating in the arena was elevated maybe 6-8 feet above the floor. There were angled corners with just a few seats. Some Capital fellows draped a sheet with some expletives about our fair school on it, over the edge. Doug comes along, just before gametime and decides to pull the sheet down. The young man attached to the sheet saw the size of his opponent and did the right thing, vacating the area for higher ground. Doug climbs up, sits in the seats, and dares anyone to trespass. Meanwhile, our fraternity group was seated about 50 feet away. A cheerleader megaphone stolen from the football game, was being passed around for fun. Our fans were hooting and hollering. Next, a phalanx of Capital guys walks in the main door and head for our frat group. Otterbein's security force in those days consisted of "Al the Rent a Cop" and probably a dean or two from the school. Suddenly all hell broke loose. Many separate skirmishes were happening. I happened to be right in the middle of this mess. Of course, Doug was too. Pretty soon we heard sirens and reinforcements were there. Somehow, enough policemen from surrounding communities showed up and the game was played. The legend of Doug went to a higher level.

After each football game, Doug and his buddies would (speculation only) get drunked up. This is where my association comes in. He (they) would return late and trash the common areas of the dorm they were in. Sometimes this even included tearing a payphone off the wall, or perhaps a urinal or two from the bathroom. I had to clean up behind these guys. It was just work to me, but Doug did make my life on those weekends, a bit more complicated.

After we graduated, we went our separate ways. Frankly, I would have only recognized his name, until I read his obituary. Sadly, he passed away May 18, 2020. If I were to have made a prediction about Doug after our Otterbein days, it would have been 100% wrong. I would have based it on the adage that; "A leopard doesn't shed its spots." People are pretty much formed in their ways by the time they are 21. Doug changed.

I am including a copy of his obituary.

Douglas Hammond; 77 died May 18, 2020. He was born in Franklin, OH to the late Owen and Alice (Combs) Hammond, just

9 weeks before his father, was deployed by the Navy to the Pacific for World War II. Doug loved sports and was Co-Captain and is in the Hall of Fame for his high school. He went on to play football at Otterbein College where he graduated with a degree in Education, was in the 'O'Club and the Pi Kappa Phi (Country Club) fraternity.

He had been drafted into the Army in 1966 and got deployed to Vietnam in 1967, soon after he married. Despite being an athlete, at 6' 2" and 220 lbs. with 16 years of education, he was drafted and assigned to be a cook. Doug (uninvited) went in to see the Commanding Officer and convinced him that he would be much more valuable to the Army as a pilot. So off he went to OCS and flight school. He served in Vietnam for 13 months and was singled out to be a platoon leader. As a gunship pilot, he flew the Huey Cobra helicopter for the 17th CAV, which sent him to Dak-To and the Central Highlands. During this time, he was awarded a Distinguished Flying Cross, Bronze Star, and many Air Medals. He ended his Army commitment as a captain and flight instructor. Doug married the late Roberta Kathleen O'Friel in 1967 during his service in the Army. Kathy passed away on December 30, 2015 from Alzheimer's.

After his service, he got a job selling helicopters for Bell Helicopter Company. He made an impression on one of his customers, Ray Kroc, McDonalds Founder of the Franchisee business, and took a job flying for him which included flying with the Hamburgler. His next career move took his family from Ohio to Bolton, Massachusetts in the early 80s. He was recruited by Ken Olsen, Founder of Digital Equipment Corporation, with the agreement to start a flight department for the company. He ended up being Global Vice President of Administrative Services, which included seven divisions including the acquisition and disposition of Digital properties, worldwide.

Doug Hammond is survived by son, John Hammond; daughter, Lindsay (Stephen) Lewis, and grandkids, Stephen "Finn", Shea, and Ashton; two sisters in laws, Sally Joranko and Mary (David) Ballinger; four nephews; Greg (Jodi) Harville, Mitch (Jennifer) Harville, David (Nora) Joranko, and Michael (Nicole) Ballinger; four nieces; Mindy Ballinger, Kelly (Chuck) Rogg, Katie (Mel) Rodriguez, and Gillian (Adam) Schoenfeld. Doug also leaves behind several great nieces and nephews.

Any obituary highlights a life, as does his. However, there was so much "between the lines" of his life.

When I decided to write about all these veterans, I didn't have Doug on my radar. Recently I was re reading his history and decided his story should be included. The main connection I figured on was his daughter, Lindsay. I looked her up on Facebook and sent her a Private Message. After no response, I realized that she rarely was on that social media. Dick Morrow from Otterbein came to my rescue. I remembered that he and Doug were close in college. I sent him a message and asked if he could help. He put me in touch with Betty Byrne, Doug's forever friend of 32 years, and after the death of his wife, not only a friend, but someone who looked after him as a caregiver would. I had a wonderful interview with her, and she was kind enough to give me a fellow combat veteran to interview. His name is Steve Davis, a retired professor at Clemson University. His insights left me no doubt that Doug was a military hero. I also borrowed some thoughts from a book by Jim Villella; a neighbor and childhood friend of Doug's until the end of his life, called "It Can Be Done." Jim interviewed Doug and 8 others to complete his work. In his prologue he states that the subjects of the book were all very successful individuals, but not famous in any way. I would say Doug fits that description very well.

Lastly, I spoke with Lindsay, Doug's daughter. She added to

his legacy of her loving father.

Here is a compilation of the information gathered.

Doug came from humble beginnings. He was born in a mining community in Eastern Kentucky. His dad was one if twelve children and like most in that part of the world, worked in a coal mine. An accident changed all that, as a coal car backed over him and broke his back. As he was young and very strong, he survived. He was able to join the Navy and served in The Pacific. Doug's mom, who grew up in an adoption center, was a talented basketball player at 5'10". She found her way; after marriage, to Middletown, Ohio, Doug's dad joined her after returning from the war. He and three brothers formed a construction company. When Doug was in the seventh grade, the family moved to Franklin, Ohio, where he would become a standout in football and basketball. He was on some very talented teams. Most notably, when he was a senior, both the football and basketball teams were undefeated in their regular seasons. After graduation, Doug probably could have played major college football (my opinion). He went along on two recruiting trips to O.S.U. and Michigan with one of his teammates, Bobby Timberlake. Bobby ended up being the starting quarterback for Michigan and is in the college football Hall of Fame. Through a local businessman/ booster, he was introduced to Otterbein College in Westerville. The booster portrayed it as a "small Christian college. Doug quipped when hearing this.

"Does that make me a small Christian?"

He went on and starred there as a four-year defensive end. That's where he and I met up.

After an auspicious .583 first semester grade average, he went on and graduated, planning to become a teacher/coach. He went back to his high school at Franklin and applied for an opening for Head Coach/football. For whatever reason, he was not hired. He still wanted to play football, so he ended up catching on with the Charleston Rockets in The Continental Football League. He soon was sent a notification from his draft board and was drafted. ***I find this part ironic in the way his path and mine then moved in opposite directions. I was hired as a teacher/coach and get deferred from the draft. His rejection by Franklin Schools paved the way for him to be drafted.

After this is also where his life changed dramatically. He was drafted in 1966. Right after he got married, he was sent to basic training, as all rookies are. I've heard about basic training. Doug and basic training scenarios would be humorous at best, to be thought of in the same breath. He talked about one instance where he challenged a fellow soldier after a training incident. An officer caught this encounter and forced a punishment on Doug. It was to wad up a paper in his mouth and push it on his hands and knees to a nearby dumpster; then return it. He remembered his thoughts at the time; "I'm not sure how this will turn out!" He curbed his internal desire to buck authority, here." He survived basic training and got his marching orders from Washington. He found that they needed cooks and that would be his assignment.

Doug being Doug did not want to be a cook. He appeared unannounced in the Battalion Commander's office and explained this dilemma. I suppose this could have been cause for a court martial (Opinion). He ran into a Sergeant Major at the desk in front. That guy heard his plea and dispatched him. He had at least had a chance to rehearse his plea.

"I'm 6'2", 220 lbs. I've had 16 years of education and I don't want to be a cook!!"

In a stroke of luck, he met the battalion commander coming in the door. He made his plea again. This time he added.

"I didn't say I wouldn't become a cook; I just don't want to be!"

The commander told him to go back to his barracks. He thought that would be the end of the matter. A few days later he was invited to the commander's office. He envisioned this as punishment for his bravado. Instead, he found that the commander oversaw interviewing candidates for Officers Training School. Wow, what a turn of events! He was accepted and assigned to an armor school. That meant he would be driving a tank. This thought almost nauseated Doug, as he was claustrophobic. He spent a trying few weeks adjusting, with little success. In another ironic twist, he was present at a meeting when an officer asked.

"Are any of you interested in flight school for helicopters?" Doug's hand flew up and he was where he felt he could thrive. And thrive he did. He went on to be a distinguished Huey Helicopter pilot and won many awards for valor. Here's where I will add in some valuable information I received from Steve Davis, who served with Doug through most of his Vietnam experience.

Steve met Doug in Vietnam. Doug trained in a troop before going to Vietnam. His unit then went by ship to the conflict. They arrived as a well-trained group and were part of the conflict as soon as they could be brought up to speed. Steve arrived about 4 months later.

"I came in as an untrained newbie. By this time, Doug had all the proper training done before, plus months of combat time as well. All I knew when I got there was how to get a helicopter from point A to point B. I was not only new, but also not wanted. The groups and men already in place were familiar with each other and what was needed to function and survive. I was a liability to that, as mistakes are easy to make, and consequences could easily prove deadly to them and to me. There were three types of helicopters. Doug was a platoon leader of one of the gunship units. Initially I got assigned to the front seat (I was there as an observer only) The first guy I was assigned to treated me like a frat pledge. He hazed me, to put it in plain terms. No respect was given. I learned zero. Clearly, I was a nuisance to him. After about three weeks, I got a tremendous break. I got assigned to Doug. Unlike my first experience, Doug was a splendid mentor. Totally respectful always. I was extremely impressed with his professionalism and his rapport with everyone he encountered. On his own, he set up additional training for his group and made sure they were as battle ready as they could be. He taught me not only the ins and outs of flying the Cobras, but also about the stuff that we might run into under battle conditions. He even let me sit in the back seat (not legal/official). I made great strides because of Doug. Later, after a while, I took over a leadership role of a troop of Huey copters. I was more than prepared because of Doug's input. Then when Doug had about two to three months left, I became the executive officer of a platoon, as I was a more senior officer by rank. That was the number two position in the whole unit. As it worked out, I oversaw the entire operation every other day, as the number one officer had restrictions on how long he could spend in his role. Doug was subordinate to me. He never let that be an issue. After all this, we became close as friends. We played some basketball on base. He was big and strong. I was not; but speedy and quick. We had some fun games for sure. I found Doug as fun loving and a prankster. Some of those even had the possibility of getting in trouble. No problem for him! I also found out quickly that he had a soft spot in his heart for the underdog. He made friends with the "hooch maids." They were locals who came in and did menial stuff for us soldiers. Even the guys who (again locals) who cleaned the latrines, were people he showed genuine respect to. They were most often ignored by our guys. He also took lesser ranked soldiers under his wing. I think I heard this from Betty but find it easy to believe. On one of his missions, he fired on and killed a Viet Kong soldier. He was aware of what he had done; so, he landed, retrieved the I.D. from the guy, and later sought out the parents to let them know how this was something he deeply regretted and ask for their forgiveness. I found him to be a rare combination. He was very self-confident but would more easily brag on his men."

I asked if Doug was in the air all the time.

"Normally our missions were for reconnaissance. Doug supervised a platoon. He would be one of two copters in the air, providing armed support for the reconnaissance copters below him. Only in an extraordinary situation would he ever land. That would be for something like helping ground troops or even picking up someone. The Cobra was small and not equipped for rescues. He usually was a thousand feet above the recon copters and provided support. Doug was an absolute whiz at firing the rockets on board. He schooled me for sure. His targets would be V.C. troops, huts, and maybe vehicles. It was not hard for the enemy to hit our crafts, as we were low enough for a V.C. with a handheld machine gun to fire on us."

I asked.

"Were either of you ever shot down?"

"For sure I was not. Doug wasn't either; however, he flew his Cobra with holes in it from being shot at by the enemy. We had friends that were, though. I learned quickly that Doug was very aware of the safety of his mates, but not necessarily of himself. I found him to be a 'larger than life' figure. Almost a Hollywood movie type. A John Wayne figure.

I said to Steve and explained some of the stuff I encountered with Doug at Otterbein.

"Steve; I caught Doug at his worst, and you caught him at his best. I also know how he treated his family and his situations later in life. He was exemplary. He had money but didn't hesitate to spend it on behalf of caring for his family in ways that almost would be unheard of. Instead of finding a facility for his mom or his wife, he made one, and cared for the largely by himself. That's different, but not unlike diving into the jungle to rescue someone. For that time period, you paint yourself out of the picture and draw in only the person you're trying to help."

Steve adds.

"He was fearlessly loyal to those he cared about." I bet if he knew you better at Otterbein, he never would have trashed the property at your dorm. He even would not attend reunions we had that guys always tried to get him to attend. He declined because he felt more responsible for his mom and wife, than of any need to have a personal leave time."

"That's interesting; Steve. I never knew that."

Steve replies.

"However, I do know he had many meetings with at least three guys he was close to that trained with him in the states before going over to Vietnam."

"Steve, tell me about yourself;"

"When I had arrived in Vietnam, I had graduated from West Point and had gone to flight school. Most of my peers were not interested in making the Army a career. I quickly picked up the moniker, 'Lifer.' I was an introvert for many years. I probably stayed in the Army because my self-confidence was not opening other possibilities to me."

"What did you do after you did get out?

"While in the service I took on some roles on, in computer science. Then I got and advanced degree in Computer Science. I had a nice second career as a college professor at Clemson. I retired in 2007.

"Anything else you can remember?"

"Doug was a prominent figure in my life. Certainly, the most prominent figure in my military career."

"Did you ever have any encounters with Doug after Vietnam?"

"Two that I can remember. We both left in 1968-69. He was stationed briefly in Georgia. I was at Ft. Benning about a hundred miles away. I was a fan of the sports teams that bases have. I went down to watch a flag football. Low and behold, Doug was a player/coach. It was a great random visit. Then, I visited him at his home in New Hampshire. This was maybe 2-3 years before he passed away. I was visiting my daughter nearby and thought I would see if we could visit. We did and had a great time. He was showing symptoms of memory loss, but still independent. I could see he was having trouble, but his core memory was still intact. He was joking with the wait staff at the restaurant we were at, and being very caring to them, by engaging them and knowing names and family situations. It was a treasured time It was truly uplifting to me."

As a quick postscript, after hearing of Steve's military background, I'm even more impressed that Steve considered Doug no less than that of a mentor and a friend during the time they served together.

When Doug leaves the Army, he is much more accomplished and self-confident than most. He shows it, as his career(s) indicate. First, he decides that his helicopter expertise can pay off. He calls Bell Helicopter Company and tells them that he's fresh out of the military and has a lot of experience with copters. After a brief conversation about exactly just what he might do, he asks.

"How do you sell helicopters?" They tell him about the several regions now and he speaks.

"I'd like to come down and talk about this." He asks for an interview. He flies down to Texas and walks into Bell Helicopter Company. He gets an interview for a sales position. They turn him down. They drive him to the airport as a courtesy. He gets a bright idea and calls his interviewer back from the airport. He spoke.

"I made a call to Hughes Aircraft, and they offered me a sales job." He was bullshitting them, but it worked. He was offered a job in Crystal Lake, Illinois. After his training, he told them he wanted to transfer to the Kentucky area. He knew that the oil embargo had driven up the price of coal immensely and that coal companies small and large would be a good target. Besides, that's where he grew up and he figured he could easily relate to them. He did and set records in sales. This success got him noticed. One day out of the blue he gets a call from a lady, June Martino. She asks him to make a pickup in one of his copters. She explained that this was a businessman but wouldn't reveal his name. Eventually her persistence and his curiosity came together, and he did it. The mystery man was Ray Kroc, founder of the McDonalds franchising enterprise. June was Ray's personal assistant. They met and he and Ray hit it off immediately. Ray wanted to use the copters to do arial photography of potential shopping areas to build on. Soon Ray bought 6 Bell Helicopters: perhaps the biggest single sale ever.

Ray was enamored with Doug. Doug was fascinated by all this and yet knew that Ray had a ruthless side because of the way he handled the original McDonald brothers. Ray soon offered Doug a position, to head up a new "flight department." Doug asks.

"Why would I come to work for you?"

He shot back.

"Why wouldn't you?"

So, Doug leaves Bell and has a five-year career with McDonalds and Ray Kroc. He became Ray's personal pilot and part of his inner circle of employees and friends. He was treated like a son and felt that Ray would do anything for him. Lindsay was young at the time. Ray invited Doug and his family to fly on the company jet to visit Disneyland. Not a bad perk for a young family; especially for Lindsay! Lindsay also remembers flying with the "Hamburgler," a company mascot at the time. At a turning point in Doug's career, his father was sick and in the Columbus area. Ray thought it would be good for him to relocate there and be close to his dad. He was teamed up with a regional manager and they began grooming him to be a store owner/operator. To most, this would seem a golden opportunity. He did not like this part of the business, for whatever reason. He decided to hire a headhunter and quickly was in touch with a fast-rising computer company; D.E.C. (Digital Equipment Company.) He met with the C.E.O. and was hired to head up their flight department. He did so. In the process, he enriched his former company by purchasing 12 Bell helicopters. He even made sure the credit for each sale went to a different guy, as he knew the value that would have. He moved his family to the Boston area. He worked there for around 15 years and ended up as Global Vice President of Administrative services. His business career(s) showed a side that would have been hard to predict from when I knew him. I have great respect for his accomplishments.

He and Kathy had two children. First, they had a daughter, Lindsay. A few years later they adopted a son; John. They loved them dearly. They enjoyed the fruits of their labors.

I also know that during the time he was with D.E.C. his family dynamics changed dramatically.

First, his mom began to suffer from Alzheimer's. He built an addition on to their house, which mimicked her residence. He moved her in there, provided in home care and only when care became too tedious, did she have to be moved to a memory care facility. In the late 90's, Kathy began to show symptoms of the same fate. She was an unlikely one to have this happen to. She was a runner, and an aerobic fitness instructor. She did everything right. Her lifestyle was amazing, comparatively. It shows how insidious this disease is. Doug retired from Digital in 2000 when it was acquired by H.P. and bought a marina on Lake Winnipesaukee. His thinking was that this would be a much lower stress position and that he could take charge of the care for Kathy and his mother, who lived until her mid 90's. He did; moving to Laconia, New Hampshire. When Kathy declined in her disease, and Doug lost his mother, he placed a twin mattress on the floor next to Kathy's hospital bed to sleep, so he would be there for her. He cared for her 24x7 (with day help) for the last 5 years; till she passed in 2015.

Sadly, Doug himself was stricken with the same disease. What a cruel twist of fate.

At this point, his longtime; and forever friend, Betty Byrne becomes integral and important to the remainder of Doug's life. She and Doug met at Digital in 1988. She was working his boss and saw Doug all the time. She was an avid runner. Almost as a tease, she gets Doug into the sport. He started out as what could be caked a" Clydesdale runner" and ended up running in several Boston Marathons, the last one was the 100th Boston Marathon. At the end of Digital (They were acquired by Compaq) Doug offered Betty a job since her boss was let go. The last two years of the company, she worked directly with him. As she put it.

"Doug literally adopted my family. He would come visit us, go to the grandkid's games, and treat us all like his own family. He not only loved us; he trusted us! He was equally attentive to his own kids and grandkids. Lindsay had a successful position, 3 kids and was living in the Boston area, a few hours away.

A few years after Lindsay came along, son John was born. The family was complete. Doug always tried his best to help his kids. He was kind and caring and loving father.

During the last years of Kathy's life, Betty began to see signs with Doug that showed his memory loss. He never tried to dismiss it but found ways (mostly through humor) to cover it up. As Betty would say.

"He did a great job of this! He was extremely creative. He made it clear that if it got to the point of seriousness, he would "Fly that plane into the lake (referring to Lake Winnipesaukee.)" Doug didn't ever own a plane or helicopter, but with his background and resourcefulness, he knew he could get his hands on one if it ever came to that. Eventually it became a problem too big to ignore. Betty was able to get Lindsay in the loop and they had a neurologist confirm their fears. The marina was not doing well. Doug's situation was not allowing him to pay proper attention to it. A decision was made to sell the marina.

Betty became Doug's caregiver and person he trusted. She helped with decisions, maintain connections with his many, many friends, from all walks of life. Betty was still working but managed her best to see that Doug was safe and received the socialization he so needed. She helped till it became evident that Doug needed to be in a facility where both physical care and memory care were available. A little over a year later, he contracted Covid and passed away. Betty added.

"Since he couldn't fly that plane, he indeed found a different vehicle to exit."

Through his life, and until the end, Doug was a truly happy and upbeat person. He was generous to a fault. Everyone I talked to, portrayed this trait of his. Betty adds this.

"He was someone you would wat to be there in a time of crisis. He was strong, able. A quick thinker; resourceful, and a problem solver."

He left a giant legacy. I have no trouble calling him an American success story. A hero in every way.

BOB CROSS

AGE WHEN ENTERED MILITARY: 19

DATE OF ENTRY TO MILITARY: 07/1960

VIETNAM TOUR DATES: FIRST QUARTER 1962

YEARS OF DUTY/RESERVES: 6

BOB CROSS

I met Bob at a conference on Evangelism that I attended a few months ago. I was deep into my research and writing for this evolving book on perspectives. His ball cap gave me a reason to talk with him. He was obviously a Vietnam War veteran. I could tell he and I were in that same age range by his appearance. He was very approachable, and we talked briefly during a break. I told him about the project and asked if he would be interested in being interviewed. I also told him that I wasn't sure I would or could interview him, as I already had several more interviews than I originally planned. He understood and handed me a card with his name and contact info on it. We shook hands and that was that.

A few weeks ago, I talked with my publisher and the possibility of a few more interviews came to be. I was thrilled because I remembered Bob and my desire to fit his story in. I called him and was pleased, as he did remember me, and we immediately set up an interview (by phone).

I was sure Bob would prove to be interesting. I got far more than I bargained for. We talked for over two hours! Each of the stories are unique. His was also. He is a very intelligent and well-spoken man. He is also not afraid to speak his mind. As in every interview, I encouraged a free mind to "tell it like it is." I hope I gave everyone that freedom. I especially wanted that with Bob, after our conversation began.

Bob is an African American. During the time we talked, I never asked him to emphasize that fact. Our conversation ended up very candid and you will hopefully continue to get more informed about what happened to him, and how his experience both mirrored and differed from the rest. Bob is also a Christian. It didn't take long for that to emerge as the centerpiece in his life.

During a text he sent me, he forwarded a video for me to watch. I thought he was in the video. As I watched, he was not. It was about origins. It was the work of a guy and an organization that wants to show the world that we are all interconnected as peoples; more than we know or have thought of.

Before we got started, I asked why he wanted me to see it. He explained.

"Larry, the reason I'm sharing this historical archaeological and anthropological kind of information is this. If you talk to the Vietnamese people; they know nothing about a Vietnam War. They will talk to you about the American war. So, all these years later, I have remained somewhat studious about such history. I see this parallel thing happening with us as American people, and peoples of the world. We have our perspective as Americans based on the way we have been taught history, our own history and world history. Now we're entering a day of reckoning and finding that it isn't all necessarily so. It never was. It's because of our position and our power in the world. I'll attribute my ability to see; and boldness to say this to my born-again experience and my Biblical studies of the past 50 years.

I've had such a deep transformative experience and I'm getting to know the God of creation as that first image bearing person created in the garden of Eden account, in Genesis. So, my whole attitude; my whole outlook on life continues to be transformed, enlightened, and clarified. Even now it continues to be, as I just yield myself to see the world and all that's in it through the eyes of the one who said; "light be." Then light took off. The speed is estimated at about 186,000 miles per second and there's no indication that light has slowed down since, because light has not been given another command. So, light continues to move, as we move through time and as we evolve. Now our physicists and other scientists are talking about the expanding universe and we're developing bigger, better telescopes that allow us to see further into the universe. However, we can only see based on the light that lights up the space that we exist in. And so, I just journey on, looking forward to hopefully build relationships with persons with imagination, like you; with creativity, like you; with obvious calling on their life as you have. Maybe, we can add something that's missing from the conversation in the public discourse today about everything that's going on for what is the future of America; what is the future of our political system.

Today we have people whom I was led to believe when I was a young soldier; when I was a young child; when I was a student; people whom I thought would be the defenders and promoters of our Democratic Republic and Constitutional government. They seem to be the party leaders now saying; let's get rid of it; let it go to hell, let this whole more perfect union experiment - just let it go. and replace it with what? Replace it with everything that I was trained that we needed to be having defenses against and fighting to keep from ever emerging and proliferating globally. The very anti-democratic systems poised to go to war against the Kingdom of God that Jesus said was at hand in His day, even as it keeps on coming to earth now.

I hope I'm not clouding the issue by; you know, by putting too much on the boil over point right now. Concerning this interview ,I think I see what you had in mind now and we will continue on that track and for sure I'm grateful for your shared perspectives because it was so interesting and something I hadn't really spent a lot of time thinking about, so we're tracking and can continue.

"Bob; yes Sir! yes Sir; great! OK so let's kind of go back to your beginning with your military service to the United States and how did you get in the service in the first place?"

"Larry, I got in the service as a college dropout."

"Well, you don't talk like a college dropout!"

"Thanks, but here's how it was at that time. I was set to matriculate at a what's referred to as a historically black college (University) and I had been raised by my grandmother. I was born in her house, and she was my primary caregiver although I lived in the same small southern town in the "Jim Crow South" that my biological parents resided in. I am an only child with 15 brothers and sisters. The way that came about was this. I was conceived by my unwed parents; teenagers whose parents were sharecroppers on nearby farms. My dad and mom never married each other. They both married different people; so, there were three living possibilities for me. One with my father and his family, a second with my mother and her family, or a third with my grandmother and grandfather. I got, I think the better of the three options, staying with my grandparents.

My grandparents were born in the first generation after it was illegal to sell Black Africans on the slave markets in the USA. They were born after 1865 so between 1865 and 1900 there were a couple of generations of people to whom enslavement was very real, albeit they were technically(legally) free, there were constant attempts to re-enslave Black Africans in America. At the same time, with all of the changes that happened and continue to happen in our human evolution and with our evolution as a nation, education was a really big deal. My grandfather made a real sacrifice for me so I could get what he never had, which was education. He stayed on the farm after moving his family to town. During the week, he worked on the farm. On the weekend he would come to town, where an older brother had settled into ahead of him. He had somehow managed to scrape up; save enough money to buy some property in the little town, on land contract. He bought a house; rather two "shotgun houses," side by side. One for his family and next door one for his parents. His mom and dad and an alcoholic sister who was a single woman lived next door to us. That was where my earliest recollections of life occurred. It was in that little rural town where the major cash crop was tobacco and none of us realized how poor we were because we all were equally poor.

My grandfather stayed out on that farm, and I was enrolled in elementary school at age 6. There was also a high school for Black students; located in our town for approximately 50 years. After the 1954 Brown v Board of Ed. Supreme Court decision our Colored High school was phased out in 1967. From about 1850 something to 1967 there had been one high school for Colored children from three counties, and I had the opportunity to graduate from that high school and enter into college as a science major at the age of 17. That was due primarily to the tutelage of my grandmother. I don't know all the circumstances of her learning to read, write and reason, but she had a very keen sense of the value of education, and she was never shy to emphasize this value. She never told me I couldn't learn. I just always knew she expected me to learn.

My mother had no formal education. My dad had no formal education. Neither of my grandparents had formal education; but my grandmother was self-taught and a very educated woman. She read every day and every day she read the Bible. Among newspapers, magazines, and other things she read I saw her read the Bible every day. I heard her singing hymns every morning and that's what I was awakened to. I was never awakened by an alarm clock to this day. It was the smell of food cooking and the sound of her voice singing hymns. At night I was put to sleep by the sound of her praying. So, I didn't see God. I didn't see Jesus; but I knew they lived in the house with us. We lived with God and the miracle of just how the material provisions that were there for us. It was a real faith experience growing up in the house with my grandmother - especially after my grandfather died when I was 9 years old.

"May I ask where that place was?"

"Yep; that place was right; it was ironically right near Fort Campbell KY, right on the Tennessee/ Kentucky border. It was in the little town of Hopkinsville KY."

"Well, sounds like you were fortunate young man! What was the Black college that you went to?"

"I went to Kentucky State College (now Ky. State University)."

"I see. So, you were there, and you ended up; I think you said you were a dropout?"

"Right; I was. I was second person in our family to graduate high school and the first to go to college. My mother's youngest brother, who served in the Army during the Korean conflict for two years was our first high school graduate. Then I was the second person that graduated high school. I was the first to attend college, and because there was no sophistication, no knowledge of the experience, it was like a whole other world to me! There was extreme Black and White ethnic segregation during that time in my hometown. in fact, in most southern towns, there were written and unwritten rules and boundaries of separation oozing from the culture. Geographically It was commonly by railroad tracks. Those tracks were the line of demarcation between the White folk and the Black folk. Interestingly and unknown to too many, there began a decline in collective Black achievement that is moving at an accelerated pace today - that was set in motion by legislated social integration. This is an important fact.

It's also a fact easy to understand. If you were Black, Colored or as they were called Negroes; or any of those terms used in that era, you had to live on the same side of the tracks with other people that looked like you. It doesn't matter. Whether you had achieved a Bachelor, Masters, PhD, MD, DD, JD, or no D at all. You would basically have to move together and live together on the same side of the tracks. You saw professional people; you saw business owners. You saw them daily, you interacted with them. You lived on the same streets with them. Yes, that's what segregation forced to be a reality for us. And so, the unintended consequence is if you can see it, you can be it. If you can't see it, the likelihood grows exponentially that you have a less chance of being what you can't see; what you don't interact with. So, if you go to a school and all of your teachers look like you; the custodian looks like; you the people in the cafeteria look like you; the secretary; the principal and all the teachers. Everybody in that building looks like you then you know you can manage things; you can run things; you can be in charge, and you can serve each other. So, that's what we have lost with the integration process. But it was still in effect for me because all of my teachers looked like my mom and dad and my grandparents until I got to college. All the teachers, professors, Dept. Chairs, Deans, and the president I had at college were Black folk also.

On the other hand, when I got to college, I met more students who looked like me who were from another economic class. That was the class difference economically, educationally, and socially. And so, it›s like being a fish out of water so to speak, a culture shock. I realize also how I understand it now, better than did then; the psychological damage that I was carrying from childhood trauma of living in a terrorized environment. Nobody talked to us about terrorists or counseling like we talk about it in the media with the advent of the Islamic terrorists, the «foreign» terrorism and a whole so called global War on Terror. During my childhood and the childhoods of my American ancestors we surely could have used a global War on Terror. And we still need to talk about it so that we can understand what has happened to people on both sides of this ghastly equation. We both have been damaged by the same system of segregation and the ideas spawned out of the doctrine of White supremacy and Black and Colored inferiority. This is still work yet to be done.

Now, I got to college because my grandmother put the fear of God in me about never dropping out of high school. She just pushed me to be this high school graduate, to stay in school and how to be a good student and how to learn. When she got me through high school and I graduated as Senior class president, I thought I was done with school. But she wasn't. So, here's what she did. She canvassed the white community where she had worked as a domestic. She started knocking on doors; informing people in that community that she had raised this little grandson of hers and, "he's really smart and he deserves to go to college." That's the script that two white ladies brought to our school who were alerted that this woman was going around trying to get money to send her grandson to college. So, these ladies made it over to the Colored high school and informed the principal and faculty there that they represented a scholarship fund, and they had been providing aid to a deserving white child each year who was financially unable to pay college tuition, to go to school, and had done so for many years. But this year they were going to expand their operation over to the colored school because of my grandmother. OK wow, so they wanted them to select one student that they thought could do college work and they would help pay for her or him to go to school.

The faculty selected me. They pulled me out of class and tested me; I think it went on for like 2 days. When they finished, they found out I had not studied a foreign language in high school. They contacted the college and found a lady who taught a French class, and she would teach me French at 4:00 o'clock in the afternoon, and I also had to work with the maintenance department M-F, and I had to carry a full load as a biology major; which was ill advised. It was too much. It was just way too much. So, when I realized the second year that I didn't have adequate money and we didn't have all the financial aid stuff that exists today, and because of human nature, there are differences today made between the classes of people, as well as the colors of people - so were there then. Had I been the son of a teacher or a doctor a lawyer; some professional person, I would have been treated differently on that college campus than I was. But I was a nobody. I wasn't you know, highly regarded. I was just there all on merit, totally all merit and GOD's grace. I just kind of got worn out. I broke under the weight of it all. So, when I got home; I'm actually in the second year. I didn't get my summer job that I expected to get. I am the walking wounded.

    I went by a pool hall and another guy, and I started drinking some inexpensive wine and we smoked one of those "no name" cigarettes and then, in the process of that negative down and depressed attitude he said; "let's join the military!" and I did something my grandmother had kept me from all through high school. I said, 'I will if you will.' She taught me to be a leader not a follower. In a flash and under the lash of intoxication I became a follower. Under the influence of this alcoholic beverage and smoke thing I weakened. And so. There we went on our way to the local military recruiting office. In our town, all the services were in the Post Office building. On the way there, we decided on the Air Force. We would join the Air Force. Having grown up right near one of America's two Strategic Air Command Army bases, it never occurred to me to be a soldier. But this day; now I'm making these bad decisions and things and I are just in motion!

When we get there, the Air Force recruiter is at lunch, but the Army guy's there. So, oh well, what the heck, we'll join the Army. I signed up for the Army, and irony of ironies I passed the exam. My buddy: this guy whose idea this plan was, he didn›t pass the first round of testing. So, there I was on my way to be in the Army. However, the recruiter guy also talked me into becoming a paratrooper right then and there. Now, because it›s an airborne base right here at home That›s the STRAC thingy. Simply put, it means, Ft. Bragg, NC. and Ft. Campbell, Ky. got paratroopers ready to go anywhere in the world 24 hours a day every day. And to ensure that he wouldn't lose me as a recruit, he told me he could set up my enlistment so I could be stationed right there at Fort Campbell Ky, and it would be like I never left home. Well, what he probably didn't know; being an enlisted person of low rank himself; he didn't know what America's foreign policy was about to be in Southeast Asia at that particular time, or maybe he did. I know I signed up to be a 101st Airborne Division paratrooper right there in the recruiter's office. That meant I went to Louisville, Ky (Saint Catherine) then to Fort Knox, Ky. There were so many troops there they couldn't coordinate basic training outfits fast enough. So, I milled around there about two weeks. Then one day they called names and we whose name got called ended up on buses and were shuttled to the Louisville airport they put us on planes and my plane landed in Manhattan, Kansas.

So, I did basic training at Fort Riley, Kansas and then after eight weeks you get a two-week leave. You go home for 14 days and then you go to advanced individual training. My advanced training was infantry training because that's part of trying to be a paratrooper. I guess my recruiter picked Infantry for me I got sent back to Ft. Riley Ks again for eight weeks of advanced infantry training and so that was the beginning of my military career.

My grandmother, who has taught me such values as; if you start something, you finish it. I realized the first night that I was away from home, at St. Catherine, before arriving at Ft. Knox, I knew I didn't want to be in the army. I really wanted to be a college student! I'm in the army but I didn't do the officers candidate training thing that I was tested for. If I had, it would have meant a lifetime commitment and I probably would not be here today. But as an enlisted person, I just I had a six-year obligation. That got divided into two terms, three years active duty and three years as a reservist. That's how I did my military service from 1960 to 1966. Six years. Honorable Discharge.

"Yes Sir; yes. So, you enlisted, as in not drafted. Did you have to get anybody's permission to do that like your grandparents or anybody?"

"Yes, to your first question and no to the second., I was well past the legal age by the time I enlisted. I graduated high school at 17 but I was 19 by the time I signed into the Army. My birthday was in June."

"So, you were good to go. Did your grandmother give you any negativity after finding out about this, or didn't that matter?"

"No. She took it quite well. Because I was clearly ready to leave home at age 17. When I got on that Greyhound bus, I was ready to go. I left home with a sense that I was going away to this college where I knew no one. Yeah, I'm here with some other kids from my graduating class who ended up going to the same school, but I didn't go with anybody. I was traveling alone on the bus and when I got there everything was; I'm on my own. But that was the whole goal of what they had poured into me. It was to have me ready to be a man. I was the same age as Emmitt Till was when he was murdered. He was 14 years old. I was 14 years old. It was a big shock. That is a part of what I talk to my psychiatrist about now in terms of childhood trauma that I experienced growing up. Because, when you know that you know what the unwritten rules are in the system of Jim Crow and that you could be taken away just any day, you don't have to do much of anything. You know that was just the way it was and so you were trained to live on alert. We went to church, and we prayed without ceasing. I realize now that the sermons and the Bible study and the Sunday school lessons and everything; it was about God's protection and God's provision. That was pretty much where we as Christians were. That was our essential theology framework. That's what shaped our society; that God was with us and if you survived from one day to the next, it was because God was blessing you and keeping you.

So, these are the kind of things that I need to talk about as I have learned and am learning about. My mind has not been idle since I came online as a 19-year-old soldier, raising my right hand and donating my life to the defense of our constitution and this Democratic Republic that we know as the United States of America. I had no reservations about that. My grandmother had no reservations about that. The only thing she told me, as a cautionary note was to stop telling her when I was going to be jumping out of airplanes that flew right over our house. She didn't want to know when I was going to be on one of those planes. She didn't want to know about that. Other than that, she never expressed any reservation, because she kept praying and trusting God. She would believe that the same God of hosts who was with David when he slew Goliath, would be with me and protecting me. And surely, HE is right up to right now.

"It must have been a great comfort to you, knowing she was always lifting you up in prayer! So, tell me how you got from your basic training and were eventually sent to Vietnam. I assume that's correct."

I got through basic training and advanced infantry training and then it was back home to Ft. Campbell, Ky. for Jump school and permanent duty assignment to B Company 506 infantry of the 101st Airborne Division and home of the original Band of Brothers. I went through jump school twice. Let's talk about that, being me from 1960 to 63 and then my view of America's southeast Asian fling.

Jump school consists of a three-week training situation, All of the elite forces that you can become a part of in terms of post basic training were now available to me. I could have gone from advanced individual training to a combat or non-combat job. However, my destiny was light and heavy weapons Infantry because of my slightly inebriated enlistment choice. After AIT it would be all voluntary and once you volunteer to get into Special Operations type units, they usually do not put you out. The only way out is to say, "I quit." So, in Jump school there's two weeks of ground training and then in the third week you do 5 qualifying jumps out of an airplane in flight. After jump number 5, out on a parade field you get wings pinned on your outer garment, kind of over your heart. You're then a full-fledged green as grass paratrooper. From there, you're ready for whatever special ops trainings in existence or anywhere you want to go.

I wish I could show you a picture of me when I went to high school. I was 4 foot 11 inches tall. I played trumpet in the high school band because I had excelled in music education from 6th grade. The school was small, and the band was small, so the band director put me and a few other students from junior high into high school band. That picture of me standing there with those taller high school size students was a sight to behold. Not only was I short, but I was also unmistakably skinny! I grew up to about 5 foot 10 over a single summer. By the time I got in the Army I was somewhere about 5 foot 11 inches tall and weighed in at a solid 135 pounds with 28-inch waist. I didn't look like a paratrooper at all. There's a movie, "Band of Brothers." It's all about the formation of the 101st airborne division from WWII. It's a good movie to watch; a good story to show how these paratroopers led and fought during World War Two. They were an all-White newly minted fighting unit thrown into combat, performing against pretty steep odds in Europe. In the beginning they experienced some epic fails There were still some of the originals on active duty when I went into jump school at Ft. Campbell, Ky.

Now I'm going to tell a story that might be difficult to hear. Some members of my Jump School Training Cadre still disagreed with President Truman signing Executive Order 9981 on July 26, 1948. My story shows that some of these guys did not want me in "their" outfit. Now had I been like Jim Brown; a big strong football type, I might have been more acceptable. But I wasn't. I was still the skinny physical specimen I was then. However, they didn't see what else I possessed. I was a guy with a super amount of inner strength. I had 10 tons of the heart of a champion and there would be no chance of me quitting! I'd been trained up like that as a child. I knew what they didn't know about me. They could not break me; they couldn't make me quit. Plus, now I have been put through the rigor of all of that Ft. Riley Kansas advanced infantry, combat readiness training. However, on the final day of ground training, after running me up to the top of the 34-foot tower to simulate jumping from the door of a plane in flight repeatedly, cutting the line ahead of other trainees and I still would not say I want to quit - two of my trainers pulled me aside and put me through an exercise that has since been banned from US. military PT. The Squat Jump.

With a main parachute on your back, and a reserve parachute on the front you lace your fingers together on top of your helmet strapped tightly under your chin. You are instructed to leap up into the air putting one foot ahead of the other before you land in a squatting position, then you spring into the air again repositioning your feet and legs each time. This crisscrossing of my legs each time; yeah, right leg in front left leg in back went on for I don't know how many times. This up and down and switching back and forth. This jumping and squatting. They did that to me until my legs just went out. Brain and body quit successfully signaling. I just crumpled on the ground; couldn't walk.

Larry, two grown men were screaming at me. They were suggesting to me that I wanted to quit. Impolitely asking me to resign. "You wanna quit, don't you? You wanna quit, don't you? "No Sergeant, I Wanna Be AIRBORNE!" They been taking turns running me morning to evening. Once in that training area I had to run everywhere I went. Everything in double time, all day long. And do pushups, all day long. So, even though it's only three weeks, it seemed like three years. The training, because it's pretty intensive, took its toll on bigger guys than me. You'd see someone giving up every day. All didn't make it. Now, I've gotten the attention of some of these contrary players, and I 've become a challenge to them. I remember being carried out of the training area on the stretcher and this guy is down in my face. He's spitting in my face and he's yelling at me saying all kind of nasty negative stuff. I really had to beat this, Larry. After I healed up, they had to put me back in Jump School because I never said, "I quit." I got in the next training class. Yes, I thought; well since I've really completed all of the ground training I'll just have to go in and do my 5 qualifying jumps and get my wings. But …. oh no. I had to go through the whole thing again! So, I went through jump school twice because I didn't look like paratrooper material. That's how much I wanted to wear that "screaming eagle Insignia" and be ready for special operations and all that kind of gung-ho stuff.

That's how that happened and as a result, here's what's really important for me to say. I need to tell people like you, guys who got deferments or like your buddy in your book who went to Canada, or somebody who served in the military in a clerical position or cook or whatever they did. If all they did was learn to march; went to the rifle range; got a marksman badge. If they hit the target the minimum enough times. You know; Larry; if they just went through the basic stuff, learned to march, stand at attention and salute. I make no difference in those persons and somebody like a high school classmate of mine who did five tours in Vietnam during the worst of all that was done in all of our names and went as far up in rank as Command Sergeant Major. After 24 years of Special Forces active duty and 20 years working in an Army hospital he's retired twice now. We talked last week because one of our classmates passed away. There's no difference in any of you and here's why.

There's a question asked in a philosophy class one day. "When is it a thief a thief, before or after he steals. Well, the real answer to that question is they are thieves before they steal; not after. A non-thief will not steal. Thinking in these same terms regarding a combat veteran. When is a combat veteran a combat veteran? Is it before or after they experience being fired upon or return fire, or get to survive a kill or be killed situation without firing a shot? My answer to that is like the thief, they prove what they are capable of once the opportunity presents itself. Military personnel do not provide their opportunities. I would add to this, that once you go through all of the training I went through and combat training from aspects for me to attain high levels of proficiency and have been through some of that training twice. Yes. Sir, that qualified me for sure, to become a combat veteran. It's the training. The exposure. Everyone has the right to change their mind. Conscientious objection is honorable and to be respected. But I digress.

Larry, what I'm about to say now is really important for this whole scenario. Here I was in the second year of my 3-year active-duty enlistment, being sent into Southeast Asia with a whole bunch of other guys from the 506 Infantry Battle Group on a TDY Mission (Temporary Duty Assignment). One day in January in1962, we thought we were going up to do a routine training jump which usually involved about four hours of flight time for the Air Force. They would fly out someplace. Maybe it was over several States, and you know, you're high in the air, you descend, and the rear doors are opened 20 minutes from the drop zone. Then we come down and we cross highway 41, focus on the white colored water tower, and receive our jump commands. Then someone is told, "Stand in the door, green light comes on and we jump, We land, gather up our chutes and do routine stuff through the rest of the day. Just doing whatever soldier stuff there was to be done. We had to do at least one training jump every three months to qualify for jump pay. Circumstances dictated that I did a lot more than 3 a month training jumps, and I loved it. I think it was for a couple of reasons. But I won't even get into that now, as I want to stay on the main thing here, as it relates to Southeast Asia.

This very cold and memorable January morning we were trucked out to the air strip and put onto planes. It was the regular time we go out; about 4:00 o'clock in the morning. So, we were sitting in the sling seats on the sides of the cargo plane and naturally, as young guys, we a lot of times had been out maybe drinking or something at night. As such it was common to doze off. But we would typically all wake up about the time the plane starts descending. But this day the plane didn't descend. We're waking up and normally we're looking out of open or opening rear doors. Where are we? can't tell anything, but we know we're not at the altitude or air speed that we jump from. This fast-moving plane just keeps flying and flying, high and fast. Next thing we know is that we land at a naval air station in California. So, we ask, what's up? We're apparently on a need-to-know basis now, and none of us possessed the need to know. After a brief time of just milling around, they march us to a barber shop and all of our hair is sheared to a basic training standard military look.

They feed us and then they get us ready to get on different, Navy/Marine commercial passenger style planes. Next stop, Hawaii. They kept us there for a few days and brought in some Polynesian girls and they danced for us. Then, the next leg of the trip they loaded us on planes, and they flew us to Wake.; then Guam. They put all the girls away someplace at that point. We didn't see any women on the island till we were leaving. Then there were girls on both sides of the tarmac waving at us, so they got us out of view. Then, our next stop was Okinawa, Japan. Now we know. Or some of us; at least; the direction we were headed might be Vietnam. There were reports of casualties coming out of Vietnam already, because we have been in Vietnam since the French were there in 1954. These are things that are not readily reported to the public. Yes, we were going on an assignment someplace in the world in Southeast Asia. We, the uniformed specialists are well on our way somewhere and have not yet been told where. The next place we were offloaded was Okinawa, Japan, where we set up camp and after about two weeks, we were back with the Air Force and on cargo planes. We arrived at an Air Force Base. That's when we start to being briefed on what our mission was. We were put in the jungles. We were put in the mountainous region above the large urban area and there organizing rebels were cut off from their objective and scattered. In the prespring of 1962 our mission was accomplished, and we returned to our home base of Ft. Campbell, Ky.

In 1962, on September 30th. we receive order to go into Oxford Ms. Out of Fort Campbell KY, I'm still on active duty. I'm close to being finished with this first three years now, 9 months and two weeks to be exact. I'm still some months away. I don't get off of active duty until July. This is September, end of September. Why am I going to Oxford, Mississippi. It's because of a young man who has served eight years in the Air Force. He's a native of Mississippi. He wants to enroll in a Mississippi State University to get his undergraduate degree. He only needs to pick up a few credit hours to complete his undergraduate requirement because he's done most of it at Jackson State. Now, the difference between Jackson State and Ole Miss. Is this. Jackson State was the Colored university and Ole Miss was the White university. There had never been a black student admitted; enrolled as a student at Ole Miss, and Ross Barnett, the governor at the time said; "There won't be one on my watch!" and so, he gets into a royal pissing match with President John F Kennedy and his brother Robert, who is the US. Attorney General. The keepers of the confederacy force the enactment of Constitutional Law.

Martial Law is declared and so we became the police. The enforcers. We became the law of the land. So, here's me. In fewer than 3 years I've now drawn 2 short straws. One put me in Southeast Asia, and the other one has me doing Civil War duty in Mississippi. The one in Southeast Asia rattled my sensibilities. The one in Mississippi tread on my sensibilities; because on the way down that highway from Memphis TN (because that's where Army logistics staged us; hoping they wouldn't have to send us into Oxford; kind of like what's going on now with this debt ceiling and authoritarian thing the current political class is playing with. You know; that that was the kind of tension that was in the air at the time for those of us on active duty. It was a little bit more intense because it was so totally wrong. Probably 30,000 soldiers from a lot of bases across the country all ascended into Oxford Ms. to get one man enrolled in school. We got there at the last minute. It was a Sunday. But the order came that " they're killing people down there. We're going in."

So, we rolled out of Memphis TN down to Oxford Ms. On the way there, we were met on the highway by guys with these long antennae on the cars and pickup trucks. they would monitor our arrival using CB radios for communication. There was a Second Lieutenant leading the section of convoy that I was a part of. He misread his map. There's a little regional airport outside of Oxford and we were supposed to turn on the road to go to the airport. He missed that road, and we went right into the heart of Oxford. In so many southern towns, there are town squares. There would be a courthouse or similar building in the middle of it. So, you can imagine trucks with trailers hung up in the town square. We had our weapons with us, but the ammunition was in the trailer. Out on the highway into Oxford we came under fire in Mississippi, by the local people; leftover from the confederacy I imagine. I started crying silently and uncontrollably. It messed me up because these trucks are clearly marked U.S. Army with the star and the large white letters always cut crisp so they could be easily seen. And those guys; some of those guys were obviously veterans themselves. They were Klan people for sure, Larry. So, that's my big war story. Not Southeast Asia, but; WOW, Mississippi. And it got worse,

Larry. We went down as an integrated US. Army. But we got re- segregated once we got down there. That was logistically and was probably most prudent. It was a wise move to make, but it was a wrong move to make at the same time. Executive order 9981 had been signed by President Harry S Truman many years before but had never been accepted fully by active-duty soldiers. So, this is what's going on now; what was going on when I put on the uniform. Your buddy who went to Canada. We were all right. I was right because I got myself into something. Then I was right to obey the orders of the officers appointed over me and go through something like hell and deal with all of the stuff that I dealt with and learned; all I had to learn under the circumstances. I learned them. And you were right to get your education for your deferment and teaching career. So, that's my take on it. But I'm just fortunate because once you raise your right hand and you let that hand down and you're in the Army or the Navy the Air Force or Marines; it's not up to you what your job is. If your job is to type on a typewriter, then that's what you do. If your job is to be in the infantry, then you go and do that. If it's to jump out of airplanes and do other kind of crazy stuff like I did, then that's what you do. But I don't think that we need to be grading people like potatoes or chickens or vegetables or something in terms of the quality of the person or based on what your job was or what you did; where you went or where you didn't go. It's so ridiculous deciding this stuff anyway; right?

My grandmother got me hooked on phonics. She had this total respect for education that's real, and how to put a value on education. Because of her, I caught it.

I hope that I›m not rambling too much; that you don›t hear that. Really what I›m saying is that I›m glad you're recording this."

"Yes Sir; Don't worry, as I am fascinated so far. I'll keep asking."

"I'm probably way too long winded, Larry."

I want to ask a couple more things about the two experiences you just talked about when you were in Vietnam. You were on the ground there approximately how long?"

"That's a little tough for me to answer. I was someplace. I was I'll leave it like this. I was someplace that to this day I don't know where I was. Because like I say, those countries; the borders; From the Philippines the terrain is quite similar all around the South China Sea, Cambodia, Vietnam, Thailand, Laos, Cambodia, and Vietnam they intersect, and you can go out of one into the other without being really aware. But because I was there before it was really legal to be there; before it was even announced; before they really started the large shipments of soldiers over there, which did not begin until 1964. Now they were arming people in the central Highlands, the Montagnard people, guys in the Marines, Army and Air Force who were already there as "Advisors" training South Vietnamese on weapons systems and tactics well before 1964 as those in the know were getting ready for this thing.

But like I say, we didn't know that all of this was going on, so I would say I don't count that I really spent any time in the actual Vietnam War because the official time of the war is counted from 1964 to 1975. I was off active duty and living in New Jersey in 1963. I don't feel sorry for me one bit. I just don't, because I have enough things to gas me up, other than this being the biggest thing of my life. I've been in Southeast Asia. I ran interference to keep dictator Ferdinand and Imelda Marcos in power, which again was a very corrupt government as I said. Then we've seen more corrupt leadership after them. and this crazy guy who succeeded Marcos now has one of the Marcos' children and one his children are in power in the Philippines."

So, you served six years. Is that right? You served three active and three in reserve; inactive reserves; yes?"

"Yes sir."

"Then once you got out completely, what was your career path?

I was buddies with a guy in the transportation unit. Matter of fact, that's who I went to Mississippi with. I went as a paratrooper with a transportation outfit; but he was from North Carolina, and he had relatives in New Jersey. So, he was getting off active duty about two weeks after I did. I hung around until He got out; we drove to New Jersey together and when I got to New Jersey, I had a lot of readiness to be a police officer. I was being you know, kind of recruited for that vocation. I looked at the police idea but decided against it. I got an opportunity to go to work at a state hospital; and get into nursing training. I got involved in psychiatric nursing and stayed at the state hospital for a while, working with geriatrics people first, and Pediatrics as well. I did the old people and children. It was the perfect place for me because it helped me get all of this airborne infantry; special operation stuff to cool down in me. The whole social change stuff that was going on; here's another piece that I want to share about what happened in 1962. Until you make note of September 30th, 1962, you may not get it. Remember November 22nd, 1963? guess what happened in the middle of a downtown Dallas TX. street?"

"Yes! President Kennedy got shot and killed."

"Right so the governor of Mississippi and all that whole Civil War revenge attitude got him back. They paid him back; in broad daylight and invited the whole town and the world to come out and watch it. And that has not been settled yet. Some of us have a clear understanding of how the President was murdered. Of course, he was shot and killed, OK. It wasn't one guy shooting from that bookstore upstairs, which wouldn't have been a hard thing to do. It just didn't happen that way. The people who said they heard multiple shots really did, because JFK wasn't intended to get away. There were other players involved. Today we ought to be able to be having intelligent conversation around that; right?

They reneged on what they put out during the Warren report. Now, you would think that; fifty years after all of the active players were dead, then we could talk about it. But we still couldn't talk about it. There are people who've been doing research. It is a known fact; but I'm just saying that's how real this thing has always been. The JFK event took place almost one year to the day, after forcing us to let this Negro come and enroll in our White school. Then five years later they got his brother, and they got Martin Luther King too. The coordination has always been there. So, when they're saying no collusion, no collusion. Well, that's stupid! There's collusion. There's coordination. And it's a tension that exists. It's what we have always dealt with. God is not going to allow the devil to win. It's just not going to happen. Good is going to overcome evil always; it's written.

We gotta learn to just be on God's, on the Lord's side, you know. We gotta choose! I'm with God. If I live, if I die, I live in him. I live for Christ. I live. If I die, I die for Christ, you know. But we don't die. We live forever; we live. There, that I wanted to stick that in there, in that that little slot. This thing: this war, is not just in Vietnam. It's all over; all the time. Sometimes it percolates up. Other times it gets tamped down. But it's always going off. "

"Back to your career path. So, you're in the psychiatric field in New Jersey?

"Yeah."

"What happened after that?"

"OK, after that I decided I'm going to go back to school. So, when you add up all my credits and all of the disciplines, I'm formally trained in, biology, psychology, and theology. So, now we're getting into the psychology piece of it, and I enrolled in Rutgers. I was going to go to school at night and work during the day. Back then we were still having manufacturing happening in America. So, a young guy like me; I could literally just walk out of one factory and go next door or down the street and get hired at another factory, any day. One time I'm working at the hospital. I'm volunteering with the group called "Welfare Rights." this was with single women who were receiving aid to dependent children. They will be organized by some people who get described today as The Dirty liberals. They were organizing these women and giving them political education and that kind of thing, to help them to make their life better and make the lives of their children better.

These were people pushing to help their children get education and go to college and help themselves. So, I was volunteering, helping these leaders, out of their office in Newark, NJ. New Jersey became one of the sites of the 1960's riots that happened, starting in South Central Los Angeles in 1965, and coming across the country two years later. Cleveland, Detroit, etc. Out of the big city slums come what Dr. MLK Jr. called the voice of the unheard. Riots! Uprisings and revolt. If you look, there's a whole lot to understand about that. All those things happen because, to this day you know; people who make kind of tourist visits to some of these communities, and remark; "Oh my God look at how these people have destroyed these neighborhoods!" Well, I know from doing a little bit of a study of Newark, Nj.

There's a lot of Black people in Newark because they were brought there to work in the factories especially during the reign of a Mayor Meyer C. Ellenstein. 1933-1941. Historians told me he brought people there by the truckloads, bus loads, on the trains of the eastern seaboard all the way from Florida. So, this is following migratory patterns of agriculture; crops from Florida, sugar cane and all, on the vegetable and fruit pickers and that kind of thing. So, you're bringing these black people; migrants on the East Coast getting greater numbers than Spanish speaking people were on the West Coast. But yes, they were from agricultural; now being moved over to an industrial manufacturing economy; steel production and that kind of thing. You start bringing these people up to fill those jobs and so the White people who had formerly bought the single-family houses in Newark, moved to the basement and the black people now live above them and then let their house be rented out to the Black migrants.

This accelerated the payoff of their mortgage because of the rent that they would charge these people to live in their houses. But here's something else they did. They told them that if the light bulb goes out just let them know and the Landlord would change the light bulb when needed. They cut the grass, painted the house and trim, they did everything. Kept the houses really neat and nice while they lived there. They put together enough money too. They created two suburban areas outside of Newark, New Jersey. One to the southwest was Livingston NJ and Netherlands to the southeast. Continuing through post WW2 times the federal government actually gave White people money to pay their mortgages, to create these suburbs. That's a part of the "red lining" that went on and the "Wealth gap" that went on. It happened under President Roosevelt, and the Federal Housing and Loan Administration. So, the conversation about reparation comes to mind. You never paid these people and then disallow them from being educated! So, somebody has to be accountable and responsible for some of this.

So, you got these two streams of people now. One has intergenerational poverty, and the others are intergenerational wealthy because one has been owned as property, and they could not own property. Then they can't, when they come into the urban areas. It's there, but they can't own it; they can only rent it. And so, when they who lives in the basement and take care of property till, they choose to move. So, these people are learning mortgage paying skills and how to take care of property. The people living upstairs think They've died and gone to heaven because down South there are white men on horses cracking whips over their back. Now they're living on top of white folk; white folk living in the basement in the house.

And so, they can play their music; they can drink their beer; they can have, and they weren't violent savages, or they would have killed each other. They would have killed the people in the basement. There's always killing and savagery. Wars and rumors of war. This is stuff that's happening in the latter time. But there is manipulation of the social order and the economic system. What was going on while they were pointing us over to Southeast Asia? It was all referred to as Indo China once upon a time. Then the middle East and its oil profits became so inviting.

These are decisions that are made by our business titans, our bankers and all those kinds of people are all in that; right? What I'm saying you know, none of this this is new. It's just that if we will allow some real education to happen and some real conversations to happen and bring the right people to the table, we can make progress. My voice can't be heard in Columbus because the Democratic Party has already selected who they choose to hear. There's a man here; a retired English professor from OSU.

He writes essays. I read one the other day that he wrote, where he referred to Columbus as (Colemanville) Ohio, which is very interesting. I'll try to see if I can get you a copy of it. Michael Coleman was a Black lawyer from Akron who the Schottenstein's brought here and made him a part of their Law office. They used him as a political figure. He became the Mayor of the city for almost 20 years. But what they've done; they created a political thing here that is nothing to nobody.

Now, here's my take. I'm the father of six sons. We used a combination of home schooling and public school. The first one did one year of public middle school, 4 years of high school, got through with our unique combination and went to Denison university. My point is we know how to educate our children. We know how to do all of this stuff. But there's a political apparatus set up;

whether it's on the right or the left, that's not going to let the working class; the people who were selected to be a permanent underclass; or their descendants, to ever rise above their knees. What is the way forward?

We're going to have to turn hard toward God. We're going to have to get really deep in Biblical training, knowledge of the Bible. And I can't give any guarantees on when this is going to happen; or how successful it's going to be. I'm just laying out the framework for how it needs to happen. Now I'm going back to New Jersey. When I was working with these A.D.C. recipient ladies, there was a lady who came over from the NAACP legal defense fund. She and I interacted some around the office and she invited me to come over to New York to interview for a job position with a consulting company. So, while I'm in school studying psychology, had I stayed and graduated with a degree in psychology I could have expected my degree to command me an annual salary of $10,000. So, she introduces me to this consultant company Executive Director. They are doing contract training, with companies and with governments. It ranged from communications to Head Start to upward mobility training with people in civil service and that kind of thing. I learned that I could make between $50 and $350.00 a day plus per diem, and I could work in an anti-poverty program which would pay me $10,000 a year.

After Bobby Kennedy was killed in 1968. his family started what was called The Robert F. Kennedy memorial fellowship. It's called The RFK Center for Human Rights now. But then, I became one of 35 charter Fellows. They moved across the country looking for young people with leadership ability, who could carry on this Ripples of Hope work. So, I got a stipend every month from them. I could go anywhere in the country to study any social program in any city, any state. They paid my expenses. For lack of better words,

I became a Kennedy. I had access to their whole deal for my time with this program. I was invited into social activities in their political circle and at their home in Virginia. It was a very promising time. It was a part of Johnson's Great Society era. All of that wasn't as bad as some people make it out to be today.

Larry: maybe another time, hopefully we can talk about and see again these dual tracks? There are two things happening at the same time. On the one side, if you were in let's say White evangelicalism, and you were in churches and you were being taught about the rapture and you have been taught just certain things from a certain theological perspective then you probably didn't even see what was going on with Black people who were just trying to become viewed and treated as human beings.

People tend to know things the way they were introduced to things. Then we know what we see the same way until we are blessed by GOD with opportunity for greater knowledge. You just keep seeing it like that until you don't. You saw the devil and you saw "them." Then they riot and now they are tearing up the street. Well, what did Jericho look like when God's people marched around it seven times, blew a shofar, shouted, and the walls fell down? There was some violence going on in Jericho. Sure, we have all of the children of God coming out of slavery way back then in a land far away. But I'm coming out of my little black Missionary Baptist situation out the South. I'm one of God's children, so if I'm in the streets protesting or marching; fitting in or where somebody whose tongue is being used as a quill dipped in God's ink and writing about what God's children are doing today and how God is with his children right here and now, what is different?

I think, though we have to take the time and look back over a large swath of time like 50-60 seventy 80 years. If so, we could understand what God was up to with these people. Right now, we're going to miss it. When I went with the consulting company, here's the opportunity I got. I not only got to work with this Black run company, with an executive director and some of the smartest men I think we had in this country at the time; but there's so many of them - we don't know their names. We will never know their names, just very smart people, and a lot of these were young college kids who were put out of Black colleges and universities of the South because they were scaring older Black presidents of the school. "You're going to cause trouble with the white folk - they're going to cut off our money."

Were you getting enough money in the first place? There're always young people who are going to move humanity forward, always. In Vietnam it was the young people; it was Ho Chi Min; his wisdom his leadership and other elders. But they depended on young people from generation after generation, to fight, to resist the French attempts to colonize them for 100 years. You see, they just weren't going to be colonized. So, this kind of picks back up on your other question of 'Did you see the enemy?' "Yes, but who's the enemy?" The person that's going to do what's necessary to run me out of his country. I'm going to call this the enemy. But in his country, he's a patriot. Then those people have a nobility about them because of what we did to their land; to their waters, to their people. Savagery that we that we executed or prosecuted in that war on those people, and we still couldn't win because they could live under the ground. We could still be dropping bombs. Then, we were ill prepared for such a time as that and so too many of us have never begun to get close to seeing them from that perspective, like the lady from the perspective of the wasp, right?

So, my understanding of what it means to be born again is unique. The transformation that I know I am undergoing right now began with me in 1973 - that's when I got honest with GOD and surrendered unconditionally to Jesus after I left the East Coast. I was earning so much money as a single guy. I had everything that I needed and so then I went to the West Coast. I got in on the tail end of the hippie movement and just in time for the Jesus movement. Some people only saw the flower people, the peace and love movement and a lot of music, jazz and gospel, all kinds of music and theater and that kind of stuff. Brother, I can consider myself very blessed. In the midst of it all Jesus saw me and called my name. Jesus wasn't lost. Bob was.

There had always been a messaging Angel with the foundation that my grandmother laid in my life coming straight out of that Bible."

"It sounds like at some point you got married; Bob."

I met my bride at a church in London, Ohio. I was speaking there in 1976. We were married in July 1977. After I got married and we had three little boys in short order, then two more came in 1985 and 1987. Then our youngest came in 1990. So, we are parents of 6 Sons. Oh, by the way, we have a 10-year-old granddaughter and three grandsons. Two are 5 and one is 2."

"How did you ever get to Columbus?"

"I got to Columbus after I surrendered to Jesus in 1973. That journey started in 1972. There's a double album recorded by Aretha Franklin. The title is Amazing Grace It's a live recording that she did at a Baptist Church in Los Angeles. Somehow, I got a hold of that record shortly after it was recorded in 1972. I had a large record collection. All kinds of music. One song on that album hooked me. "Give yourself to Jesus, you don't have much time, Give yourself to the Master, He'll make your life sublime" God used that to get me headed in the direction of Columbus, Ohio via a circuitous route.

I was living in a big three-story house in San Francisco and had a lot going on. It was just really kind of; I don't know! It was just a great nonstop party situation, and in those days, partying wasn't that hard to do anywhere in California really. Up and down the whole coast. It was 500 miles between San Francisco and Los Angeles. Then you go down to San Diego and you could just go back and forth across the border in and out of Mexico, without any trouble at all. Marijuana was very plentiful. Cocaine was plentiful also. So were psychedelics and alcohol. I found out that there were some scientist type guys who were working for the US. Government. They revealed that the government had LSD in 55-gallon drums. Put a pin in that right now, Larry.

Fast forward to 2003. We got propagandized about Iraq but now our oligarchs had decided that we're going to go ahead and turn over these seven nations in five years in the so-called Middle East, beginning with Iraq. After a group of Saudis knocked over the world trade tower, suddenly Afghanistan became the first thing we must do, after we create pretext for the creation of an enemy. We gotta dirty up Saddam Hussein. So, what was pitched to us was that he used chemical weapons on his own people. Well, we here in America use chemical weapons on our own people too, because those 55-gallon drums of government LSD had been experimented with on soldiers, military people and other people in confinement that could be used as experimental targets. And so, it was. I know there were parts of California where I witnessed in my own life, where this stuff was just spilled out into the streets. I saw the effect that it had on White children. This stuff wasn't just dumped in the black ghetto. They just delivered the heroin and the crack cocaine in the black ghetto, but they did the LSD to the White kids. Chemical warfare was used against these young people that were determined to be an enemy because they were coming with too much pressure on the status quo for change. These young people were saying we're not sure we want to inherit the company business and we're not sure we want to inherit even these blue-chip stocks, you know, if you can't treat Black and brown people better.

Right now, these are children who go to school with black people. Now the Klan is saying, "We told you not to do this." I'm saying even to those who claim to be God's children, talk about obeying God. And so, I would say my brother, when I talk about going to the East Coast where I didn't have any relatives. I wanted to try out my survival stuff; my military stuff; my social skills that I'd been trained and raised with, to see can I get along in this world and live with all the people in the world, out of a military uniform; without carrying weapons of mass destruction; just seeking and spreading the truth."

"Now, if it's okay with you, I wanna change gears just slightly. A lot of the guys that I interviewed had lots of ill effects from their service in Vietnam. Chief among them would be the effects of Agent Orange. Also, PTSD. Things like that. Now because you were there so early, you probably were not there when Agent Orange was used. Would that be right?

Yeah, Larry, you're absolutely right about that. I didn't experience any of that."

"Then what about the PTSD part? I'm curious about that, because again your experience was different than a lot of soldiers. By all means, the stuff you related to me could lead to PTSD. Do you have that?"

"Yes Sir. I do. I'm on that spectrum. I keep regular appointments with my behavioral health department, at my local VA clinic here in Columbus. And have a very good psychiatrist who I've been working with for about 10 years now."

"Good. From what you've told me, I would have every reason to think that the derivation of that was your service experience; correct?"

"Well, I would say it was exacerbated by things I experienced in the service, while I was on active-duty military. As short a time as those three years were, I refer to it as three very exotic years of service There was an actual attempt to medically discharge me for psychiatric reasons. I'm convinced that the reasons were based purely on the doctrine of white supremacy and racism. Because remember I'm coming from college. I'm coming from being an intellectually gifted child. I didn't even know that term until I started working with the consultant company I worked for in New York. Never heard it before. We worked with kids in "Head Start," and those kinds of terms; that terminology started to percolate up. But that's who I was and that accounts for me adapting to science. I had a great guy who was my science teacher. He taught biology, chemistry, and physics. I took all three of those classes from him. As busy as I was; I had to work. That was taken into account during this senior year testing period; to see if I could do college work. So, the teacher said that my GPA potential, which was a great lesson for me, and I still live by that as I deal with people. Everybody, including you right now. I saw something in you, Larry from that one day we talked on the phone a couple times. I'm a great believer in you. You demonstrated to me, just who you are. I know that there's no measurement of the depth of who God is in you, and what God might do with you. So, I just approach all of my optimism. My outlook on life, and people like that don't count people out, don't give up on people, that kind of thing and so this is my laboratory experience for my sociological survey that I'm still engaged in that I started back at that early age when I was on active duty in the military. So, when I say without attributing all of my PTSD to what happened in the military it is because it would have happened to me in civilian life because of the causation assailed me in and out of uniform. If I never enlisted in military service of course I would have encountered a racist supervisor or foreman on the job. I wasn't, I wasn't going to be the kind of Negro that he was accustomed to dealing with; that he's going to just in his mind be comfortable extending that lower expectation attitude and behavior towards. I'm just not anyone's low expectation Negro and yet I have equipment to work with. I have tools in my in my toolbox that are not going to allow me to play into racist traps and end up in handcuffs. At the end of the day, I want to go in to prison and jails to visit inmates, not to be one. I'm a hard target for these folks. They were attempting to not promote me and to force me out of the military, because they couldn't put me in the stockade. I had a Sergeant from Macon GA. He was my platoon Sergeant, very unfortunate fellow. He'd been captured in Korea, but he couldn't; he didn't have the wherewithal to be thankful of the fact that he'd survived. He wasn't born again. He didn't know who Jesus was; so, he couldn't be thankful for surviving that and being home. So, when he gets home; what does he do? He gets with his buddies; his little, small minded White racist friends, to see if we could find a little brown bug to step on. Somebody to taunt and humiliate, intimidate, right? Someone that they could have authority over. Those guys back then, and still to this day they could be promoted without knowing what I was forced to know. At the same time, I might still not be promoted or respected. I had to know twice as much; be twice as good, to get a fraction of respect and or promotion and pay; that's the downside of the foolishness of the doctrine of white supremacy.

After I became a Squad Leader and it was time for me to be promoted to Sergeant E-5, I recall they put a kid in my heavy weapon squad from a rifle squad that I was leading. Heavy weapons are your mortars; and in the old days they had a weapon; it was a Jeep mounted tank killer; It was a recoilless rifle. They called it 106 recoilless rifle, or 105 millimeters. But it was a four-man operation. The team consisted of a driver, a loader, a gunner, and the squad leader. So, when the guy who was in the Sgt. E5 position, the guy that was in the squad leader position decided not to reenlist, he caught platoon leadership by surprise because he didn't tell them in advance. That meant that I moved up from gunner to squad leader. So, I'm the top gunner in the battle group. I'm always working to be the best. Somebody gotta be the best, might as well be me. You're not going to you get counted out. So, I'm always going above and beyond to be the best. So, they didn't want to promote me. I don't have any reason not to be promoted, though. So, they brought this racist kid down and put him in my squad. He'd been born and raised in Alabama. We're still stationed right there in Tennessee/Kentucky. We were in the field playing war games. We get everything dirty and muddy together. We come back in. We clean it up together, so that everybody can go to town have off, do what you wanna do. New guy kept walking off the detail going upstairs back to be with his buddy upstairs. Now He's been put in my squad for a reason. I realized that reason. I'm a young guy. I'm like twenty; barely 21 years old at the time. I am being tested. This kid pushes me to the limit. I sent somebody to get him twice. The third time, I went to get him myself. We were outside of where everybody was, so nobody could hear what I am saying to him but me and him. I asked him; "Why is it so difficult for you to stick to the task after I explained how we do things here? You know in this squad, we get it dirty together, and we clean it up together. We do everything together here. He looked down. He studied the top of his boots. He studied the top of mine, and I could almost feel his eyes coming up my body, my ankles my shin, my knees, my thighs, my waist. Then he locked his eyes right in mine. He looked in my eyes he said, "Well, by God, I tell you I just ain't used to taking orders from a nigger." Right now, this is leaving no doubt to me what has just happened. The order to integrate all branches of the military armed forces had been signed years ago by President Truman. But it has not been accepted by these people on active duty with me. I do not see things having changed at all on a certain level. There is always going to be those who don't know who God is; who need to know who God is; who don't. We just do not know enough of anything. We do not. None of us should think, we know enough. I can stop learning if I choose to. I do not feel that way about; you know, with what I know about humanity. I know about the devil and our promised future of eternal life, but that is some of the stuff that I experienced. I am finding out now that we're learning that epigenetically it has an effect. Trauma leaves tracks. That is what one psychiatrist weighs in with. So, every time you have experiences; unjust, unfair on things that you are just not ready for; on things that that we should be past; we should be over. But you still have to deal with it. Trauma nurses trauma Doctors, oncologists; people who deal with cancer patients, you know they are psyche is different. You know your life is different. You gotta get up with a different expectation every morning when you go to work. An introvert and an extrovert; the only difference in them is one has to put forward extra effort to present themselves. That is the basic difference. But when you are putting forth extra effort it's like being on alert all the time. So, that is what brings on the P.T.S.D. stuff. It did not have to be in a war situation; understand? "

"I do. Let me tell you that you are giving me infinitely more than I bargained for, Bob. I love that! I am so happy that I got a chance to talk to you. Now what is your situation today? Are you retired, or are you still working?"

"I am retired, and I'm still working. It is because I picked up a lot of skills. I picked up construction skills, after the consultant stuff, which still goes on. I have had peer support training because I picked up addiction. So, in recovery from substance use, or substance abuse disorder, and dual diagnosis psychiatry on the psychiatric side. I have the truth Behavioral Health refers to as depressive disorder. I do a lot of work in the recovery community. Mostly on me. Recovery. That is where my heart is towards. Recovery is possible! People can recover from anything. One thing I want to say, before I make this the worst interview! I just want to; brother I want you to know man, that I am proud of you for being an educator and for not going to Vietnam as a soldier. I am proud of you, and I want you to be proud of yourself.

"I appreciate that. I have become; there is nothing more I have become much more the purveyor of a broad perspective that I had before and you have added to that immensely, my friend."

Please forgive me for being so long winded. I got all this stuff in me, and I do not get the opportunity to talk in depth with many people about it.

"I am glad you did. I took the time I had the time. I wanted it to happen and so you and I are definitely on the same wavelength."

Hey man; my dear brother and may we both go forward in this world making God more famous.

Postscript to my interview with Bob.

He sent me an excerpt from a letter he sent to his six sons. He sent it around Father's Day. He granted me permission to use any part, with discretion. It showed me in so many ways, the kind of man Bob had become. I have never met any of his sons. If they read what I did, I know they would see that their parents set the bar very high for them. I hope they turn out as good or better than their expectations!

Excerpt: After a year of being engaged and now sort of ill prepared newlyweds from Jim Crow south and Ohio dysfunctional and traumatized childhoods, your mother and I jumped into the political, religious, and psycho/social equivalent of a four-engine prop blast at 2,000 feet in the wintertime. Hey! I am an all-in paratrooper. Let Us Go.

Over a period of 12 years, six sons were born, with 5 of those years separating the birth of son number three from son number four.

Although each of you were too young to now remember the intentional joy filled early preparatory days for your lifelong success, those days are forever etched deeply in my brain. You all mastered the language arts basics quite handily. Like gaining balance on the two-wheeled bicycle, you were launched into the diverse community of literate, semi-literate, illiterate, functional, and dysfunctional American Humans, to live and learn and grow and thrive.

How It Happened.

After the birth of son number one and one year in Columbus, we moved to your mother›s birthplace and hometown of Washington Court House, Ohio. I became a U.S. Postal Service Civil servant and served the people of rural Washington Court House for 7 years. We briefly lived in a nice newly built apartment complex, then into our first Cross family single family house, mortgage, double digit interest rate and all. I also became known as the Senior teaching Pastor of a fast-growing local New Testament Church community.

Fifteen months after the 1978 springtime birth of son number one son number two was born on June 11, 1979, and on 12 October 1980 son number three arrived. As the Biblical book of Genesis creation account says of GOD›s sixth day sabbatical - your parents followed GOD›s example. We rested. Three healthy sons well provided for experienced 5 years growing up together before another brother was added to the Cross household on June 19th, 1985.

Surrounded by age appropriate spoken and written words, music, and childhood activities, eventually, six young sons would be encouraged to practice and gain proficiency in Human communications and necessary social skills, using proven successful resources and methods. I know the thoughts I thought toward you.

As the sole bread earner and one of a very few non-White men in a very White small town in rural south-central Ohio, I budgeted for 4-year-old son number one's private piano lessons and an 8:00 AM swimming class for three little guys who did not know how to be afraid of swimming pool water. By that time, the first three of you were learning to be brothers together and becoming known in town as the "Cross boys."

Your mother who lived with us in the best house on our block; built with 2x6 framing, an underground two car garage and centered on a manicured double lot surrounded by gated 4-foot chain link fence in a quiet residential neighborhood. Our house had complete brick exterior. When the grass needed to be cut there was a riding lawn mower in the garage and when your mother needed to transport you to wherever for whatever, she had her own new car in the garage for that. I saw to it that your mother always had her own car. As the family grew, we got bigger cars.

Your mother was not asked to chip in for rent, mortgage, car payments, fuel, maintenance, insurance, utilities, groceries, clothes, transportation, entertainment; nothing.

After saying, "I will," your mother was allowed to stay home and help raise children for 16 years. After saying, "I will" your mother was encouraged to have her own library card, to vote and to assist me with the processes of home schooling you until each of you entered public school at various ages. I know the thoughts I thought toward all of you before I physically saw you, and during your formative years. Your mother was also encouraged to interact and share knowledge and personal growth with female peers outside her first family of blood relatives.

GUY GRUTERS

AGE WHEN ENTERED MILITARY: 17

DATE OF ENTRY TO MILITARY: 06/1960

VIETNAM TOUR DATES: 03/1967-RELEASE DATE 1973

YEARS OF DUTY/RESERVES: 13

GUY GRUTERS

When I decided that I needed to interview a P.O.W. from the Vietnam War era, I knew immediately who I could contact. My daughter had done a team building exercise with her company, where a P.O.W. spoke. I called her, got his name, and began a quest to contact him. That was not as easy as I thought it would be, as the number that I found in Google gave me a lady on the other end. She was nice enough to tell me that she had purchased her cell phone from Guy, and that she also had a new number for him. I called him that evening. To my surprise, and it gave me a chuckle, the first thing he said was.

"Is this a sales call?"

I laughed and spoke.

"No, it isn't." He immediately began to talk to me we actually spoke for almost a 1/2 hour that evening. He was so kind and very engaging and had no problem talking to me about my book and about what I was doing. I asked him if it would be all right if I came to his town and interviewed him. I knew that he lived in Sidney Ohio, which was near Troy, OH. I had been there many times, as my wife Barb was from that town. We agreed on a date, and I got his number down in my phone contacts. We texted back and forth a few times about the date and time. As we got close to the date, I began to realize that he was not answering them. I was not sure exactly why, and the day we were to meet had come and gone without him responding. I was dejected about this, of course because I was anxious to meet him and finish my effort. We were to meet on a Monday. By Tuesday night I decided that I should give him a call. I was concerned that something had happened to him and that is the reason that he wasn't responding. When I called, he answered immediately and related that his phone capacity of receiving and sending texts sometimes was experiencing difficulty. Once again, he was extremely kind and cordial. He asked me if I could come on Thursday. Luckily, I had an opening and I said yes. And so, on Thursday, June 8th, I got up early and drove to Piqua Ohio where we met in a Cracker Barrel restaurant.

After briefly explaining to Guy about my project, I gave him free time to speak. Here is what came out. I stressed that I was looking for a broad perspective on this era. As soon as he heard me say this, he chimed in.

"Larry, I have got a perspective for you. It is totally different than anything you've heard. It is called, God's perspective, on Why Vietnam? And what Vietnam really did."

I responded back.

"OK; wonderful."

Guy then adds.

"Larry, this is my take on the Vietnam Era you are talking about.

From the United States of America, you know; you have got the mainstream media. You have got the liberals. You have got the anti-war mongers, OK? And they were really against it because they did not want to go over there. You have got the media saying they're very much against it because we weren't fighting it to win it; OK? That it is just dragging on, in effect. Then they turned on our Vietnam soldiers. After all they did; their training, their efforts. Now they were told that they were not good. In fact, the opposite. They were portrayed as evil, even as baby killers. Larry, that is not true. Brainwashing is real. If you are told something often enough, you start to believe it. I was in a brainwashing environment myself, so I know. I also studied the Nazi and other efforts in the past. They (The media) had the soldiers and the American people believing that the war was bad, and our soldiers were as well. Now, Larry, let me show you another perspective. You have got a Cold War now starting. It started in the late forties. Basically you have two protagonists. You have The United States of America, and you have the Soviet Union. They've both got nuclear weapons. We had it first but through a treasonous act the Soviets had nuclear weapons as well. The Soviets now had both the atomic and hydrogen bombs. At the time, Eisenhower was the president of the United States. Dwight D. Eisenhower was a devout Protestant man. So much so, that he had the Bible; the entire Bible memorized by the time he was 13 years old. Don't you find that amazing? My dad was on his staff in World War Two, so he knew him well. Eisenhower was a tremendous Christian leader. Now in the early part of the Cold War we are in a fight, and it is like nothing ever before. Here we are facing the potential of an all-out war with nuclear weapons that would be unlike the ones that were dropped on Hiroshima and Nagasaki. They were many times the power of those. With a war that included those, the entire world as we know it could have been wiped out. The difference could be as much as forty to one compared to those early bombs. So, Larry, it is easy to see that this era was a dangerous one. Now Larry, here is something about Eisenhower that you should know. He installed the wording; "Under God," in the Pledge of Allegiance. He made sure that became important. So much so that he put it into law. In the end of the Korean war, he helped institute the "code of conduct." It became the mantra of the military, and especially guided soldiers that were captured, on what to say and do. It ended with; "I will trust in my God and the United States of America." That is what got us (me) through the prison camps in Vietnam quite successfully. It was our mantra. We started with it in our services every week. We included the Twenty Third Psalm and The Lord's Prayer. Also, Larry, Robbie Reisner, a poor sharecropper, who rose through the ranks; was the overall commander of all the prison camps in Vietnam.

"Guy, go back to Eisenhower."

"So, we have got the two powerful nations; both with mega powerful nuclear weapons that could ultimately lead to the total annihilation of both. Not only that, but it could also lead to the dying off of the whole northern hemisphere. They were both in an all-out arms race. So, with that as the perspective, you had Eisenhower in charge. He puts "Under God" in place, as well as the code of conduct for our troops. In 1956 he files a bill to make it the national official motto of the United States. It passed 435 -0 in the House and 96-0 In the senate. (Remember we only had forty-eight states then.) So, we have us with this motto and the Soviets with a motto; "In Government we trust." So, what's God going to do? Is He going to let us get into an all-out war with the Soviets who do not believe in Him? And even if we win; do we? He does not do that! What does He do? He has a guy named Khrushchev get into power, in the fifties. He was bringing a lot of bluster to the fray. "We are going to bury you! If you give us any trouble, we can blow you up!" Meanwhile here is what really happened. He says to all his military and Politburo members (in the mid-fifties) "We do not have the money to do this. The people hardly have enough money for a pair of pants or a decent shirt. We have got to cut this military down. So, there is over 5 million men in the Soviet military. He cut it down to less than three million in 1964. Plus, he scrapped the entire Navy. His argument was to his admirals; "Are we going to match the US Navy? No…we cannot do that. So why try. Why have a little "piss ant" Navy. We only have a couple of ports. The U.S.

could knock them out in a flash. We just do not have it! So, he scrapped not only the construction of new ships. He had the ships they already had scrapped for the iron. His generals, of course were not all in agreement. There was even an attempted coup. But Khrushchev was ruthless and savvy and was strongly in power at this time. He had all the plans to take the Navy completely down to zero. He surmised that all they needed was a few ballistic missiles and powerful warheads. That would effectively keep the U.S. off their backs. We are not going to get in a war! That way, we can get a little bit of economy, and get the populous off our backs, so they will not revolt. So, he is generally getting away with this and nobody is fighting…. until the Gulf of Tonkin incident, August 2-4. 1964. Now you have got to understand. These Soviet Generals, with Brezhnev in charge. They had been through World War Two. The US lost around *four hundred thousand* men during that time. The Russians lost over twelve million. Larry, that is no comparison. Plus, many millions of civilians were lost. The basic idea was that that they wanted nothing to do with such a fight with the US over Vietnam. Also, Khrushchev did not want to put a penny into Vietnam. All he had was a big mouth, However, North Vietnam kicked out all of the Russian ambassadors from the embassies. So, they got Khrushchev out; immediately, with a coup. October 14, he was replaced from the coup. Now between early November, and Christmas of 1964 there is 18 *missions* of USSR military and civilians and the Russian buildup in North Vietnam starts. At that same time, China offers North Vietnam an obscene amount of money to allow them to come in if they could come in instead of the Russians. They were turned down. They knew that China did not have the wherewithal or the weaponry that the Russians did. The Russians immediately brought in massive amounts of antiaircraft weapons alone. Plus, they supplied all the uniforms, even food and supplies. They brought it all in through the port of Haiphong. This was directly different than what Khrushchev wanted. Worse than that, we are going to get in a huge fight with the US. This could lead to WWIII. They took all their top scientists, all their R & D and switched them from civilian to military. This is why the time became known as 'The great stagnation" period of The Soviet Union. There was no more advancement of the economy. It all went to the military. At the time, Gaidar, was the prime minister. On December 25, *Khrushchev* gets on the phone with President Bush and announces that the USSR is no more. Larry, I want you to see the irony. It is Christmas!! The very next day, the all-powerful USSR is now reduced to a bunch of smaller bankrupt nations. They are now all start from nothing. After 5-6 years of this, the errors of the recent past become evident. Gaidar later writes in a book; "In 1990-91 they tried to get three hundred banks worldwide, to lend them money. He said they did not care if many banks just lended a little. They just need the money. They were looking for $50 Billion. Larry: do you know what it was for? It was to buy flour. To make bread. The people and the cities were so broke that they did not have bread. Gaidar goes on; "We could not pay the military. We could not pay the Communist Party members. We could not pay anybody or for anything. All over the world where we had embassies. We could not pay the taxes. We could not even buy gas for the workers cars. They had to walk! We were totally finished." *Gorbachev* had no choice. He (they) had to dissolve the USSR. He called it that "Mad militarization" from 1964-1991. He could not stop it. He said, "What good is it. We have 60,000 tanks. We have 10,000 missiles being manufactured (which almost matched the US). They typically had 820-830 consumer goods items in their stores. Now they were down to one item: salt. There literally was no food. The whole system was bankrupt. And it was this "mad militarization" that did it. Gaidar, their top economist said that the military part of the budget should have been around 10% Instead it was more near 25%. No economy could survive that! They gave too much credit to building tanks and such. Tanks cannot feed the people, Larry! But during this time, the Communist regime felt such a threat of getting into all-out war with the US through Vietnam, which led to all the lopsided spending they did. Larry, my feeling is strong here. Now who would put that kind of belief in the minds of our biggest enemy? To me, it was God Almighty. Our God set this all up as punishment. Remember in WWII, who got punished the worst? It was Russia and Germany. Even further back, in WWI, it was Austria. Before they started that war, they were extremely powerful. It was their motto to 'rule the world' before that. They started that war. See what God can do. They went from 50milion to 7 million. From one nation to thirteen or so nations. In history, the countries that started these big wars got smashed the worst. Anyhow, with that as a backdrop, the Soviets were not going to let *Khrushchev* get them into this big war. No sir: it was gametime. Get him out of here! So, do you see the effect Vietnam had here? Also, another perspective…. If Nixon had lost to Humphrey in the presidential election, Vietnam would have been over just 4 years into the buildup. While that would sound great to some, here is the rub. That did not happen. There was a guy I knew, Pat Mahoney. Larry he was a character. I learned quickly that he was adamant about the pronunciation of his name. To him, it was Ma'Hanny. Anyhow, he was in Vietnam for 5 years. He volunteered. At the end, he was a Master Sergeant E8. He was offered E9, but he turned it down. He wanted to stay. At the time he was in control if all *"out of the country"* operations. But he was in that position in 1968, when the presidential election was going on back home. On October 1, Johnson is the outgoing president. He saw the impending political disaster for Humphrey. It looked like he was going to lose by 20-30 points. Nixon had announced that he had a secret plan to end the war and it looked like he was a shoo in. So, Johnson decided to do him one better and stop the bombing on October 1. There would be strong negotiations then to go on that would end things. Pat Mahoney had a huge part in what happened next. He had thirty-two-man teams on the ground. Each one had a Special Forces soldier from the US and a teammate of a Special Forces soldier from the South Vietnamese Army. There were there to locate the enemy convoys. Those guys would mark the locations so we could find them and bomb them. So, when the announcement came down, Mahoney asks; "What about my teams. If you stop the bombing, what happens to them?" The answer he got was that they would not be supported. They would not be picked up. They were just going to be collateral damage of this move. The sixty men's lives would be doomed. They were all good soldiers, Larry. They would just be written off! Mahoney says to his commander; "You do that, and I'll go back to the United States, and I'll get ahold of every newspaper, TV, Radio and any kind of reporter that I can find and blow this up in a way that will be as bad as something could be!" It was a strong enough threat that they did not do it on the first. They did it three weeks later, after they got those thirty teams out of North Vietnam. Even after this, Humphrey almost won the election. Those three weeks, and what happened, would have turned the election if things had gone as planned. Also, if Humphrey wins, the buildup stops. The Russians could effectively move on. Nixon comes in and says, "Bullshit; we are not getting out, at least until we get all our POWS out. Larry, do you know about the Tet offensive? Well, I knew a guy who was a right-hand man to Kissinger. Stearman was his name. He was in the foreign service; you know in the White House for the last 20 years and was on the ground in Vietnam. He was in the first wave of eight Navy invasions in World War 2. What he said, Nixon knew that the TET offensive had completely destroyed the guerillas. The media in Vietnam did not know anything. They were all back in the bars. I was out on the with the *173rd* airborne for seven months in *Doc To*. I was in all the hot fights. I never saw one reporter in seven months. They never came out they were always back in the damn bars in Saigon. Stearman asked them; "Why in the hell do not you tell what's going on out here? You know; there is a lot of good things going on out here!" Larry, there were reporters from all the networks and papers. We cannot do that; they tell him. They tell us we are finished if we do. They said they are not gonna publish anything. They only want negative stories. OK that is what they told Stearman. Do you know in the White House; Hey, what's wrong with you guys? He is saying that there's a lot of positive stuff. Now because Nixon is staying in the fight; that is up through 1973 when we were released. Remember, they (The Russians) had to keep building up. This is all draining the economy of The Soviet Union. 1975 is when they finally built up their forces again. Our Congress stopped the supplies of the South Vietnamese forces. They won militarily in 75. They did not have any money. The Soviet Union is still being drained all the way. Finally in eighty-five they said, "We have nothing left." They stopped supporting him in eighty-five. The last hardline communist was kicked out of Communist Party in north Vietnam; now all of Vietnam. They started their turn around to capitalism. By 1986 every family in Vietnam were given one acre, half a *hectare*. A little different than an acre, but about an acre was given to each family so that there would be food! By 1991 -1992, each family had a full hectare. I went over there a year or so ago, for the first time in 50 years. I was ecstatic. I was in North Vietnam in the war. There was not one vehicle: even a bicycle. In

South Vietnam it was just end to end bicycles. Bikes, cars. Shoot, it was more dangerous than being in a war. Now this is in sixty-seven. But in north Vietnam; Holy crap! I went across the whole country. It was nothing but military vehicles. I stayed in one of the villages for four days. The food each day was a pot of rice cooked on a stick fire. I was with the mayor of this little town, and his wife and four kids. Now this is after being captured. The first four days I am in this little hut. The wife makes a fire with sticks and leaves on the dirt floor. There was no stove. There are no cabinets. We only have two sets of pajamas for five years: two pair of pajamas! On Sunday, they let us get to a cistern to wash. Larry, this is the mayor, his wife, and kids; you know, from 16-17, down to 8. There is no kitchen. There is no ice box. There is no electricity. There is no radio; OK? And they have their extra pair of pajamas on a hook on the wall. Six times a day that woman swept out that dirt floor with a handmade bamboo whisk broom; bent over as she swept it out six times a day. She worked harder than any woman anywhere in the United States. I'm just trying to tell you that's the way it was. Now, I just went back this year. It is free enterprise. I think everybody is doing great. I went back to that same village in which I was captured. One of The Mistys made a lot of money. He spent a month or two each year for the last 15 years building libraries and schools for those little villages that we flew over. The seven hundred miles of North Vietnam. or so and just north of the DMZ. We were knocking out convoys. OK, they were going back into Laos, coming South down through Cambodia supplying that million-man N. Vietnamese army. It was all with Russian supplies coming through Haiphong, not through China. You know, I was interviewed with interrogation in prison camp by a top guy. He became a premier in the Communist Party. When he came in, here is what he did. Generally, there are five guards behind you. This guy says to them; "get out of here." Then he says to me.

"You know; just tell me. I want you to speak, frankly. Tell me what you think. Do you think we are winning the war?" I tell him.

"No; you do not have a chance. There is no way in Hell. You do not have the firepower. You do not have the artillery. You are trying to fight our infantry with artillery. You do not have that support. You cannot do it. We just sit there and wait from here and kill you with our firepower, you know."

Anyway, I am telling the guy who's eventually a premier. We go back and forth on this. He speaks.

"Yeah, but we are doing so and so "He's not giving me any arguments. He is not saying anything; not really fighting hard. He then says.

"*We beat the French army at their own game. We can beat you!*" But what he did not understand is that the fight wasn't about Vietnam. The fight was about the Cold War between the U.S. and Russia. Another perspective; God's way the hell above what we are looking at. Do you see that, Larry? OK, here is another thing on Vietnam… Larry, you hopefully can see God at work. He does not want the entire northern hemisphere wiped out by 20,000 nuclear bombs. What I say is… if I can talk to any Vietnam veteran that died or was in prison camp, which is easy by comparison. I know they would all agree that their sacrifice was worth it. I was a survivor. I was with a really good guy in captivity. He was a fire weapons school instructor. He was like Top Gun, but for the Air Force, not the Navy. He was my instructor. I was shot down with him and we were together for the first 2 1/2 years in a number of prison camps up there. Anyway, he said.

"Well, this isn›t as bad as a stick in the eye."

We were in an absolutely hopeless situation, but he says it is not as bad as a stick in the eye! He is right that we could have seen the worst and given up. I am just saying that anybody that died would be happy to be part of the sacrifice that likely prevented another war between the USSR and the United States, Larry, I'd easily do it again. Are you kidding me? Keep the United States from nuclear war. You know, nearly 60,000 men killed; another 100,000 horribly wounded. But we saved hundreds of millions of people in our countries along with the rest of the world. You, see? I'm trying for you to see, Larry. This is my take. He made a wonderful thing out of something that was disastrous at the time. Instead of the Russians being able to keep getting more powerful, they sapped all of their resources in Vietnam. I think so! Here is another perspective. This is from Bill Stearman. The prime minister of Singapore was Lee Kuan Yu. He wrote a book called "From Third World to First." Larry, you really wanna read it! I think it should be mandatory to be studied by every person on earth! He was neutral; he and his country had the guts, according to Bill Stearman, to taking on Communist insurgencies and beat them. It was because of our guts and efforts in South Vietnam. In other words, here you have got Russia and China still; but they didn't have the extra wherewithal to keep supporting their communist guerrillas. In short, Yu said himself; "All of Southeast Asia owes a blood debt to America." Larry, when we were winners in the other big wars, we went in and helped the people of the countries we defeated. They, on the other hand went in and raped and pillaged. We did not. Remember how we were criticized at home for Vietnam? Well, here is me. I went on a 300-mile convoy across South Vietnam. I went with other troops and branches. Everywhere we went there were tremendous crowds. They are all saying the same thing, you know. They did not know how to speak English, but here's what I heard; "Chocolate!" I am not kidding; "Chocolate, Joe!" So, these mean American servicemen; characterized by the press as so mean. These guys are taking not just the chocolate out of their packs. They are taking their C-rations, and even clothing. The Vietnamese do not hate us! They love us! When I went back, I went back to the village where I was captured. Here is a quick story if I haven't told you. I was tied up and basically helpless. A mob with machetes appears. Hundreds of people coming in. We have seen 2 pilots cut to pieces the previous month. The militia commander that saved my life was there. Larry, I got to meet him. So, we are about to be killed. All of a sudden, this guy gives a command. His soldiers obeyed and drew their bayonets. Then they made a path through all those angry people, and we walked unharmed right through them. It was truly amazing. We walked for about two hours to a hut. I did not find till now that this hut was a schoolhouse. Then this woman cooked me a *Casaba* meal (potato like.) This woman turned out to be that militia commander›s wife. The Misty had done all this work for them you know, so he knew somebody who knew somebody. When I was there on my return visit, they found this guy. They found that militia commander. They took my *son›s wife; my daughter and myself out* there. It was a wonderful afternoon. Twenty people from the village were there as well. His wife was still alive. He was still alive at 84. He had eight kids. His youngest kid was a Down syndrome child. She was 60 years, a beautiful soul! Also, the two guys that found me in my hiding place were there. I›m buried into the jungle, but they find me. They get me and I am stripped down. Now I am in boxer shorts My ankles are bound together. I can only hobble. Now all these years later, he is dressed in the uniform that he was in when he captured me 56 years ago. His wife is there. She fixes the same meal, Larry! There are twenty villagers there including another soldier that captured my instructor. That was this year, and God is so good! I did not think much of it, but the trip was scheduled at the same time as the 50-year anniversary of my release on March 14th. 1973. On March 14th, 2023; fifty years exactly, Larry, I was in this militia commanders house for the afternoon."

"Guy; that can only be God; it can only be God!"

"Are you kidding me? People say… I mean you talk about perspective. Let us talk about the courage of that militia commander. Oh yes; holy crap, I don›t think there›s one in a 1000 that would have had his courage. These are your own neighbors. And you say, no, it is not right. We are not gonna kill this guy. I was amazed at the time, and I have been amazed ever since. I mean; "Who the Hell is this guy?" He is just like a Midwesterner. A guy like you and me; just trying to do the right thing. We capture this guy. He is helpless. We are not gonna just cut him to pieces."

"Guy; he was an Angel."

"Yep! He was my Angel." I told my friend. I sent him a letter. I said thank you! I got to have my family. You got eight kids; yes, I wouldn't have any of that if it weren't for you. Thank God! I would never have had those five years. Because of you! Because you did the right thing. I thank you so much I do not know how I could ever repay you! "

"Guy, would it be all right if I switch gears for a bit.? I want to make sure I cover all the things I drove over here for."

"Of course."

"First of all, get yourself from a young man. How did you get into s the service. How did that happen?"

"That was my mom. She saw this article. We were in Sarasota. We moved there because of my grandparents. They lived in New York. They were getting sickly. My dad moved them down to Sarasota, which added 5-10 years to their lives. So, I was down there for my senior year in high school. My mom saw this thing. The Air Force Academy is having three days of testing up in Tampa, at MacDill Air Force Base. She wanted me to do this. "Guy, if you could get into the Academy; what a great way to start!" I told her that I would not have a chance because you had to be sponsored by a congressman. She really wanted me to do it, so I did. I got in as a "qualified alternate." They take the one the congressman picks. *Of the other nine, a few more get in.* Anyhow, I got in! I always wanted to be a pilot. I never thought I could. My dad was in the army, but you know when I was young, I did a lot of trapping. You know, muskrat trapping. I did not do sports. I was always trapping. Oh yes; that's how I made my money was muskrat trapping. I was always in the woods. I loved the woods. I loved animals; except for the muskrats, hah, ha… but I still liked them, I really did."

"We have another thing in common. I trapped rabbits. I was different in that I used humane traps that kept them alive."

"Anyway, that is what happened. With that money that I made trapping, I subscribed to Flying magazine and the Air Force magazine. In high school I would look at those magazines without ever a hope of being able to fly. And you know later on I was a pilot."

"So, you got in the Air Force. Keep telling."

"I was a top engineering graduate of the Academy. Then I went to Purdue. They had an astronaut program where you get a Masters in astronautical engineering, which is rocket science. Then right out of that, instead of being an engineer in the Air Force they put you right into pilot training. From there you go into combat if there was any combat going on like Vietnam. You were an Academy graduate; you had a Masters in astronautical engineering and rockets. You were a fighter pilot, and you have combat experience. That would put you on a fast track after coming out, to be an astronaut. And I was, but I had all kinds of physical injuries after being shot down twice and had gone through a lot of torture. I simply couldn't do the astronaut program. They tried to get me into it afterwards, but it just did not work."

"So, once you got in the Air Force and through all of your basic stuff, what was your path to Vietnam?"

"I did very good in pilot training, so I got to do *F-100 single* seat fighters Then I went to F100 training at Luke Air Force Base in Arizona, which was for six months. I did good there as well. Then they had you take your choice of units. The F-100 was the standard of fighters back then. This was before *105's*. In this jet there were 2,500 fighters from 1956 to 1964-65. That was standard tactical air command. So that was the standard. If you did that, you had to stay out of Vietnam for two years, because they did not want you going into the ground on a dive. You get "target fixation," you know. We are gonna hit that target. And you do not pull out in time. You are moving down at 600 miles an hour. If you do not start to pull out. If you are not careful. If you are a young inexperienced pilot, you could easily crash and lose your life and your plane. So, you have to be in a peacetime unit on gunnery ranges where you do not get target fixation on the enemy, we're gonna kill him no matter what. But here is me, Larry. I wanna go to Vietnam. So, I was told that the only way it is happening is if you join FAC (Forward Air Control). They were in smaller, non-jet planes that flew and did reconnaissance. Most fighter pilots did not want to do that. I signed up immediately. My honest thinking was this. I wanted to stop Communism. I'd read all kinds of stuff on communism. I knew that they are saying that Americans don't the guts to fight us. You will never stop us. We could take all these little countries all over the world. This was Stalin's philosophy on the 1920's. You take all these little countries all over the world. You surround the US and Europe, and they will all fall like ripe plums into our arms. So, I knew that is what they were after. They would eventually try to ruin our economy and Vietnam was just a step they were taking. That was my philosophy, Larry. That is what I was willing to give my life for."

"So, how long were you in Vietnam?"

"I was in Vietnam about 10 1/2 months; four hundred combat missions and was shot down twice. Two out of the last three missions. The first time I was rescued just offshore. The second, I was captured like I mentioned to you."

"So, the second time you were shot down and captured, correct?"

"That›s right."

"And you were shot down in north Vietnam. So, Guy; this is just a question if you don't mind my interruption. I have read that there were 700 or so POWs. Is that accurate?"

"Well, that is a good perspective too. You can look this up. Less than seven hundred came home for release. Out of those seven hundred, 472 were in North Vietnam and there have been 3550 air crews shot down and not rescued in North. Assumedly, the Russians and the North Vietnamese tortured to death or killed; in one way or another, six out of seven. 15-16% came home. Out of Germany 80%. 472 came home. The seven hundred you mentioned were from all over, Laos, Cambodia, and South Vietnam and all the services. But in North Vietnam, it was 472 out of 3500. We lost over nine thousand airplanes. Just giving you some good perspective."

"Sure; thank you."

"Most of those were fixed wing aircraft; you know, like thousands were lost over North Vietnam. That is where the 3500 came from. Generally, the jets had two-man crews. So, every time there was a shoot down, you see the loss. So, that›s North Vietnam. Now in South Vietnam it was mostly helicopters. We lost over; and these are the official figures… 5600 Huey helicopters shot down. Most of those I believe; this is my figure we are "dust offs." Do you know what dust offs are?"

"Please tell me."

"Dust offs were where the combat search and rescue, in the army; you know. You and I are fighting somebody over here. We're in a company maybe 150-200 men. We are in the jungle. Trees all over the place, and someone gets shot and critically wounded. How is a guy like that going to get rescued? They send in a helicopter. He hovers just over the trees and the cover. He lets down a gurney on a rope and the guy gets rescued. Then they haul him up with a hydraulic hoist. Meantime, the helicopter is just hovering.; just sitting up there. They were easy targets, Larry! These firefights were going on all the time. It was not just ten minutes or even an hour, like you see in the movies. Some would last all day! So here are these helicopters. Then, you got these enemy guys over there. They have got machine guns and any other weapon they had and were shooting holes in our copters. To me, of those five thousand or so helicopters shot down, most were shot down trying to get our wounded soldiers out. That is a hell of a story. In North Vietnam, they rescued *2500 fighter pilot crews*, like me, OK? That was my first time. Rescued by one of those Jolly green helicopters. They would go into North Vietnam, where we have been shot down. They could only go about two hundred miles an hour. Once again, they were very vulnerable to being shot down. 832 of those Jolly Greens; rescuing those 2500 guys. We called them the bravest men in the world! It is like the first responders here. Our first responders to do their work. They are always putting themselves in the path of danger. So, Larry, there's tremendous stories on Vietnam, you know. People do not know. Most Vietnam army guys do not know that they lost 5600 helicopters. Not everybody knows these things. Like you mentioned the number seven hundred. It was probably more like 3500. It could even be more."

"Yes, that makes sense now, Guy. So, in North Vietnam, you were in captivity six years did you say?"

"I was captured December 20th, 1967, and came out on March 14, 1973; five years and three months. But I had been over there for 10 1/2 months. I got over there like about the 1st of March, so I was over there from the 1st of March 1967 till the 14th of March 1973. Just about six years. My Sandy waited for six years."

"Give me a couple of things that happened to you when you were first captured."

"Larry, I don‹t mind. I learned forgiveness up there. I got it. It took me six months of prayer to forgive. I got into suicidal thoughts. They killed my friend in front of me. I got into horrible stuff; *22 tortures and interrogations*, you know. Larry, I never hated anyone till then. It wasn't me! It was the devil talking to me. Every day I'm praying God let me see. I was blind to everything. I was in the worst horrible hatred no doubt of it, so I said to myself. 'I got to live. It was terrible! I gotta stop these voices. I'll forgive them. I tried for a couple of weeks to forgive em' and I couldn't. So, I got on my knees right out there. Jesus, please help me forgive them. I can't stop this. You gotta save me. And after three months of praying hard to Jesus. he gave me the thought in my mind; forgive him. But I didn't mean; it was a lie. But Larry, just being able to form those words in my mind. I was never able before. I would have not been able to do that; and I knew that he was changing my heart. And three months later I was praying for those torturers and interrogators. I kept that up for the next 3 1/2 years. It literally transformed everything. next 3 1/2 years in prison camp you know, were probably the most joy filled and peaceful moments I've ever had in my whole life because I really was praying for my enemy! It's true. You're praying for your enemies. It really gives you a warm heart. It's amazing you know!"

"Guy; was every day at these camps the same routine?"

"I was in six different camps. So, no; every day wasn‹t the same. But for the first year there, it was really scary until the Son Tay rescue raid, which was considered a failure, you know. In late November, which was about three years into it. What that did; generally, you›re in one- and two-man cells. OK, your communication is through the walls. Have you ever heard of the "tap code?"

"No; can you show me?"

"Yep; here are the basics." So, the alphabet is set up in a 5x5 grid. The letter K is removed to make that work, K and C sound the same, so when you hear the tap for one, you know it's either. Call up on the wall by tapping lightly, We had to do it that way, as if the guards heard us, it would be bad, really bad with torture! We had typical call ups that we would be aware of. This Larry was a daily routine. Here's an example. After the alert, I would here the greeting 'Hi," (second row, third column; second row, fourth column.) Make sense? Morse code doesn't work here's the dash; here's the dot. They both sound the same. Morse code simply doesn't work. You can't do it. With the tap code you can't, you never make a mistake. I tap "Hi" then stop. On the other side, he gets it. Texting one word at a time. If he doesn't get it, he sends several taps. That would tell me to re-tap. One word; one word for hours at a time! You got your cellmate. He's looking out under the door for any movement. There's no windows inside. It's like a master bedroom closet. everybody's in our master bedroom closet. But you can see under the door, see? So, you got half the guys looking under the doors, and the other half tapping on the walls. If anybody sees a guard moving close by, he slams the concrete. That tells everybody, and you immediately stopped communicating. Everyone in the cellblock can hear that."

"So, if that happened, you stopped; right?"

"Yep; that's right. Then after, we would get an "all clear signal and start back up again. That›s what you did all day long. That was "Code of conduct, Larry. That let us have a team, command, and control. The code was a wonderful thing! Date of rank; date of rank. Doesn't matter the service. Date of rank; first guy there, he's in charge of each cell and cell block. nothing else matters just date of rank. You've got a boss to make the decisions, Larry. Worked great!"

"So, you had cell blocks with two people in them?"

"You know; the cells would be you know 1- 2-3 man. Cell blocks might have 5-15 cells. Then a prison camp might have 2,3,4 cell blocks in them."

"And you saw the other guys on a daily basis?"

"You could see them under the door. Otherwise, no. There's no exercise outside. There's nothing like that. But on Sunday alright; they would bring one cell room out at a time. There was a series of five small washroom three or four feet square. Each had a cistern. They'd lock you in there and you could throw water over yourself. So, as they're bringing the cells; Larry, they went to unbelievable efforts to keep the solitaire effect on us. Unbelievable! OK? The interrogation… you have to go through the interrogation. They're screaming at you. They're beating the hell out of you. Here's an example; "Buttermore, you're the only guy; you're the only guy that's not giving us what we want. Everybody else is answering these questions, but you're not. You know we should kill you! You're the only one that's not!" But you know better. Because of the tap code, you know what happening. But it's very convincing the way do it. "Larry, you're not giving us what everybody else is. You're not giving us Larry; what everybody else is. What's wrong with you?"

"Were there guys who caved?"

"Oh yeah; but very few. Then if/when they actually get to you; you just lie. To me, they never got anything worthwhile. But you do cave in from the tortures. The rope torture was one of the worst. They would hang you from your elbows, from behind your back, from the ceiling. They did those 18 cycles a day, until you agreed to answer the question. The thing that was most dangerous was meeting delegations, like Jane Fonda. One guy; blinked out T.O R.T.U.R.E. during the interrogation in front of worldwide press coverage. They got all that on camera. I think it was another Navy guy. He was brought out in front of 20 or 30 reporters from the major newspapers and networks. They wanted him to bow to them. He did a real number, Larry. He looked like a robot. Lots of cameras were on him. Can you imagine the crap that caused.? Can you imagine watching an American officer looking like a robot? That really hurt me.' Remember me telling you about the multiple interrogations all the time? Usually, through the tap code, we knew what to expect and how we should react. If we ever had to make our own decision, we would answer in the most "hard line" that we could. Then the moment you got back, you used the tap code and told all you fifty or so buddies in camp, the questions, and your answers. so, you got 50 guys giving the same freaking 5 answers: all hard line. We had to be driving them crazy! So, we never had a weak link."

"How interesting. You guys through your own ingenuity were outsmarting them big time."

Larry, it worked pretty darn good. It was all communist leaning interrogations, like Jane Fonda. They were Communists; they only let the communist sympathizers in. They give them five questions. Always one was "Should we be in Vietnam? All lies Larry! You've got these five answers; induced by the agony you've been through. All the tortures we've been through, nobody knew about. They never made a mark or a scar that anyone could see. "Oh, we treat them great! We treat them very humanely."

"I never knew that. I'm guessing almost nobody did, as the press and TV suppressed most of that."

"Are you scarred up at all, Guy?"

"No. Generally I have bad joint problems from the tortures. A lot of guys with those scars from cigarette burns; not on their hands, but on their arms and torsos. A lot of guys with bad scars around their ankles from the irons and stuff. I had an ankle iron on for weeks, but I never got any scars. The guys I had didn't make it to where they cut into my legs. They were tight they didn't cut me open. but generally, they try not to leave scars. The classic torture was to tie your elbows touching behind your back. Now that can easily dislocate your shoulder. Your elbows are touching behind your back. Then they take a rope over your shoulder. You have your ankle iron on. They took the rope over your shoulder and around the ankle iron. Then they would pull up on it till your head is between your knees. You're in absolute agony, Larry. They would tie you off and just leave you like that. Sometimes all day and all night. Twice a day they would untie you for five or ten minutes. During that little time, they would feed you bread and water."

"How in the world!! I can't even imagine the idea of being hungry all the time. How did you do it?"

"Larry, we all started off around 200 lbs. We were solid. This is very interesting. Your weight depends on how much you eat; the number of calories you take in. We all saw it. Basically, when you don't have enough food to support your weight, you get hunger pangs. Really bad hunger! What happened to us; we were getting 6-800 calories a day. Then you go from 200 down to; in my case, 120 lbs. Well now, those same 600 calories will support that kind of weight. Larry....no more hunger pangs! So, if you say wanted to get from 350 lbs. down to 250, figure you're going to be hungry till you get down to that new weight. So, you can't keep eating the same amount of food as always, or you'll never lose the weight."

"Am I right Guy; you were already married and had two kids by the time you entered the service; right?"

"Yes; we were married and had two little girls. When I got back, we had 5 more children."

"Now during all your captivity, did your family even know if you were dead or alive?"

"For the first two and a half years they did. After that, our code of conduct told us that we were to take no special favors." Our interrogators would bait us. "You answer these questions pal, and we'll let you write home." But I (we) would have none of that. So, Sandy didn't get another letter and I received none for a long time. Sometime after the Son Tay raid and after the death of Ho Chi Minh, somebody said it was now okay to write home. So, our commanders said OKAY you Can, but only 6 lines. Until then, our wives and families were completely in the dark."

"So, you were released in 1973; correct?"

"That's right. On March 14th."

"Did you come home right away?"

"Larry; what they did first was take us to the Philippines. They got us uniforms. Then we stopped at Hawaii for fuel. Then we went to one of seven bases. Ours was Montgomery, Alabama. They had the families come and meet us there. Sandy, my kids; my mother and father all came up there. We were there about two weeks. We were examined and tested and questioned there. We had three months leave from active duty. I took an airline job with Eastern Airlines in August. So, for the next 17 years I was with Eastern Airlines. I was with them till they went out of business. Meanwhile I started up my own software company, which still exists today. Then I took a job as MIS director for Pearl Vision, eyeglasses. I had my first job was with IBM for five years and I had really good training with IBM."

"Guy; this as after the service; right?"

"Right. When I first got my job with Eastern Airlines, I was laid off in just a few months, with the fuel crisis. That was in late 73; remember?"

"Yes, I do; that was a big deal nationwide."

"So, I was laid off for 7 years. During that time is when my brother and I had our company. Eventually I was called back to Eastern. I was able to keep on part-time with my brother."

"Guy; in 1973, when you left the service, were you totally out or did you have a reservist status?"

"I effectively resigned my Commission in August of 73. I had a lot of physical problems. I couldn't even look behind me. I simply wouldn't have worked as a fighter pilot. My neck and back were relatively shot. My joints weren't on good shape."

"When you worked for Eastern, you were a pilot; right?"

"I know what you're getting at. Working as a commercial pilot was much easier. Larry."

"Is Eastern the only airline you worked for?"

"Yes; I worked for them till they went bankrupt. Then I got the very good offer from Pearle Vision. I was offered jobs by other airlines, but I would have had to start over as a copilot. I decided the Pearle path was a better one."

"How did that happen? Did you have an agent?"

"Larry, as I remember, they contacted me. Maybe I had some conversation with them in my computer business. They heard that Eastern was going out of business and just asked me if I wanted to come out there."

"What was your rank when you came out of the Air Force?"

"I was a Captain."

"So, if you were never captured, wouldn't you likely have been a higher rank?"

"Actually, they promote you based on time served. So, if I would have stayed in after getting released, I would have been a Major."

"When you were done in 1973, the Vietnam War was either over, or about to be over; right?"

In 73, the war was over as far as US involvement. Right after that Congress passed the Church amendment and cut off enough aid to the South that The N.V.A. were emboldened and quickly moved to conquer. That happened by April 1975 when Saigon fell to the North and the last US personnel were evacuated.

But again, Larry; as a perspective, it kept the Russians involved and tied up their resources and not giving them the foothold, they wanted against us."

"Guy, how did you meet Sandy?"

"I met her on a blind date when I was at The Air Force Academy."

"Oh; nice! So, you met her in Colorado?"

"Nope; I was home on leave. She was a college student at FSU."

"I believe you said you had a Sarasota connection, right?"

"Yes, my dad moved us there to allowed him to take care of his parents in their older years. I only spent about a year there before going to The Academy."

"So, it was I Sarasota where you met Sandy? How long did you court her. We dated and were engaged until I graduated. Then we got married."

"Then how long after you got married do you go to Vietnam?"

"About 3 years. I graduated in 64 and went in 67."

"So, I think I understand about your successes after you got out of the service. Now, let me ask this. A lot of the guys I interviewed that were "boots on the ground" were exposed to Agent Orange. Were you?"

"I'm pretty sure I was when in the Central Highlands. But I never got cancer, or any other symptoms related to it."

"That was a good thing sir!"

"Agreed."

"Then, any other health maladies from your war experience?"

"For sure, I had joint pains and arthritis problems, form the crazy positions I had to endure when they tortured me."

"What about PTSD?"

"Larry, I think so. As I see it, this condition happens in life to many people when things go different than they expect. It's a lot different being a soldier than being a student. With me, the biggest thing that happened initially was that I lost faith in the human race. I once was totally trusting. The something happens and you get kicked in the teeth. With prison camp that happened to me, in spades. Here's a perfect example. Remember my friend Mahoney? He got there before me. He became a postman. He found that position okay, but his desire was to be in combat. He volunteered to be with a dust-off chopper unit. After his day job, he would do these rescue missions at night. He did 40 or so of these and probably rescued between 40 and 80 soldiers. He asked me if I wanted to go and visit some of the guys he'd rescued. Of course, I said yes. So, we went to this hospital. The first guys we saw were hurt, but not so badly that they couldn't talk to us. Then he took me into the 'head wound' ward. Now I'm looking at 50-60 guys; each in a separate bed. They all have a blank stare in their eyes and none of them are moving. They had to be soon fed. I saw this and was in total disbelief that anything like this could ever happen. I (we) was just 24 years old! How could this be? These are real people. I'm not looking at a book or a movie, Larry! So, I ask a nurse if any of these guys ever recover. She tells me that a few do snap out of it. Somehow the brain can repair itself and they make it back. Some of them got shipped back to the states after 6 months, as there is I no improvement. They did that to get them back near their families in hopes that would help. Nobody wanted anybody to die! Larry, I couldn't go back to that ward ever again. I've talked to many professional nurses. Even ones here that never had combat experiences. I don't see how every nurse manages not to have PTSD!

"Guy, I've taken up a ton of your time. Any last thoughts for me to ponder? Either way, I know a lot of the guys I've talked to have formed lifetime bonds with fellow Vietnam vets, through clubs and organizations. They have reunions and other get togethers. How about you? Any experiences like that; especially with your fellow POWs?"

"Yes, Larry. In fact, we just had a 50 Year reunion. It was at The Nixon Library, on May 24th. Nixon had a White House dinner for us back then on that same date in 1973. We got to see Bob Hope and Clint Eastwood and John Wayne. Back then it was the biggest ever such event. Then 10 years ago, on May 24, 2013. On both occasions, we were served the same wonderful dinner and at both we had many guests and dignitaries. A little more than 150 of the POWS from the 473rd. are still alive. Ross Perot Jr., the Governor of California (where the Nixon Library is) and Tricia Nixon was too! Even a direct descendent of Dwight Eisenhower was there.

"Anything else?"

"Larry, I think that our time together should give you what you came for."

I totally agree and can't thank you enough for your service and your legacy. You're a true American hero."

CLOSING AUTHOR'S NOTE

So, there you have it. My original epilogue to a novel, became a book! I hope it was significant. It certainly was to me. It took me from a position of narrow mindedness, to one of strength. I never went to Vietnam, or any war. I consider myself lucky and blessed for that. I lived most of my life not thinking much about this, until I embarked on my project. The project forced me to see many perspectives. I saw how the era, and in particular the conflict affected people in and around it. I was honored that so many people were willing to talk to me about their unique experiences. I truly want to bring attention to this time period and how our nation has dealt with it. To me there were direct casualties; 58,000 plus that died in the conflict. Then there were the indirect ones. Many more than that number of loved ones were left to grieve. Then there's the shrapnel; the collateral damage. Of the millions that directly participated, many have since died because of this collateral damage. Some by the ravages of Agent Orange. Many by suicide. Many by the 24/7 effects of P.T.S.D. Many that had side effects of the conflict that caused other physical ailments such as Diabetes, Skin, Prostate, and other Cancers. Some from …… you get the point. The 58,000 doesn't scratch the surface. From my position now, I wish I had been more aware. I wish I could have done more. I can't make the past change. My perspective certainly has. I hope yours has too.

I'm compelled to donate a portion of the proceeds from each book sold, to a special charity. I've chosen Vietnam Veterans of

America. My brief research shows it as the only such national organization that is congressionally chartered and exclusively dedicated to Vietnam-era veterans and their families.

Also, I'd love to hear from you personally, on if/how reading the book affected you. Also let me know if you have a story as well. I hope to have enough success to get a follow up published. My email is larrybuttermore@gmail.com.

If you would like me to personalize your book; send me an email. I have made a special insert I will personalize and send to you. Please include your home address.

Thank you so much.

ACKNOWLEDGEMENTS

First and foremost, I give My Jesus the credit for any thought and thought process that went into this book. It started out as the epilogue to my recent novel; "Over and Back." Somehow, He placed a small cartoon in front of me that led me back to the Vietnam era that my novel was set in. I was a young adult when the story began. The main character was a "draft dodger," and I was a teacher. Neither of us set foot in Vietnam. The cartoon I spoke of brought me to the conclusion that should have been obvious to me. I was presenting a very narrow perspective of this important time in our history. My good friend, Bob Kuhn became the catalyst of how I might broaden my own, plus every reader's view of the Vietnam conflict. He is a hero. He has endured just about everything that Vietnam offered. He went. He returned. He married his sweetheart and became a successful part of society. That's the best part. He was not welcomed back with the high regard he deserved. He eventually accumulated many health problems associated with Agent Orange. He has what became known as P.T.S.D. That's the worst part.

He was kind enough to allow me to interview him. Our talk was very much an eye opener for me. It spurred me to want other such interviews. I thought I'd end things with four interviews. One from each of the major services. Then I met and talked with Wendy Roush. She recommended I do a story about her cousin, a casualty of the conflict. I knew him from our days at Otterbein and said yes. My brother reminded me that Cousin Fred was there and that he had a compelling story. After this, I thought eight interviews might be the number. I got those in and was about to say; "done." Then I met Steve Morris in my local Kroger store. He was unmistakably a Viet Vet. I made contact with him, and his story added a great deal. An Otterbein Magazine obituary led me to Doug Hammond. After reading it I knew I had to include him. Dick Morrow, a former classmate from college, was my resource. He had maintained a connection with Doug. He put me in touch with Betty Byrne. She was able to add to Doug's wonderful life story and made the process easy. Lastly, on a short vacation, I picked up a USA Today newspaper. It had an entire section devoted to the era and conflict. It was also done through interviews, much like mine. It made me aware of two important categories that I had not considered. This led me to Bob Cross; an African American vet, and Guy Gruters, a P.O.W. from Vietnam.

This Epilogue had now become a volume. I reasoned that fitting it in at the end of my novel would be a bad idea. Who's going to read an epilogue that's nearly as large as the book? I presented this to my publisher, and they agreed.

I thank everyone for the inspiration and encouragement.

ABOUT THE AUTHOR

Larry Buttermore is a retired but extremely busy resident of Apple Valley, Ohio. He grew up in Connellsville, Pennsylvania, and came to Ohio to attend Otterbein University. Larry became a published author in 2009. His first book is called *Switch Hitters*. The book is an example of autobiographical fiction, drawing on memories of a childhood softball team he was on. In 2019, the COVID pandemic had him at home with lots of extra time. He took some loosely organized thoughts and completed a story. His novel called *Over and Back* was published in 2023. After completing it, he became aware that the main time frame of that novel was the Vietnam era. Also, the two main characters Trey, and Larry himself, were both of draft eligible age, but never served. This led to his realization that a wider perspective might be in order. His first thought was to expand this in his epilogue. He started with four interviews with actual Vietnam combat veterans. The project took on a life of its own and four led to thirteen. He decided that it would be too big for an epilogue and that it deserved to be its own book. His publisher agreed and thus *Every Perspective has a Voice; Every Voice has a Perspective* became a reality.

www.ingramcontent.com/pod-product-compliance
Lightning Source LLC
Chambersburg PA
CBHW030819090426
42737CB00009B/789